Peace Talks

An Anthology of Peace Region Stories

Edited by Ronnie Roberts

Edited by Ronnie Roberts

Cover Art by Darcy Shawchek

Cover Design by Kristen Designs

Published by Pajama Therapy Books - 2016

Paper Book ISBN: 978-0-9958025-1-3

Forward

By Ronnie Roberts

When I attended the first ever meeting of the Writers of the Peace in the Fort St. John public library, I had no idea how impressed I would be with the talent around that table, how long we would stick together and how close we would become. Over the years, we've grown to trust and rely on one another for raising our knowledge and writing skills, for feedback and critique, for a pat on the back when needed and the occasional gentle kick in the rear, also when needed. Over time, we've continued to expand our numbers, welcoming newcomers, regardless of where they are on their writer's journey, and are the better for their presence.

Our open meetings are biweekly, casual—no dress code required—and beyond acceptance and respect of others and no politicking, they are a wonderful couple of hours in which we can immerse ourselves in the craft we love with people who understand our passion to record our stories. We catch up, we commiserate, we celebrate, we learn, we grow, and we go home refreshed and inspired. Pretty perfect, as far as I can tell!

The idea to put together this anthology came to us as a group, a thunderbolt of 'why not' hitting us at once, it seemed, and we were off to the races. The Peace Region literally oozes creative talent, whether it is writing, painting, acting, photography, sculpting, weaving, quilting—you name the art form; it thrives here in the north. Our 'why not' question—why not present a sampling from our local writers on the subject of our region and the subject of peace itself?

The writing and publishing experiences among our group is varied; some having traveled further down that road than others, but everyone was eager to try their hand at producing a regional anthology. Being the acquiring editor, I didn't know exactly what I would be receiving as submissions, but I was hopeful. I love the Peace, and I love these generous, giving writers.

So the submissions began to trickle in. Oh my goodness.

The book you have in your hands represents the blood, sweat and tears of eighteen local writers—writers who care very much about the words they've assembled and the message they're sending out into the world. These are heartfelt, sometimes funny, sometimes heartbreaking stories. These stories will make you think, make you grateful, make you laugh, make you humble, make you see yourselves and your neighbours in a true, unfiltered light.

We also decided we wanted to feature a local artist on our cover, and as you can see, we were extremely fortunate to have Darcy Shawchek's brilliant photo (one of so many!) as our face to the world.

All in all, this anthology has been a positive experience for everyone concerned, even with some more nervous than others to expose themselves to the world in this way. Publishing your work is a brave act, and these writers are brave indeed. I am so very proud of them, and of this book. I hope you enjoy the stories and poems herein. I know their contributors loved creating them for you.

Table of Contents

In the Region of Peace

By Lily Chen

A voice beckons me from a thousand miles away;
I fly to the north with my wings wide open.
I cross the mountains, land in the region of peace,
and begin my life on the northern side.

Butterflies dance around to greet me;
the aspen trees sing their welcoming songs.
The perfume of wild flowers linger in the air;
a deer prances by, light and carefree.

I wonder if a great artist lives nearby,
scattering millions of paints to colour the land.
The country breeze whispers to me on my morning runs,
while the sun warms my face with its summer smile.

Where are the seeds of the northern lights?
Their roots must be deep, to climb high in the sky.
How can I count the shades of the northern lights?
I will paint my life with the aurora and the star lights.

Lily Chen has just recently moved to Fort St John and loves being a permanent resident of the Canadian north. She hails from China, and has published works in Chinese. This is Lily's first published English Poem.

Fort St. John

By Kevin Buchholz

Hello and welcome to the City of Fort St. John. It is the busiest small city you will probably ever find yourself in. In our small community, you will find many of the amenities of bigger cities. The city seems to be growing pretty fast. Some might think almost too fast, for there are things here that you would be right in thinking the city is too small to have.

As you sit there reading this brochure, you might find yourself asking, "What is there for someone to do in this fair city?" And to tell you the truth I'm not entirely sure what to say. I guess I can start by asking you how long you're planning on staying? Are you happy to find yourself here? What is it you like to do?

If you're only passing through, then I guess that Cheers or The Dill is where you can find what it is you're looking for. Though don't be surprised by what you find there. Our fair city does have an earned reputation. But I'll let you know that the people who call this place home have this weird pride when it comes to The Dill. Everyone you ask will have an unbelievable story to tie themselves to that place. I, myself choked a bouncer out there for throwing a man half his size across the floor for no good reason. Cheers has good TV screens for when you've seen enough dancing and believe you, me, that totally can happen on a slow day in Fort St. John.

On a slow day. That's almost too funny a phrase. There are very few people that have a slow day in this wonderful northern city. Everyone on the roads here seems to have this desire to be wherever they need to be—first. The traffic is scary; you need to always pay attention. Every second person seems to be talking on their phone as they drive to wherever they are headed.

If you're here for more than just a night, you're either in jail, or been asked to come here to work, temporarily, of course. Ha-ha, that's almost a motto up in the energetic city. You see, most people here are "only here temporarily". They are either here because they were needed to help some company, save money to go to school, or make money to pay off debt. There is nothing here, if not opportunity, to be almost anything you want to be. And you will be paid handsomely to do it.

Anyway, if you're planning on being here for a week, or a year, again, let me direct your attention to those two aforementioned establishments. Seriously, if you get a couple of your friends to go there with you, and you find yourself in the right state of mind, all manner of fun can be found in those places. We also have a leisure pool that you can frequent to get yourself some extra exercise if you have a job that isn't too physically demanding. There are also many gyms in the city to help you get or stay in shape. As a matter of fact, there aren't too many activities you can't find. Baseball, hockey, basketball, skating, soccer, running. The only thing that is curiously absent is football, which is a shame because it truly is a wonderful sport.

Oh, and if your planning on staying any length of time might I suggest you find a place to stay right now. No, do not wait a month or two to start looking. You have no idea how much things change in this city "in a month or two". In a month or two there may be no place to rent. Or what there is will be really expensive—like stupid expensive. But hey, again, that's part of the charm of this city. If you want to be here, you will find you have to work really hard just to live here. It's almost as if everyone is waiting for some sort of payoff to come rolling in. At the very least, living here will make you appreciate the warm weather we do get.

It can get cold in Fort St. John. Like cold cold. Imagine the coldest you can. Now stop crying, you pansy, because it will get even colder than that. Bitching about it will neither change it, nor make it go away, so you may as well embrace it. Fool yourself into thinking you like it. Some days it literally is the only way I can make it through a day of work. If you need to, just watch the smoke coming from the furnace vents of all those houses and let yourself imagine a warm place. The way it just floats above the houses when there is no wind. And the hoar frost that grows on the powerlines, trees and chain-link fences is too beautiful to even describe. When it gets really cold, you can even watch as it forms.

There are weeks where it is so cold outside, that it seems as if the rest of the world has gone silent. You walk outside and the only sound you'll hear is the sound your boots make as you walk across the freshly fallen snow. You will spend an hour just digging your car out of your driveway, the only sound you'll hear will be your breath behind your scarf. And the thing that is more amazing is that even though it will get cold enough to freeze the balls off a brass monkey, the people here still go about their day doing what it is they do. There's seldom ever a cold day that stops us up here. Work needs to be done, schools need to be attended, groceries need to be bought, and meals need to be prepared.

If you're lucky enough to find yourself living here for years on end, you may also find locals who will embrace you for who you are. Though do not be offended if it takes you more than a couple of years to feel any sort of welcome. You see this city is very transient, and no one knows this better than the locals. There are many who come here and realize soon enough they can't hack it. Many a day I still ask myself what it is I'm still doing here. But if you let it happen, you can easily fall in love with this strange crossroad of this planet.

If you look hard enough, you'll find boundless adventure and exploration for sure. The local geography has just about everything. From rivers and lakes, to hills and valleys, forest and mountains are within an easy drive to find. So please be sure to take the time to explore and appreciate this actual paradise on earth.

So welcome to our fair northern city. May it provide you with more than just a paycheck. May it grant you all the peace and adventure you choose to find here. And may you yourself add to the stories that are written here.

Kevin Buchholz was not born nor raised in Fort St. John, but he has been happily living here for a few years now.

Fearless in Peace Country

By Ronnie Roberts

Here is the boy, taped to the pipe. Three rolls of tape, it had taken, and three of their burliest, toughest men. They allowed him to first saunter into the nearby woods to relieve himself. When he returned, trudging back through the clear-cut between lengths of pipe resting on cones and skids to his left, and a six-foot-deep trench to his right that stretched for miles into the wilderness, they fanned out and came up around him. By the time he sensed danger, his brown eyes widening in alarm, it was too late.

"No!" He lunged to his left, but his boots slid in the slick clay and he was down, narrowly missing the trench. Rolling on his back, he pulled his banana knife from his grimy overalls, skidded back onto his feet and slashed at thin air.

Cautiously calm, steady like land sharks, they closed in.

Too late, and too young, and against men who could toss and tie a calf in twenty seconds, the wise-ass kid from the city was hung in the air, each man struggling with a grip on his arm or leg. He bucked, he twisted, he even got a punch off with his left fist, smacking Russell, the spread boss, on the side of his head, and a decent kick in the stomach to Surfer Jimmy. It didn't stop them; it didn't even anger them.

They hauled him up so his body lay parallel to the pipe and produced rolls of tape. "Come on now Rob, no sense fighting it. You know you're not gonna win," Surfer Jimmy ground out through clenched teeth, whipping the black tape around the kid's legs and the pipe with the precision of a surgeon while Russell worked on his shoulders. "Nobody here's gonna help, neither, so don't bother yelling."

Keith, who rounded out the four-man shrink crew, worked on taping the boy's mid-section. He wasn't so intent on his work he didn't have time to cast his eyes with fear to the edge of the dense and dark old-growth forest. "I wouldn't be big on the yelling if I were you. It'll only disturb the bears, and I hear they're ornery this summer. Not many berries around." He looked at Surfer Jim. "Didn't you say there was a rogue black bear in this area about a week ago?"

"Yup, a mean one, but he's deaf as a post. He can't hear a damned thing 'cause of the rock blasting, so you're safe on that account." Surfer Jim produced Rob's cellphone, stolen from his lunch box while he was in the woods, and snapped a few pictures of the men posing around their quarry.

"But, that ol' bear can smell fear ten miles away," Russell said with admiration.

Surfer Jim tossed the phone and Rob's banana knife to the ground. "There it is kid— freedom. All's you gotta do is get one arm free, and you can cut your way out. I hope you do better than the last guy."

Russell shuddered. "I told ya' I don't like you talking about that guy."

"Sorry. I forgot it was you who found him."

The men backed off and moved west along the pipeline.

Robert craned his neck. "Found who?" he demanded. No one answered. "Who'd you find? What guy?" He strained against the tape, trying to keep his crew in sight, knowing they had to come back. “Come on, guys, you can’t seriously leave me like this, my plane leaves at nine tonight!” No one cared. Switching tactics, he bellowed, “You’ll never make today’s target without me and I know you’re counting on that bonus!”

Laughter drifted back toward him, then silence. He struggled furiously against the tape. Nothing moved, not even a fraction of an inch.

“Come back!” he yelled at the sky, his voice bouncing from newly blasted rock face, and absorbed by the towering trees that stood silent witness along the freshly scarred landscape. “Cut me loose!” he yelled again, then stopped, seeing for the first time the dark clouds moving in from the west. And why would today be any different? Of course it’ll rain. Damn, damn, damn.

He tried flexing his knees to stretch the tape. All he needed was a little wiggle room. He shrugged his shoulders, flexed forward, arched back. There. Was that movement or just wishful thinking? Deciding it could only help, he continued the shoulder action, backward, forward, feeling the tape beginning to move with him, just a little. Glancing down, he saw the banana knife, so close, so very, very close, yet it might as well be in the next freaking county. And his phone. Yeah, he had wanted a record of his first summer up north, earning the big bucks, but, man, it didn’t come easy. Had he only been here eleven weeks? It felt like a lifetime.

He’d arrived in Peace Country—that was rich—the gateway to the northern oil patch, on the sixteenth of June with a plan; a plan to earn enough money to buy new goalie pads. They didn’t come cheap; two thousand, at least. He’d added a good four inches to his height over the last year, topping out at five-eleven and his old pads just weren’t doing the job; he'd caught himself flinching in net and that was the death of a good goalie. A goalie couldn't afford to fear mere mortal hockey players—a goalie had to know he was invincible.

His part time job as a cashier at Super Store wasn't enough. If he'd stayed there and saved every dime over the summer, and that meant no movies, no gas for his beat-up truck, and doing nothing with his friends, he still couldn't have earned enough for the pads, so here he was, swallowing the garbage the pipeline crew dished out. The truth was, he'd hated working at Super Store and when he'd heard about the money to be made up north, he'd quit, and not in a quiet way, singing "*Ground Control to Major Tom, I'm stepping through the door…*" before he'd cartwheeled out the automatic doors to unemployed freedom.

He'd had just enough cash to buy a pair of steel-toed boots and plane fare to his sister Deena's place in Fort St. John, only to find when you're seventeen and fresh out of grade eleven, the pipeline companies don't meet your plane, shake your hand and offer you a job when you hit town. Too late to go crying back to Mom, who hadn't liked his plan to go north to start with.

Every day, he'd gotten up from a lousy sleep on Deena's couch, packed himself a lunch and hitched a ride with her neighbor Trevor down to Tyson's office. Well, office was being kind. It was a human corral, and he and a hundred other men were the cattle, waiting for someone to walk in and choose them for a job, any job, on the pipelines.

Of course, he was never one of the chosen. He was the youngest, the smallest at one-seventy, soaking wet, and the most obvious newbie. The men didn't talk to him; their gazes simply passed him by, like he wasn't there. It was humiliating. He felt like he had a red 'x' on his forehead for all to see he had no clue.

The thing was–he had talked up his summer job opportunities back home and he couldn't go back with his tail between his legs and ride out grade twelve a broke-ass loser, and there would be no going back to Super Store.

So, he'd brought the same lunch four days running, was never a chosen one, returned to Deena's apartment by ten every day, put his lunch back in the fridge and played video games until she came home from work. It was depressing and getting harder to look cheery, pretending his ego wasn't taking a beating everyday he stood amongst the more experienced, bigger, heavier men, pretending he didn't see the scorn or pity in their eyes.

Day six he decided it was time for a fresh lunch.

Maybe his old lunch was bad luck, and a new couple of sandwiches and row of cookies would make him a more appealing employee. He walked into Tyson's with the new lunch and what he hoped looked like a new attitude. Throw me a bone, any bone.

No work; not for the Newbie.

Home again, video games again.

Maybe if he gained some weight, looked bigger?

He ate nine corn dogs from Deena's freezer. Naturally, when she got home, she'd kill him, but as of this moment, it seemed a viable alternative to his current unemployed state.

Next day, six in the morning, he walked into Tyson, his new, luckier lunch tucked under his arm, found himself a deserted seat, keeping the expression on his face blandly expectant, like this wasn't the fiftieth time he was about to be smacked down as useless in front of everyone.

Then he heard a strange thing. Someone over by the coffee machine murmured "Hey, the kid's back."

A grisly man in worn overalls gave him a barely perceptible nod of acknowledgement; if Rob blinked, he'd have missed it. His body went almost rubbery with gratitude. Someone here didn't think he was a total waste of space after all. Of course, he didn't work, but, hey, it was a start, wasn't it?

The lucky lunch was trotted out every day that week until it too was retired and replaced with another luckier-yet lunch—this one cold wieners in buns with mustard and two pudding cups. Each day, at six a.m., Trevor dropped him off at Tyson, and each day it seemed more of the men actually saw him there, and nodded at him, or grunted a few words. Some even knew his name, and it felt like Christmas when he walked in the last day of his third week, and Tim, the guy behind the Tyson counter said, "Hey Rob, how's it going?"

Fighting the urge to jump up and down with glee, Rob nodded. "Can't complain."

To appear needy was death. That much he'd learned by watching the other men, who also showed up with what he guessed was their lucky lunches, lucky hard hats, lucky underwear? Something that got them work every day. Or maybe it was all about the swagger.

Six o'clock the next morning he walked in with purpose and didn't wait to be greeted by the others. Instead, he nodded first, receiving several nods from around the room that swelled his heart. He went directly to the coffee machine and poured a cup of the grim black liquid and made himself drink it; made himself like it.

As usual, Tim yelled out assignments, men picked up tote-bags that Robert knew contained safety goggles; hard-hat; gloves; fire-retardant overalls with yellow and gray reflective tape; a lunch; smokes. They left in groups of two, six, sometimes as many as fifteen. By seven-twenty the room had emptied, and he was left alone again. A torturous hour passed. His shoulders wanted to sag with disappointment, but he glanced at the scuffs on his boots and reminded himself it wasn't over 'til it was over.

Tim met his eyes and smiled. "Better luck tomorrow, maybe?"

The main door crashed open and a big man with a huge shiny bald head burst in, disappointment registering across his meaty face. "Great." He strode to the counter. "Hey Tim, I'm short a man. My helper's wife is down with appendicitis. Tell me you've got someone you can call up."

Robert saw Tim nod in his direction and watched with disbelief as the man turned to look at him, grimaced as if he was in pain, then jerked his thumb over his shoulder. "You win. Let's go."

Robert grabbed up his tote filled with the second-hand gear Deena had found for him and followed the big man out of Tyson's, Tim giving him a thumbs up as he passed. Outside, he swallowed a lump of fear and climbed into the truck; the guy was backing out before he could even close the door.

"What's your name kid?"

"Rob." *Don't screw up, don't screw up.*

"I'm Joe. We're working Tumbler Ridge. Been a welder's helper before?"

"I'm a fast learner. You won't be disappointed."

They roared out of Tyson's yard and hit the highway pavement at an angle. Still grappling with his seatbelt, Robert's head smacked the roof of the cab.

"What have you done?"

"Farmhand."

When Joe nodded as if satisfied, Robert decided against mentioning his year as a check-out clerk at Super Store, where he could reel off all one hundred and thirty-seven product codes for bulk foods and fresh produce.

Good thing Joe wasn't a talker. Robert was still stunned to find himself in the truck, going somewhere he'd never heard of before, to do a job he had no idea how to do. As the noisy diesel ate up the miles, Robert could hear Deena warning him, "Whatever you do, don't talk back. Take what they dish, keep your eyes open, your mouth shut and learn. Learn, work hard, don't complain, and you'll get a call-back."

They made Tumbler Ridge by ten–late. Joe hit the ground running, hauling Robert in his wake, barking instructions as he set up near a length of four-inch pipe that was laid alongside a deep trench. As far as Robert could see pipe lay ahead of them, a long disjointed row leading through a ridge of blasted rock. In the distance, he could make out other workers and a crane picking up each pipe and swinging it into place beside the trench.

"No time to gawk, kid. The shrink crew is only a day behind and we have to make up this morning's lost time." With quick movements and few words, Joe showed him how to grind slag from a pipe.

Robert caught on and worked hard, imagining himself the best damned slag grinder Tyson had ever hired. The work was tough, the pipes heavy, and he found no matter how fast he worked, Joe easily kept up with him. Soon his feet were wet, right through his boots. He slipped and slid in the mud, moving Joe's equipment, running ahead to grind the pipe clean of slag, and back again to move the welding truck forward. As the day wore on, his feet began to burn, each step fiery torture. By four, Robert had no feeling in his feet, and he'd established a rhythm with Joe, anticipating his needs, his next move, and accommodated him with equipment, space, and muscle.

At six, he was ready to drop in his tracks, but kept moving along with Joe, who seemed untouched by fatigue and relentless in his pursuit of fresh joints to weld. They worked until darkness fell and Joe declared it too dangerous to continue. Robert didn't protest, his limbs were jelly, with the inner hum of exhaustion revealed in the trembling of his hands he could no longer hide. He fought the need to sink where he stood, knowing if he did, he'd never get up again. Instead, they gathered up the equipment, stowed it on the back of the truck and headed into town.

When Joe pulled into the parking lot of Deena's apartment, he turned and looked at Robert. "So you worked as a farmhand?"

"Yup. My grandmother's farm." Robert didn't add it was only on weekends, driving the tractor as he and his Dad paced and repaired the fence lines. Pretty tame stuff compared to today.

"I can tell. On a farm, you never stop. Today you never stopped."

Robert opened the door and slid his stiffened, sore body painfully to the pavement. "Thanks Joe." He pulled his bag from the back of the truck, slapped the cab with his palm and watched it roar away. It wasn't until the taillights had disappeared around the corner that he turned with a groan toward the yellow light shining in Deena's kitchen window. A bullet to the head would be merciful.

Like all bad news, five o'clock the next morning came too swiftly. The blisters on his feet were drained and gauzed with care, his feet packed tenderly back into his boots. Opening the door to Tyson, he stopped hobbling, but couldn't help laying each foot onto the cement floor gingerly. Every face in the place seemed trained on his entrance, wicked grins blooming across craggy features; wolf whistles and chuckles followed him to the coffeepot. He gritted his teeth and grimaced at the monstrously bitter liquid, but recognized at once the benefits of caffeine to his bruised and battered body.

The first job and group was shouted out. Men gathered up their belongings as their names were called and they piled into diesels, crew cabs, long boxes and headed north. As the crowd thinned at its customary rate, and Robert considered the shortest route to hobble home, Joe smacked the door open, and the same as yesterday, it cracked against the wall before springing back against his hard, calloused hand. He glanced around the room and so did Robert. There were twelve men left, all of whom were bigger, tougher, and more experience than he. Here it comes, his ninety-ninth humiliation.

Joe's eyes landed on Robert. He jerked his thumb over his shoulder. "Rob. Let's go."

Relief, gratitude, pride, hell, even a swell of warm affection for the tough old guy flooded Robert, carrying his tortured body across the floor and into Joe's truck like he had wings. Returning to Tumbler Ridge was Christmas morning, a second date with a girl you really liked, and a shutout game all rolled into one.

All day he whistled as he worked, drowning out the screams of protest his soft body emitted as he dragged it protesting through the tough, take-no-prisoners world of pipeline construction with the big boys. He knew anything that slowed down a welder was reason to be yelled at, so he made it his business not to slow the welder. That meant anticipating Joe's next move and keeping all supplies within reach. For six days straight they worked steadily, hardly speaking, each knowing the next step in their gold-sparked dance along the pipeline. By nightfall, he and Joe had caught up with the main crew and Robert felt easy in his own skin.

Day seven, Robert shifted a new weld too soon, resting the seam against his neck. Hot metal seared into his skin with a hiss; his skin tore apart, fried to the pipe when he lunged away.

Joe dropped his torch. "It get you?"

Robert grimaced, his hand hovering over the wound, wanting, but not daring to touch. The smell of burnt hair and hot fat lifted his stomach to his throat. Gagging, he barely registered Joe hurrying to the truck and coming back with a flat round tin.

"Here." He tossed it to Robert then reached down and fired up his torch again. "Cooling Gel. Keep it covered all the time."

Robert scooped some gel, applied it gingerly–the relief was immediate–and went back to work, his neck still on fire.

When Joe's regular helper was back, Robert returned to Tyson's morning cattle call with something to offer. He'd paid his dues. Work came his way in sputtering waves; a day here, three there. He kept his mouth shut, his head down and learned. The thick black scab on his neck fell away after a few weeks, revealing a pink six-inch long double line down his neck.

While hauling propane tanks by hand up a long muddy hill (what the men called neck-down work) he passed the brain-numbing boredom of this particular job by making up bizarre stories about his new scar to tell his friends, or adding up how much he'd made so far and how he'd spend it when he got back home.

It was pure luck he was at this jobsite. He'd been swapping stories with the usual suspects down at Tyson, when Gary Farmer came over, blowing on his hot coffee. "Man, I can't believe it. Some idiot just got offered three weeks work out in camp and turned it down."

Robert's head shot up and he scanned the room. "What idiot?"

"What, you interested?"

"Damned right, I'm interested. Three solid weeks means I'd work right up to the start of school."

Gary nodded. "Hang on, let me see what I can do."

Robert watched him make his way through the crowded room and lean over the Tyson counter. When Tim looked up at him, Robert just had time to nod his acknowledgement before the milling crowd blocked his sightline. Tim called out names and assignments and all around the room men tossed away coffee cups, bent to lift gear bags and plodded out the door.

"You Rob Baxter?" A skinny man wearing a brilliantly flowered shirt had materialized beside him.

"Yup."

"I hear you're interested in camp work."

"If it's legal and it pays, I'm interested."

"How long will it take you to get ready?"

"Ten minutes."

"I'm Surfer Jim. Let's go."

Four hours later, as the newest member of Surfer Jim's shrink crew, Robert hauled his suitcase full of unwashed clothes into Room 12 of the Rapids Motel, and headed out to the new site. Surfer Jim drove the diesel and yammered about extreme sports and Russell the spread boss promptly set about rolling a supply of joints for the day.

The fourth man in the truck was Keith, an apparent crossword fanatic, who never once pulled his huge honking nose out of his book. This would be Robert's crew for the balance of the summer, and as the newest man, he inherited the jobs nobody wanted.

That meant carrying propane tanks or huge rolls of rock guard, two on each arm, up the line, dropping one tank or two rolls beside each joint. Russell, the spread boss, was all over the place, checking with the consultant; checking everything was moving according to plan and each crew kept up their part on the massive assembly line. Jimmy and Keith worked at each joint, with Robert helping out once he'd delivered the needed supplies.

He soon learned this site was different. These men weren't like quiet, relentless Joe, where the job was everything. Here, the guys liked to play a little.

The first day, he was told it was now his responsibility as the new guy to do the spark tests. He was given a Styrofoam coffee cup and told to hold it close to the heating torch to collect sparks to be tested. This was news to him, having worked with Joe, who never seemed interested in spark testing during the initial weld. Surfer Jimmy assured Robert this was because Joe was so damned good at his job, he didn't need to test anymore, whereas Jim had only a couple of years in the business, and wasn't sure enough of the final seal to drop the testing altogether.

It was damned near impossible to catch the sparks. Feeling like a tool, Robert looked up at Russell to see if he was pissed, and caught sight of his lazy smile as he took a drag off his joint and held the smoke in his lungs.

Man! He was being had.

He flung the cup to the ground and the guys burst out laughing and he found himself laughing along with them–he couldn't help it; it *was* funny. There wasn't much beyond relentless, heavy work out here on the pipelines and a prank or well-told joke was highly prized by the men.

For the next few days Robert learned all about protecting the welds before the long pipe was shifted into the trough like an impossibly huge line of spaghetti. When he wasn't hauling supplies, he helped with the joints. They cleared debris from the inside of the pipe by dropping a piece of cork, called a pig, inside through a valve in the flange and shooting it down the pipe to the next flange with air compression. Robert practically jumped out of his skin when right beside him, that first pig burst out of the pipe with the sound of a freight train. The guys thought it was great fun.

Next came the layers of protection the pipe needed before being buried in the ground. It had to be heated in order to melt on a black plastic, tar-lined sleeve. After the black sleeve cooled, a second sleeve of Styrofoam, then a third, this one yellow, was wrapped around the joint and all along the pipe, followed by a thick wrapping of rock guard.

They were in their third day of drizzling rain and the road had become impossible for the big supply trucks to climb without ruining the roads. This meant below-the-neck work for the construction crews. By now the hillside they were working on was slick with mud and hauling the propane tanks and rolls of plastic, Styrofoam and rock guard was taking its toll. As the day wore on and with each subsequent trip Robert's arms seemed ready to leave their sockets.

He dropped the last two rolls of rock guard beside Keith who was holding a large umbrella over Surfer Jim as they struggled to keep the joint dry while they worked. Just then a man on a four-by-four ground through the mud, spackling Robert from head to toe. "Hey!" Robert yelled after the guy, clearing his eyes on his sleeves. To his crew he said, "Who's the loser on the four-by-four?"

Surfer Jim craned his neck to look up the pipeline. "That's Shit Head."

"No, what's his name?"

"*La* Shit Head." Jim was smiling.

"Real nice guy."

"We all think so."

Robert worked until lunch, hauling gear through the slippery muck, then huddled under the trees with the rest of the crew, grateful for the hot coffee the motel kitchen had packed in his lunch. He was starting to shiver; thanks to his mud bath. It felt like he would never be warm again. He wrapped his hands around his cup, absorbing the heat it gave off. With chattering teeth, he said, "Well, in just a few weeks, gentleman, I'll be back on my ass in a nice warm, dry classroom, complaining how hard school work is."

"What, and leave all this?" Keith looked injured. "You could ditch school and take it easy up here with us."

"As good as that offer sounds, I think I'll pass."

Surfer Jim waved his half-eaten sandwich in Robert's direction. "How in the hell will he ever be a lawyer if he doesn't get his ass back to school?"

Keith laughed. "You mean how in the hell is he gonna spring your sorry self out 'a jail after he becomes a lawyer, if he doesn't get back to school."

He tossed the rest of his coffee into the ferns. "So what are we gonna do about that last pipe. It's just not long enough."

Surfer Jim pressed his lips together and shook his head. "It's a friggin' amateur show around here. We'll have to get a sky jack, that's all there is to it."

Keith nodded in agreement. "If they even have one out here. I heard they're using pipe stretchers now. The sky jacks are always breaking down in the rain."

Robert finished his coffee and packed up his lunch. Sitting was a mistake; he'd have to keep moving to stay warm. "Should I go up the line and see if they have one?"

Keith looked at Surfer Jim like Rob had had the best idea ever. "What's better, a sky jack or pipe stretcher?"

Jim packed his lunch up. "Either one'll do."

"Okay, I'll go find you one." Back on his feet, Robert grinned down at them. "That means one of you gentleman can do a bit of hauling while I'm gone."

"It's a dirty job, but someone's gotta do it," Keith smirked.

Seeing La Shit Head headed back down with the four-by-four, Rob signaled for him to stop, which apparently necessitated a florid curve to the left that splattered more mud across Robert's overalls. He was past caring.

"Hey, do you know if there's a sky jack or pipe stretch…" Hearing the words coming from his own mouth, he stopped and spun on his heel, looking back at his crew.

Surfer Jim was doubled over, laughing his guts out.

"Oh look!" Keith chortled, pointing to the gray

clouds above them. "The sky is falling. Everybody run."

"Loser," La Shit Head spat, gunned the four-by-four past him and continued down the line. Robert stomped past his crew, pack-mule once again. Neck-down work it was. He shook his head in disgust. How long was he going to keep falling for this crap?

At the bottom of the hill, La Shit Head was doing donuts in the muck while Robert threaded more spools of rock guard onto his arms and grabbed two propane tanks. Just as he was about to heft the whole load and start back up the hill, Russell showed up.

"Hey, hey, hey. That's too much." He turned to La Shit Head. "You, Sperry. Off the ATV. This isn't a damned trail ride." He turned back to Robert. "Pack the equipment up on this for the rest of the day. That's what it's for. When you're done, help Jim."

Robert couldn't help grinning at Sperry's dark look of resentment, saved especially for Robert when Russell wasn't looking. He quickly loaded up the four-by-four and headed up the hill. The four-by-four was a dream come true. He waved as Russell passed him in the diesel, headed further up the line. Yuppers, this he could handle.

His crew was hard at work under the ungainly umbrella and surprised to see him back so quick. He unloaded and headed down for more.

At the bottom of the hill, Sperry was waiting for him. Robert got off the ATV and was surprised when Sperry helped him load it up. But, at the last minute, Sperry jumped onto the four-by-four. "I'll take over this job now," he said, gunning up the slope, and showering Robert in his wake. La Shit Head, indeed.

'Keep your mouth shut and learn', Deena had said. He picked up another load and started back up the hill. Fearless.

By the end of week two, Robert had developed a healthy dislike for Alan Sperry. The guy was a bully and a loser. How he weaseled his way onto the four-by-four day after day could only be seen as an art-form, and his ability to drive around the site without actually doing anything was a mystery to Robert. All day long, Sperry played in the rough terrain, grinding up and down the hill with the four-by-four empty while Robert hauled every load by hand.

Dropping the last of his load beside Keith, Robert watched Sperry climb the hill toward them. "How the hell does he get away with it?"

Keith glanced back then said, "I've got it down to one of two things. Either he's got important relatives or he's got something on the boss."

"So there's nothing we can do about it?"

"Not a thing. Don't it make you feel so much better?" Keith's grin was wicked.

"So, we're just the grunts who have to suck it up. And you're telling me there's no sense even thinking about bringing him down a notch or two?"

"Well, then, my job is done." Keith began winding rock guard around the pipe.

"I think you're wrong–I think he's all talk, no action."

Sperry careened to a stop beside them, his skinny, unshaven face a mask of fury. "Get back to work, you moron! This isn't a kindergarten class, we're not playing here, boy! You can't keep up, get your sorry ass off site!"

Robert crossed his arms and looked back at Sperry. "What's up, somebody important around you're trying to impress? You don't give a rat's ass what the hell I do, as long as you've got a motor tucked up between your legs, ain't that right, Shit

Head?"

The colour drained from Sperry's face. He looked to see if Surfer Jim was listening. Jim was intent on heating the pipe up, and seemed uninterested in the exchange. Keith simply adjusted his hardhat and kept on wrapping.

"I don't have time for your mouth. Get back to work or–."

"Or what, you'll tell on me? The fact is, I'm leaving in a week, and an endorsement from you, I don't need." Robert turned away and started down the hill. What an ass.

Sperry gunned the four-by-four and roared off. Surfer Jim yelled after Robert, "Hey kid. You're gonna be some kind 'a lawyer when you're done!"

Robert smiled at the sound of Keith and Jim's silly giggles drifting after him, raised his hand in salute without turning around and plodded on, the mud sucking his boots with each step.

The next time Sperry cruised by on his four-by-four, Robert was ready. "Keith!" he yelled over Sperry's ATV's engine. "Jimmy doesn't like the look of that last flange. We don't have the right cuddle ring to use for an expander. He said I should take the four-by-four and get one from the consultant." He knew Sperry would never give up the four-by-four.

Keith was slow to answer. "Well, there's the four-by-four. Jump on and go get one." He asked a question with his eyes—what are you up to?

Robert smiled. "So, just one cuddle, or do we need two?"

Understanding blossomed on Keith's face. "Oh, one will do the job, absolutely. Hey, Sperry, let Rob have the four-by-four. He needs to ask the consultant–."

"I heard," Sperry cut him off and revved the

motor. "I'll go get it."

Robert shrugged. "If you insist."

Sperry drew his lips back in what, for him, passed as a smile. "I *do* insist."

Robert bit his lip to keep from grinning.

Keith nudged Surfer Jim. "Hey, want to have some fun?"

Jim's mouth turned up into a bow. "Always."

They watched Sperry roar up to the crest of the hill. Warren Petrie was the consultant on this site, and always up for some fun. They saw Sperry jump off the four-by-four and swagger over to the consultant. Russell and two men who were looking over a diagram with Petrie parted, allowing Sperry to interrupt whatever they were discussing. Now the center of attention, Sperry tipped back his hard hat and said something, then turned to point in their direction. Petrie looked down at them then said something to Sperry. Sperry pointed at them again and talked some more. They waited.

"Here it comes," Robert said in a low voice, not wanting to jinx it.

Suddenly, Petrie opened his arms and advanced toward Sperry. Sperry scrambled backwards, landing on his butt in the mud. Now Petrie was bent over, holding his stomach and by the looks of Russell and the other men, they were all busting a gut. Petrie wiped his eyes and pointed down the line to Rob, Jim and Keith and waved. They waved back.

"He actually went up to Petrie and asked him for a cuddle," Keith gasped. "Aw, ain't that sweet?"

Without taking his eyes off the scene before them, Surfer Jim said, "Ah, Rob, I think you just lost a friend in La Shit Head."

"Do I look like I give a rat's ass?"

The last week in camp passed swiftly, with Rob's crew breaking up the tedium by confessing with great sincerity, "Hey guys, I'm feeling a little vulnerable right now. I could use a cuddle," to get them all giggling again.

Robert was no longer whipped after supper and aching to lay his weary body in bed. Now, he played Frisbee with Surfer Jim in the park across from the Rapids Motel, battled nightly over Wheel of Fortune with Keith, and talked hockey with Russell.

The night before Rob was due to leave, the guys were all sprawled around Russell's dingy motel room as usual, like they didn't see enough of one another all damned day. Surfer Jim was jammed into the only upholstered chair, looking like he was boneless, and had been closing in on never solving the battered Rubik's cube someone had left under the bed before he'd nodded off, his mouth slack and emitting an occasional snore. Keith was busy coaching a woman on the television screen to buy a 'y'.

Talk of hockey had changed to Rob telling Russell about his father, who'd died two summers ago, and how he and his mother struggled, and why with university just around the corner, new hockey pads weren't in their budget.

"And so you're going to become a lawyer?"

"That's the plan."

"Right after you buy your new goalie pads."

Rob bobbed his head.

"'Cause goalies know no fear."

Now Rob grinned. "No fear."

Russel pulled out the worn photo he kept in his wallet–it seemed to Rob that he'd seen Russel take it out and stare at it a thousand times–and handed it to Rob.

A pretty, dark-haired woman with two little

carbon copies of Russell by her side smiled up at him. "Nice family."

Russell stretched his calloused and knobby hands out before him. "See these hands? This is why I'm out here. My two sons' hands will never look like mine. My sons are going to have a chance at a better life. That's why I'm out here; missing them, missing Meggie." He took back the picture and carefully placed it inside his wallet.

Robert looked down at his own hands, and was surprised to see callouses. He barely recognized them as his own. The images of missed sons, missed fathers, and soft and calloused hands turned inside his brain.

Russell murmured, "They'll never have these hands," then leaned back on his bed and closed his eyes.

Keith threw the channel changer across the room. "Buy an 'm' already, will ya!"

***

By the time Sperry showed up, maybe an hour had passed, and the rain had been coming down on Robert pretty steady. The tape was loose, loose enough that he listed to one side, and was now achingly close to the banana knife.

"Well, well, well, what do we have here?" Sperry's tone was thick with satisfaction. Apprehension spiked through Robert. "I hear you've been here for almost an hour. Looks good on you." With lightning speed, Sperry brought his knee up into Robert's face, slamming his head back against the pipe.

Pain exploded in his head; he tasted blood.

"Oops, sorry, did that hurt?" Sperry adjusted his body. "I meant to do this." He drove his knee into Robert's abdomen, driving the air from his lungs, leaving him sucking for oxygen. "So you wanna cuddle?" He raised his hand. "Here's a cuddle!" He backhanded Robert across the face, then brought his knee up into his stomach again. Robert gagged, and fought for air.

Sperry raised his hand, prepared to slap Robert again. He was grabbed from behind.

"Hey there, sweetie, no slapping our guy, now." It was Surfer Jim, his words coming in short gasps. "We can't have that. We have to return him to his mother in the same shape as she left him."

Sperry yelped as his arm was twisted behind his back and he was forced to his knees in the mud.

Through clenched teeth, Jim smiled mirthlessly and said, "Mothers are funny like that."

Keith dropped his hard hat and hurried to Robert. He cut through the tape and lowered him carefully to the ground.

Robert coughed and noisily dragged air into his body, slowing the sound of his racing heart that pumped blood into his throbbing head. The rain was coming down hard now, but it felt good against his burning skin.

"You okay, Rob?" Keith wiped his shirt across Rob's face, wiping snot and blood off with the tenderness of a woman.

Rob nodded. Talking wasn't an option at the moment.

Keith stripped the bands of tape away from the rest of Rob's body and rubbed his limbs to get the circulation going. "Jeez, Kid, we didn't mean… We were just… Oh jeez, we're sorry, Rob. Really sorry."

Robert spit out red and pulled himself into a sitting position. For just a moment the world turned a little too fast for his senses. "That's alright," he croaked, turning his neck gingerly from one side to the other, testing. "I'm still here, spittin' and grinnin'."

He felt his lip swell as he spoke, making his face feel odd. This was different. He stretched his arms out into the rain, flexed his fingers and tried to smile at Keith and Jim, stopping when his lip cracked.

"What's going on here?" It was Russell, and it was the first time Robert had heard him angry. His face was dark, his eyes narrowed as he assessed the scene before him. From where Rob was sitting, Russell looked every inch the six-foot-four spread boss that he was. By the expression on Sperry's face, Russell looked terrifying.

Jim spoke up. "Ol' Shit Head here thought he was in for a treat, finding Rob tied up, sitting pretty for his brand of justice."

Robert lurched to his feet and shook his head clear; shaking water away from his now-overly-long hair like a wet dog. Suddenly he felt totally and completely alive, so alive that every nerve was free and on alert and poised to spring into action. It was like he'd been training for this moment his whole life. "I'd like the opportunity to even the score."

Russell's eye brows shot up in surprise. "You've been tied up. You know what you're doing?"

Robert moved restlessly, rolling, shrugging his shoulders, shifting his feet, testing the ground. He spat out more blood then nodded to Surfer Jim. "Let La Shit Head go."

Jim yanked Sperry to his feet then released him. "It's up to you kid."

Sperry's eyes darted around the circle of men which had grown in numbers and saw there was no escape. Robert could even see when he considered, then discarded the idea of running. His black-marble gaze returned to Robert and hardened. Bringing his fists into the air, he hunkered down. "All right, kid, let's see what ya' got."

Almost before the words were out of his mouth, Robert shot out his fist in a quick, double jab at Sperry's face. Sperry staggered back, raising his hands to the sudden bloom of blood that flowed from his face onto his grimy overalls. "You broke my nose!!" he wailed, fear and indignant accusation battling in his eyes.

Robert faked a left at Sperry's soft gut and pulled back just short of contact, then watched with disgust as Sperry fell to the ground as if he'd been struck, his arms wrapped around his body for protection. He was crying!

Surfer Jim said, "You'd better find yourself another jobsite to work, Sperry. No one here wants to work with you and that's not good, not good for anyone."

Standing over the crying man, Robert stilled; the pleasure of revenge draining from him as quickly as it had come. What was the point? Where was the triumph of hitting someone until they fell down? Did it make the man standing right, the man down wrong? Had he come all this way and worked this hard to end his summer like this?

He looked at his friends, standing protectively around him and knew they *were* his friends. "I'm not here for this. I'm here for goalie pads."

Russell's intense expression cleared and he became the easy-going spread boss Robert had come to know and trust. "You're right kid. It's all about the goalie pads."

He laid his arm across Robert's shoulder and paced him away from the whimpering Sperry. "I came up to let you know the guys worked their tails off so you could get your bonus. I have your gear from the motel stowed in the back of the truck. I'm taking you straight into town to the airport. You're going home, kid."

Keith and Jim fell into step with them, then waited by the truck door as Robert stood on a piece of cardboard and leaned against the seat, pulled off his boots and wrestled out of his overalls. "Hey, guys. What can I say? I didn't know anything when I came up here... and you guys..."

His throat had closed, making words impossible. From the driver's seat, Russell handed him a pair of jeans and a clean shirt. Robert made a business of putting them on while getting his emotions back in check.

"Yeah, yeah, we know the drill. Off to La La Land, with your pockets full o' cash." Keith punched him in the arm for emphasis then handed his boots back, one at a time. "Maybe stomp off most of the mud before you get on the plane."

Russell grinned. "He isn't the first pipeline worker to muddy up a plane heading back south, and he won't be the last."

"Oh, I almost forgot." Surfer Jimmy dug into his pocket and pulled out a tattered paper and shoved it into Robert's hand. "Here, kid. You come back next year, you give any one of us a call. We'll pick you up at the airport and bring ya' straight out to Paradise."

Robert looked at the paper and saw their names and phone numbers listed in thick gray pencil. Not trusting his voice, he bobbed his head, climbed into the truck and pulled the door closed. Keith and Jim slapped the cab with their hands and turned back to the pipeline.

Russell started up the noisy diesel and swung the big truck away and up onto the company road. "You know what they say, don't ya?"

He glanced at Robert with a mile-wide smile. "A goalie's got to be fearless."

Ronnie Roberts is the tireless, talented leader of the Writers of the Peace, the literary glue that holds us together, showing us the way to better writing while having fun doing it." Okay – so Pat made me say that.

Glue, huh? I can be sticky, especially after eating caramel popcorn, (which I hardly ever do!), and writing is fun (and maddening, and rewarding and sometimes reduces me to tears of frustration), and I did write a book for fiction writers entitled Complete Boot Camp for Fiction Writers.

Besides that, I've published six novels – The Wedding Dress Promise Series and the Poet Oregon Series and numerous short stories in magazines and anthologies. What I'm super excited about now is the three book Sci Fi series I'm currently writing, Earth Survives: Lost Sentinel, Cursed Apprentice and Deadly Messenger. What's not to like? Time travel, a post-apocalyptic world, a telepathic heroine, a battle between good and evil? Yup, Pat is right, writing is so much fun!!

Oh – and my family came to Fort St John 'temporarily' in search of work ten years ago. We fell in love with the people and seasons of the Peace and stayed.

Old Welder

By Brian Kelly

He's an old half blind welder
Who's seen better days
Mostly seen a walking
In an alcoholic haze
His knees are shot and crippled
Arthritis settin' in
The hands are gripped like talons
The old geezer just can't win
He's chased those rigs and pipelines
On each and every coast
And sucking fumes and whiskey
Is what he loves the most
There's four kids and two old ladies
Scattered 'cross the land
And money pissed out the window
Like raindrops in the sand
And he chases all those big jobs
Just to stay with his old crew
But the body's almost wore out
And his mind won't take the truth
Yet his cronies keep him going
On the job and in the bar
Till at last he draws his last breath
Holding an empty whisky jar
Did you ever stop and wonder
What makes a man go on
It's not just for the money
It's to show that you belong

Brian Kelly is a self-employed welder who grew up in Hudson Hope, met his wife (from Cecil Lake) at the FSJ dormitory, raised two kids in Fort St. John, and when not entertaining his gregarious grandchildren, can rarely be seen without a book in his hand.

North Peace Blues

By Glenn Palmer

This isn't a musical piece, but it is a blues.
The blues are the songs we sing and the stories we tell
When life deals come from the bottom of the deck,
When everything we touch seems to turn to shit.
Things will get better if we just hang on, tough it out,
But that isn't always true,
Sometimes at the end of the tunnel, there is no light.

ONE
Lunch at the Mondo

If Greg Jensen had gone to McDonald's for lunch half the troubles heading his way could have been avoided. Not all. Fate had already cocked the fickle-finger pistol and pointed it in his direction, but he probably wouldn't have met Jacob Running Feather.

Instead, he was attracted to the bright yellow restaurant with the 'Mondo' sign on one wall. There was a parking spot at the door, so he pulled his RAM 2500 to a stop and climbed down from the cab. It was the seventh of February. Snow on the ground reflected bright sunshine and suspended ice crystals glistened in the air.

Breathing the crisp, fresh air made him realize that for most of the trip he'd breathed a miasma of dead cigarette butts, cold coffee and stale farts. *Is it safe to leave the windows rolled down while I eat? Probably not.*

He walked to the end of the street, checking out

the scenery, hoping the bit of movement would undo the kinks the long drive had left in his back and thighs. His butt was numb and he gave it a vigorous scratch hoping to restore some feeling before propping his ass on yet another seat.

When he got back to the Mondo, a young native fellow was sitting beside the door beating a small hand drum, 'pung, pung, pung.' The drum's tone was much richer than he'd have expected from such a small head.

The door opened and an older, red-headed lady stuck her head out. "Jacob, remember our deal. You can sit here as long as you're polite and don't go nuts with the drum."

"I know, Bonnie, I'll be good," the young man said. Jacob flashed a smile that could comfort small, frightened animals, or melt a maiden's heart; a smile that said he was very happy to be in the world and especially thankful to find you there with him.

Bonnie went back inside. Noticing Greg, he said "I'm a twoney short for lunch. Can you help me out?"

Greg had a set response whenever a panhandler wrapped his plea up with a desire to eat: he always offered to buy them a meal. Seven out of ten stormed off in a huff. The three who took him up on it had provided some of the most interesting conversations he had taken part in.

"No money, but I'll buy you lunch."

Jacob squinted in suspicion. "You queer, whitey? Is that what this is?" The question hung there just long enough to be offensive, then he cracked that million-dollar smile again. "Nah, you ain't queer. Just fuckin' with you man. Sure; feed me. Why the hell not?"

Greg pulled the door open and went inside while Jacob gathered his gear.

Bonnie was behind the till just inside the door.

She handed Greg a menu. When the door opened a second time and Jacob appeared, she moved to intercept. “Now Jacob,” she began.

Greg interrupted, “It’s okay. He’s with me.”

Bonnie looked like she was going to argue, grabbed a second menu and thrust it at Jacob. “Sit wherever you like,” she said.

Greg liked a small table by the front window. He could watch the traffic patterns and get a feel for the new town. Jacob sat down opposite him. He piled his stuff on the window sill, an over-the-shoulder white cotton bag and the drum he’d been thumping out front.

Greg thrust his hand across the table. "Bonnie called you Jacob. I'm Greg Jensen."

"Yeah. It's on your jacket." Jacob gave Greg’s extended hand a hesitant shake. "Greg Jensen, Safer World Security. Never heard of that outfit. What are you doing up here?"

"We're doing some of the security on the new dam."

Jacob shook his head. "I heard the Guards had that whole thing sewn up."

“My partner, Jimmy, is a bidding genius. The Guards forgot to specify a couple of functions. We bid on them and won before they realized what had happened. What's good to eat here?"

"Don't ask me man; I've never been inside. They don't let me in and even if they did, I wouldn't have enough money to buy anything."

He said this as if it was just a statement of fact, without a trace of self-pity or any sense of being persecuted.

Now that Greg had a better look at him, he couldn't even be sure he was native. Jacob was a little under six feet tall, slim, with long hair. The hand drum and headband had made him seem Indian, but now it seemed he might be white.

"Jeez, man, take a picture. You're peeling the skin off my face. If you want to know something, just ask."

"I was trying to figure out what tribe you're from. I have a pretty good eye and ear for this stuff, usually, but I can't peg you."

"I'm Ojibway, from northern Ontario. Adopted when I was three and raised white. Here's a tip for you, though. You shouldn't talk about this kind of thing with somebody you just met. Say this stuff to the wrong person and it gives them a good excuse to thump you." The smile flashed out like the beam from a lighthouse, warming and welcoming, then passing on.

"Fair enough. Any idea where I can find a place to live?"

"Who do you think you're talking to, man? I'm Jacob Running Feather. I live on the streets or at the Sally-Ann. I steal, panhandle and pick bottles. I'm not a nice guy." Again the brilliant smile.

"How bad can you be with a smile like that?"

"'A man can smile and smile and still be a villain.' That's Shakespeare."

"Hamlet. I know."

"Don't look so surprised, man. I finished high school. Wasn't top of my class, but I was close. Some people you meet stumbling down the street had a pretty good start and a good education."

"Sounds like you had more education than I did," said Greg. "I only made it to grade ten."

"You like to read, don't you? And you spend a lot of time trying to make up for not finishing school. I bet you have a subscription to National Geographic."

"You think you know me?"

Jacob nodded. "I know the type: intelligent but

short on schooling; genuinely nice and generous, which is why we're here. Hard worker, honest, independent. Right?"

"I like to think so."

Jacob smiled again. "See? I know you but you don't know me. That gives me the advantage. Sizing somebody up at a glance is a survival requirement where I live. Want to know what my motto is?"

"Sure."

Jacob frowned and his voice was very deep and serious. "Never look back; somebody might be gaining on you." As he said it he tapped himself on the chest. Greg felt a sudden sense of dread and sat back in his chair to create as much distance as possible between them. As soon as he drew back he saw the serious expression fall from Jacob's face, replaced by a slight grin. "I didn't make that up, just heard it somewhere." His voice was back to normal.

A server appeared just then and took their orders. Greg ordered an omelet, 'Mondo Supreme.' Jacob settled for bacon, eggs and pancakes. They were delivered almost at once.

When they were alone again, Greg asked, "What did you mean when you said you have the advantage?"

"Knowing you makes you my natural prey. Now I just have to figure out how to play you."

Greg cut into his omelet. "That's pretty blunt. And I'm not buying it. I think you're just acting like a tough guy to impress me."

"Don't think that. I *am* a tough guy. This, what we're doing here, is a new technique I'm trying out. Complete honesty and lots of winning smiles. I'm telling you the absolute truth, but you don't believe me. One of the seven main ways of lying is to tell the truth in an unconvincing manner."

"So you're just picking me for information that will let you rob me?"

"A blind man could take you." Jacob nodded and pointed his finger like a pistol. "You got no idea of what goes on or how to protect yourself. You're a little lamb, ready for the shears. For a security guy you got no street smarts."

An underlying menace had crept into the conversation. Greg had to resist the temptation to pat himself to ensure his possessions were intact. His omelet tasted like sawdust. "Maybe you should pay for your own lunch," he said.

Jacob laughed. "That ain't you, man. A deal's a deal, even if it breaks your heart, 'cause you're an honest guy. Anyway, I'm just messin' with you. Those things I said? That ain't me. All I want is to drink my wine and beat my drum."

He drowned his pancakes with syrup then grinned at Greg. "What I said at the end is true, though. You're awful simple and you need to be on the lookout for scams and hustles."

Greg's Mondo Supreme tasted good again. The egg was moist. The meat and cheese tastes blended perfectly. The peppers and onions were just cooked without being soggy. Cholesterol perfection. "Okay," he said, "Tell me what to watch out for. I'm from Vancouver. I know most of the scams."

"Heard of ain't the same as recognizing a scam when it's coming at you. A really good scam is one where you never catch on. You'll even defend the guy that's hustling you; you keep coming back for more."

Greg was sure that he was street wise and capable. "Tell me one."

Jacob put his fork down and gestured to the server with his coffee cup. When he was ignored he continued, "Okay, the scam you're most likely to run into up here is 'repentant addict.' The player presents himself as a basically good person that has been tripped up by drugs or alcohol. He's been down for a while but now he's trying to claw his way back. You get to know him. He never asks you for anything, but you admire his struggle so much that you want to help. Maybe you drive him to meetings first, just when it's raining or snowing. The rest of the time he gets there himself. "

"Sometime later, when you run into him, he seems really sad or down. You ask him what's wrong and he tells you his daughter is sick or his dog needs an operation, or his mother needs a new walker. Whatever it is, there's now a big need in his life to do something you really agree with, but he doesn't have any money. You give it to him.

"Here's the thing, though. He never asks you. He doesn't even want to talk about what's wrong until you drag it out of him. When it comes to the money, you have to force it on him because he's too proud to take your charity. It won't even be a loan in the end, because there's no way he can promise to pay it back the way things are."

Jacob stopped talking and mopped up the remaining syrup on his plate with a piece of toast. Greg waits for more but Jacob seems to be finished.

"What's the next step?"

Jacob puffed his lips and shook his head. "I was just thinking that the addict scam is pretty complicated and there are lots of others that are really simple and fast that you need to be on the lookout for."

"Fine, you can tell me about them later. For now, tell me what comes next in this game."

"It can go a lot of ways from here. The important thing is you gave the player a fair amount of money with no conditions and it was your idea. Hey, can you wave Bonnie over? I could use another coffee and she looks away every time I signal."

When Greg signaled, Bonnie brought the coffee pot around and refilled their cups.

Jacob waited until he'd sugared his coffee before continuing. "There are two main ways this con plays out, short and long. In the short version, you get to know each other better over a period of time, then one day there's a disaster that needs a major pile of cash to fix. You pay up and the player disappears. You never see him again.

"In the long version, you become very good friends with the player. Occasionally you give him some money for something. Sometimes he even pays you back. What it comes down to is you've become his cash cow. As long as he behaves a certain way he can count on you to kick him some cash when he wants to get high or visit his girlfriend in Dawson. See how it works?"

Greg nodded slowly. *I'll be damned. I've had people in suits suck me in with that one and never spotted it.* "Yeah, I got it. Tell me another one, Jacob."

"Okay. A different version of the same thing is 'look how hard I'm trying.'"

"I think I see how that one plays out."

"Yeah, it's pretty much the same thing. Hey, what time is it?"

"Just after two."

"Shit, I'm late. Got things to do. Thanks for the meal." Jacob got up and pulled his coat on, then threw his bag over his shoulder.

"It's snowing pretty hard now. Do you need a ride someplace?"

"Nah, I'm fine. This is my country, remember. Maybe we'll see each other around sometime.

Macintosh is a small town."

"You sure you're okay? You don't even have a hat."

"You've done enough for me already, Greg. I really appreciate it."

"It's been an education. Probably saved me a lot more than the price of the meal. I owe you."

"If you want to square up, there *is* something... I haven't had a smoke for a couple of days. Buy me some smokes and we'll call it square."

"Sure." Greg pulled out his wallet and handed over ten bucks. "Here you go."

"Smokes are twelve bucks, but I got the twoney. Thanks man."

"No problem. If we see each other again we'll go for coffee."

"Sure." Jacob made for the door and disappeared into the blowing snow.

Greg pulled out his debit card and waited at the till while Bonnie rang up his bill. She handed him the receipt and said, "Check your pockets and the fillings in your teeth. If you spend much time around Jacob Running Feather, nothing you own is safe."

"He seems nice enough."

"Yeah, he does. That's the problem."

TWO
Jacob At the Library

Jacob walked through the falling snow. He pulled a toque out of his bag and covered his head. The snow was a nuisance. It cut down on the places he could go. When the sun was shining it was possible to find a place out of the wind to hang out with his friends. Snow meant you needed to find real shelter or at least an overhang to block the falling flakes.

One of the biggest downsides to being homeless

is needing to fill the empty time. Food wasn't as much of an issue. There were kitchens open at various times where it was possible to get food. Lunch at the Salvation army was simple but good and a guy could meet up with his buddies and hang out in the warm. For breakfast on weekdays there was the Native Friendship Center. In the summer, they set up a van in an empty lot and gave out bag lunches to anybody who needed one. In the winter, the center served breakfast between seven and nine on weekdays.

Pickings were slim on Saturdays. Sunday you could get breakfast at the mission church, and the Baptist church had a soup kitchen in the middle of the afternoon. The first thing that anyone on the street did when they got to a new place was find out where the free food was. The availability of food became fixed points in the day. In between there were empty hours to fill.

The only place he could really go was the library. There wasn't much room to sit, and you couldn't talk and grab ass in there, but at least it was warm. Jacob always tried to find a seat at a computer station. Once you got yourself planted in front of a computer you were good for hours. Most guys couldn't actually do anything with a computer. Jacob was a rare exception. His normal drill was to surf around a bit, check CNN. There was a local classifieds site that sometimes advertised events. They were good to know about.

Today, Jacob did a quick search for 'Safer World Security'. It had a small, simple website. The company seemed to be new with only two permanent employees, Greg and some guy named Jimmy.

Jacob didn't visit any more sites. His mind began to wander and his gaze drilled through the screen. He was trying to develop a plan, but his belly was fuller and more comfortable than it had been in a long time and he found himself nodding off, then catching himself back into wakefulness.

He recognized that he had a high-quality mark on the line. Now he had to figure out how to play him. He briefly considered getting Greg to hire him as a guard. Wouldn't that be a hoot? But no, that wouldn't work. Even if he didn't have to be bonded there would, for sure, be a CRC, a criminal records check, that would set off bells right across Canada. He wasn't a big time bad guy, but he did have a petty record that stretched from Ontario to British Columbia. Nothing heavy enough to justify arrest and transport, but he didn't want his whereabouts widely known and that was one of the very real consequences of a CRC.

So, no security job for Jacob. What else could he do?

The guy was really gullible, that's for sure. Jacob could shear that sheep over and over for years. Like the way he'd just forked over the money for cigarettes. Jacob smoked, but he never bought them. He bummed off other people or stripped down butts from public ashtrays and rerolled the used tobacco. It wasn't that bad, once you got used to the bite. So, thanks to Greg, he had enough money to buy a mickey of vodka. With any luck he would be able to keep it to himself. Maybe chug the whole thing right off the bat and toss the bottle. Yeah, that's the ticket.

Anyway, as far as Greg was concerned, there were all kinds of ways to suck him dry. The trouble was they all took time and Jacob really didn't like Greg. *He's a pompous, do-gooder prick, acting all hoity-toity just because he shelled out for a meal. Bastard. What's it like to live on the street, Jacob? Fuck you, I ain't your pet monkey. You want to know what life on the street is like? Maybe you should find out. And fuck you too about knowing anything about Indians.*

Jacob couldn't come up with any ideas for what to do about Greg. He checked in on the CNN site, but couldn't concentrate. The meal he had shared with Greg now squatted in his stomach like a stone.

What is it about that guy that pisses me off so much?

Jacob alternated between two states. In one, he was filled with despair, unworthiness and guilt, like he should be doing much more with his life and just wasn't bothering. In the other state, which he usually entered when he had some wine or drugs to enjoy, he felt like he had life wired, and all the people running around to their jobs and shopping in stores were just stuck in the biggest sucker trap ever. That's what society was, just a big trap to keep the little rats running on their wheels, throwing money out behind them to benefit the ones in control. What a bunch of suckers! Work their guts out and worry all their lives, never having enough money because they had to have the house and the cars. It's so simple if you let go of ambition and wanting stuff. If you dropped down, all you really needed was a place out of the weather to sleep. There were people who would feed you if you showed up. When it got cold they'd give you clothes and blankets. Hell, in some places people hunted you down on the street to give you stuff. There were always ways of making a little bit of money so you could get a bottle of wine. Staying alive wasn't that hard for the smart ones who had things figured out.

Jacob was too restless to stay in the library. Outside he saw Mealy Pete and Blue Dog sitting at one of the tables in the hallway. Jacob walked over, told Mealy Pete to take a hike and took his place. "What's up guy?"

Blue Dog was a short, stout fellow. Today he was wearing a new, bright red ski jacket. Jacob saw he was wearing the fancy sneakers he'd scored the other day while binning. They had been bright blue high tops when he'd pulled them out of the garbage and found they fit him. Now they were ruined from being soaked in the snow. The Dog's feet must be freezing. He wouldn't give them up, though. He thought they still looked sharp.

Blue dog had a cup of coffee in front of him, so Jacob grabbed it and took a sip. It wasn't that he wanted a drink. He was just signifying the relative position between the two of them.

Blue Dog looked different today. "When did you get the new haircut, man?"

Blue dog was sporting a truly magnificent haircut. His hair had been long, hanging down in two braids. Now it was cut like a samurai warrior. The back and sides were shaved tight to the skin; the hair an top had been left long and braided into a queue that hung down his back. It wasn't a flat braid, either. It was a round one that Jacob had never seen before. The braid was tied off with a bright blue ribbon at the tip.

"My auntie. She got some new clippers, wanted to give me a new do. How did it come out?"

"That cut is bad-ass. All you need now is a sword and a bathrobe."

The haircut *was* pretty cool. Jacob considered making a visit to the Dog's auntie to get one of his own. Nah, that wouldn't work. One way Jacob kept his status was by never imitating anybody else. People imitated him. That kept him high on the totem pole.

Anyway, auntie would have made him pay somehow and he didn't like the haircut that much. It looked good on Blue Dog, though.

Funny thing, the new haircut made the Dog look like a warrior when he was actually one of the kindest hearted people Jacob knew, one of those people who were truly gentle. One night, he and Jacob had been hanging out behind a hotel and some guy came staggering down the alley. He was obviously lost, wearing a very nice overcoat. Jacob decided he wanted the coat, so he rolled the guy: took his coat, wallet and watch. Blue Dog wouldn't do anything to help. When Jacob broke the guy's nose and the blood splashed out, Blue Dog started to cry. What a wuz. If he didn't man up soon he wouldn't survive out here very long.

THREE
The Bomb Drops

Greg was cold. The coat he was wearing wasn't up to the job, but he didn't want to take the time to get a better one out of the truck.

First day on the job, February eighth, Thursday. He had been on duty in front of the hydro offices since eight o'clock. That was what the manager he had spoken to the afternoon before had told him to do. After leaving the Mondo he drove past the Hydro office and decided to introduce himself to the management. He wasn't due to start until tomorrow, but showing up early and seeming eager could earn him some valuable points.

The manager he spoke to was named Gord Sulley. Gord was an affable fellow, and very rah-rah about the new dam. He showed Greg scale models of the dam. It was late in the day so Gord had told him to set up on 100th Avenue the next morning.

It was almost nine now. The sun was just coming up. Traffic was moving pretty well. He was used to Vancouver traffic patterns. The idea of a rush hour seemed to be foreign to Macintosh.

The coat and hat he was wearing would have

been good enough, but for the wind. There was a thirty km/h wind blowing and it cut right through the floater coat and down vest he was wearing.

"What are you doing here?" The woman posing the question was just under six feet tall and looked like she would tip the scale at around 210. She was just wearing a light coat and didn't seem to be bothered by the temperature. Her face was pinched and angry, but for some reason Greg felt that was just the way she viewed the world and she didn't have a particular target.

"I'm Greg from Safer World Security. I'll be providing for your security needs today. This is our first day on the job."

"This job belongs to The Guards. Who brought you in?"

"The contract was signed in Vancouver. I spoke to Mr. Sulley yesterday and he told me to set up here at eight."

"Sulley's an idiot."

"And you are?"

"Shelley Turcott. You're supposed to be in the alley in the back. Nobody is going to storm the front of the building where people can see them. Get around there and watch for people trying to get through the back door."

Greg moved to the alley that ran behind the building. He didn't want to stir up any trouble when he didn't know who was who in the office. Besides, it gave him a chance to bulk out his clothing and put on his heavy down parka. Macintosh residents seemed to be fine with light jackets and scarves, but Greg needed major protection.

At ten-thirty the back door of the office opened and Gord Sulley came out. "Greg, you're here," he said. "I didn't see you out front and thought something was wrong."

"Didn't anybody tell you I was here?"

"Not a word. If you've been back here the whole time, there's no way for anybody to know you're here."

"Ms. Turcott knew I was here. She's the one that chased me around from the front."

"She didn't pass it on to me. She was in charge here for a while until I was sent up to take over. Shelly was none too pleased about that. Now she's keeping secrets, spreading chaos and confusion in an effort to assert some kind of authority."

"She did a good job as far as I'm concerned."

Sulley nodded. "I just came out to get something from my car or I'd still be in the dark. How are you doing out here, anyway?"

Greg laughed. "I'm not as tough as I thought I was. Not doing well with the cold yet."

"Come inside for a couple of minutes, maybe grab a coffee."

"I'll come in for a bit to warm up, but I have lots of coffee with me, thanks."

Sulley brought Greg in and introduced him to the other employees. Shelley Turcott didn't join in the introductions, choosing to stay at her desk and glare instead. Sulley told him to send a text to the lady seated at the desk closest to the backdoor whenever he wanted to warm up a bit. Greg went back out to the alley.

This was actually a better set-up from Greg's point of view. He was closer to his truck and could get his hands on anything he needed.

He was sitting in his truck eating a sandwich at two when a big Hummer with the logo of The Guards rolled down the alley and parked near the office door. The man that emerged from behind the wheel seemed impossibly tall. Greg's grandmother had a saying, "The man could hunt geese with a rake!" and that applied here. The giant had black, shiny hair. A gray goatee framed his mouth. He stared across at Greg while he pulled on a wedge-shaped fur hat, then walked over to the truck.

"Do you always stand watch from inside your truck?" he asked. His voice had a sneer of condescension. Greg held his hand out to shake. The stranger just stared at Greg's proffered hand. "Don't get too comfortable," he said and walked away to knock on the door of the office.

I guess we aren't going to be buddies. Condescending bugger.

Greg made a point of finishing his lunch before resuming his post by the door.

The giant emerged from the office forty minutes later, brushing past Greg without a word of acknowledgement. Just before climbing into his Hummer, he looked at Greg and snapped a quick salute. The expression on his face was a cross between a sneer and a smirk. Greg's stomach lurched and felt empty.

That guy just changed the game somehow. What the hell is going on?

The next hour sped by. Lots of people walked through the alley and he was surprised that many of them stopped to talk. That wouldn't have happened in Vancouver. The people who stopped to chat thought Hydro was being paranoid to hire security for their offices. There weren't going to be any riots or anything like that.

Greg was on the lookout for potential Safer World Security employees. He had set up a deal with the local employment center to fast track training on the promise of a job. At first, there were no prospects.

Then an old guy came by walking a little white dog. He stopped and chatted until the dog barked in shivering protest. When he went on his way, Greg had two potential hires in his notebook. Things were looking good for a first day.

He had just finished another sandwich when his phone went off. "Answer the phone, it's Jimmy! Answer the phone, it's Jimmy," delivered in a loud parrot squawk. Jenna had loaded his phone up with custom ring-tones last year. It still made him smile.

He pulled his phone from his pocket. "Hey Jimmy, what's up?"

"Checking in. How was the first day?"

"Nothing to it. Biggest problem was staying warm. People are friendly. Oh, and I set up the training at the employment center and came up with a couple of potential hires."

Long silence at the other end. Greg thought he heard Jimmy swallow hard a couple of times.

There's bad news in the wind somewhere.

"What's up Jimmy? You don't sound good."

"I'm not, and you won't be either in a minute."

"Just spit it out Jimmy. How bad can it be?"

"You tell me," said Jimmy. He swallowed again, then said "We lost the contract, Greg."

"How could we lose the contract? We just got started."

"Hydro gave the job to the Guards."

Greg climbed into his truck to get some privacy. "They can't do that. We have a signed contract," he said.

"Guards played real hardball. They asserted that their contract was comprehensive, whether every function was specified or not. They undercut our price by twenty-five percent, and will be losing money on it. Finally, they said that their contract was voided if we came on and they'd drop out of the whole thing if they didn't get their way. Hydro caved. End of story."

And that's it. Screwed, blued and tattooed.

"Are you there, Greg?"

"Where else would I be? Do you know how screwed I am? I'm stuck up here in the snow. I mean, this place is north of the wall. Almost expect to run into a White Walker. I deferred my child support and my mortgage to come up here, borrowed against my house. Things couldn't get much worse. Are you going to get me out of here?"

"Nothing's changed here, Greg. There's no money until the end of the month."

Both were silent for a while. Jimmy was waiting for Greg to speak and vice-versa. The silence stretched out. Finally, Greg said, "Jimmy, I don't know if we come back from this. I know it's not your fault, but it feels like it is. Next job you come up with better be written in blood and sealed in stone. Otherwise get yourself another site tamer."

Silence from the other end.

"Did you hear me clear, Jimmy?"

"Yeah, Greg, I got it."

"Alright. I have to find some way to dig myself out of this hole. Don't call me unless you come up with a solution. You are so on my shit list. I'll probably forgive you by the time I get back to town, but for now I only want to hear good news from you, okay?"

"Yeah. Greg, I'm really sorry. If there was any—"

Greg disconnected and didn't hear what else Jimmy had to say.

After talking to Jimmy, Greg went back to his post by the door. He had a half-hour left in his first, and last, day on the job. Night was coming and it was already darkening in the alley.

One thing I won't do is go into the office and beg. I think I'd puke if I had to watch Shelley Turcott gloat, or listen to Sulley explain that he didn't really have any choice. Just let this bloody day be over.

Greg was as punctual with his stop time as he had been in the morning. It was precisely five when he climbed into his truck and drove South on 100th street. His plan was to drive until he ran out of road and hope it was a good place to come up with some out-of-the-box thinking.

FOUR
The Lookout

It didn't take long to run out of road. Greg pulled his pickup to a stop in a parking lot overlooking a canyon. It was a small lot and had a chain link fence between the pavement and the drop off. The nose of the truck just touched the big concrete no-go that saved vehicles from a quick plunge into the canyon. The Peace River rolled along in the canyon bottom, the water foamy and brown.

There was some daylight left in this dark, cloudy day. Snow was falling and a wind was whipping it sideways. Greg couldn't see much beyond his headlights, so he turned them off. The whole reason for coming down here was to check out the scenery and think about what he could do next.

Let's face it, boys and girls, he was in a terrible spot. Everything he'd done and planned on was dependent on running the security job on the new dam. That was now gone. That meant he had three thousand dollars and a truck. Against that, he had negotiated a skip on his mortgage payment and on the child support he owed Jenna. Without that job he could lose his house and the respect of the woman he couldn't seem to get along with but still loved. Of course, there was also the matter of his respect for himself, but that didn't seem important in the grand scheme of things.

The air in the cab suddenly smelled toxic to him, the confined space closing in. He got out of the truck, put on the parka he kept behind the seat and grabbed the big nine cell flashlight that was clipped to the dash. A patch of brush growing outside the fence looked like a good place to meditate.

He found a nice little shelter under a bush, crawled in and settled down, cross-legged. The wind was at his back, blowing the snow directly away from him. The parka would have been too much of a good thing if he were moving around, but it kept him toasty and comfortable now. It was soon so dark that he couldn't see anything in front of him and he began to drift in a near-complete trance of sensory deprivation. Time's passage became imperceptible. At some point, day punched it's time card and night took over, but it was already so black that Greg wasn't aware of the transformation.

He had intended to meditate on some way out of the mess that he was in. Instead, he found himself in a sort of dream state and the visions that came to him were all pleasant. The first time he realized he loved Jenna and that there was at least a chance that she loved him back. Finding the house and getting approved for a mortgage. Playing with his dog, Ben, in the park on a foggy morning.

The chain of pleasant memories left him with a feeling of hope and security. Hell, he'd been in tough spots before. This time he was actually better off. At least this time he had his truck and the three thousand dollars hidden in the safe that was built onto the rear axle. Soon the daydreams and visions became real dreams and he drifted off with a smile on his face.

Something woke him. He wasn't sure what. Sitting on the ground had left him stiff. That was just as well. His inability to move gave him time to realize where he was. If he had simply jumped up and started to move he might have stepped off into emptiness and wound up at the bottom of the canyon.

He got his legs straightened out in front of him and started jiggling them to get the blood moving again, groping for the big flashlight. Noise was coming down from the parking lot, laughing and banging.

He made it to his feet, flicked on the light and searched for the trail he had come down. His tracks were barely visible, winding their way between the bushes. It didn't take long to make it back up to the parking lot.

The sight that met his eyes was exactly what he'd feared. A bunch of young rowdies had shown up and they were going through his truck. One was in the box, another was in the cab, visible in the dome light. A couple of others were staggering around outside. They seemed to be pretty blitzed, having a tough time standing up straight, but they were still in control enough to start trashing the truck with random sticks. One guy worked on smashing the passenger side mirror while another positioned himself to start in on the windshield.

Greg stepped into the parking lot and blasted them with the big flashlight, hoping to blind them. "Fun's over, guys. Get back in your car and beat it so I don't have to shoot someone."

Maybe they'd believe he had a gun. If they didn't, he could be in serious trouble. With at least four opponents against him it was just a matter of time before they pulled him down, no matter how stoned they were.

The guy in the cab climbed down and swaggered over to Greg. He seemed to be the leader and he wasn't staggering. "You don't got a gun, and get that light out of my face, honky," he said.

Greg took a step back. Out of the corner of his eye he saw an old black Honda Civic parked beyond his truck. The doors of the Honda opened and a couple more young guys climbed out. Bad situation. They moved slowly to surround him. He backed away. Something hit the side of his head with a crack. Stars. Pain. Down he went.

***

Somebody was shaking his shoulder. "Greg. Wake up man, wake up!"

Consciousness returned, but it was a mixed blessing. He rolled over, got to all fours and vomited. God that hurt. Somebody had put the boot in a couple of times. He spat blood, then just sat there in the snow looking around. Nothing made sense yet.

What happened?

Oh yeah. The truck.

He looked around but the parking lot was empty. Who'd been shaking him?

Now he remembered and recognized the voice. Jacob. Jacob was lying in the snow. Greg crawled over and pulled him to a sitting position. Jacob's left eye was puffed shut, his nose was pushed sideways and there was a knife wound on his right cheekbone. "What are you doing here, Jacob?"

"I was with those guys who worked you over and took your truck. I tried to stop them when they started in on the truck. They probably would have just broke your mirrors, but you didn't lock it, man. I did what I could, but they didn't want anybody to spoil their party."

Greg wasn't sure how this made sense, but his head was only firing on a couple of cylinders. Mostly he just stared off into the darkness and ached.

At some point, he and Jacob managed to get to their feet and started back to town. Greg hoped somebody with a car would give them a lift, but there wasn't much traffic and anybody who slowed down to get a look at them sped off in a hurry.

It seemed to take forever, but they eventually made it to the Blueberry Motel. The muggers had taken his key, so he had to get another from the office. The manager offered to call the RCMP, but Greg said he would do it himself after he cleaned up.

When they got into the room everything was still there. Surprise. Either the boys hadn't thought to steal his gear from the room or they didn't want to show themselves in the light and risk being recognized. His first order of business would be to transfer to a different room.

By the time they had gotten cleaned up, Greg was thinking more clearly. He couldn't do anything about Jacob's nose, but he was able to butterfly the knife cut on his cheek.

FIVE
Taking Stock

Settled into the new room, Greg got down to business.

"All right, Jacob, talk. How did you happen to be down at the lookout when I got the shit kicked out of me?"

"Got anything to drink, man? My face feels like it got stuck in a blender."

"Let's talk first and maybe drink later. What were you doing with those guys? Who were they?"

Jacob mumbled something under his breath.

Greg waited, watching the wheels turn slowly in Jacob's head.

"I got my bell rung pretty good, Greg. Give me a second to get my thoughts together."

Jacob wrinkled his forehead and his lips moved a bit as he put a story together. "Okay," he said at last. "Here's what I remember. My cousin and I were out picking cans and he said a bunch of guys was in from the reserve and just got their gas cheques so they would be partying pretty good. We went out looking for them. All we knew was they had this old Honda; wasn't hard to find them. They were parked at Humpty's." He stopped and flexed his jaw experimentally. "If you aren't going to give me a drink, at least give me a smoke. I'm all out."

Greg passed a pack of Camels and a lighter over, but didn't say a word. Jacob lit up and contorted his face. "How can you smoke these things? I for sure believe they came from a camel."

"In future I'll try to keep a better brand of smokes for you to bum. Keep talking."

"Story's pretty much what you'd expect. They had a gallon of Logana, a half-gallon of Applejack and a lid of dope. I managed to weasel my way in with my smile. They didn't like my cousin, though; chased him off."

Long drag on the cigarette. He was trying to give the impression of remembering through a fog, but Greg had the feeling that he was making up the story as he went along.

"We were getting too rowdy and the guy from PetroCan came out, said we could leave or he'd call the cops. No, he said he'd called the cops and we better go before they showed up. That was probably bullshit, but we all piled into the car and took off."

He stubbed out the smoke and shook another out of the pack without asking. Greg tossed the lighter over when Jacob raised the eyebrow that still worked.

"And that's pretty much it. They didn't know any good place to party. I suggested the lookout. Off we went. You know the rest."

"You could have done something when they started beating on my truck."

Jacob look down at the floor and muttered something. When he looked up there were tears in his eyes. "You don't get it, man. You don't know what it's like. They had all this wine and they were sharing. I'm trying to get better man, but the pull was just too strong. I didn't even recognize the truck, just waiting for the Applejack to come my way again.

"First I knew it was you was when you showed up, waving that big Maglite around and threatening to shoot somebody. Never do that if you can't back it up. It's like blood in the water to guys like that.

"Anyway, I tried to cool things down, especially after you hit the ground. You should thank me; I wound up taking the rest of your beating. You'd be dead now if it wasn't for me."

Greg blew up. "Thanks very much. I lost everything. Truck, wallet, ID, phone."

"Lucky they didn't take your coat. That's a nice warm parka. What are you going to do now?"

God only knows. I'm screwed if I can't find that truck. Nobody can know how important it is.

"I'll call the cops and get them started tracking my stuff down. Maybe you can give some kind of description that will help them catch these guys."

"Ain't happening, man. I'm taking off and if they want any statement from me they'll have to arrest me first." Jacob was up and pulling on his coat as he headed for the door. Greg managed to get there first, and held out his hand. "Leave the smokes and lighter." Jacob handed them over. Greg stepped aside.

"You don't have to mention my name at all," Jacob said. "I don't know those guys and everything would have happened the same if I wasn't there, 'cept my nose would still work and I wouldn't have this cut on my face. Just leave me out of it, Greg, please."

Greg watched Jacob go out the door. A puff of cold wind and snowflakes had blown inside, dusting the floor mat. Something about the snow on the mat made Greg feel guilty. He pulled the door open and stepped outside. Jacob had almost reached the highway. Greg called him and he came back.

"What's up?" asked Jacob.

"Where are you sleeping tonight?"

Jacob pulled his toque off and banged it against his leg to dislodge the snow. "Probably behind the old hospital. There are a couple of holes there out of the wind. It's not bad."

"If you don't have a curfew, why don't you come in and help me tame the bottle of spiced rum in my suitcase?"

"I thought you didn't trust me."

Greg shook his head. "It's the damnedest thing. After the day I've had, I have every intention of getting hammered. For some reason, I'd rather have company than sit in front of the TV drinking like a lush. What do you say?"

"I don't know, man. Is it a full bottle? I don't wanna waste my time with a mickey."

Greg held his hand up in an affirming gesture. "Virgin 40 pounder. Worth your while."

"Well, hell, bring it on then," said Jacob. He stepped back inside, hung his coat on the rack and pulled off his boots. "Don't bother with the TV," he said. "Picture's all grainy when it snows this hard."

There was only one chair in the room, so they both sat on the floor. Greg broke the seal and poured rum into a couple of coffee cups. The rum was smooth as silk. "You'd better not ask for mixer, Jacob, or you're out the door."

"Nah man, don't wanna spoil this. It's like nectar." With the curtains open, they watched the snow falling outside.

Greg saw Jacob's cup was empty, so reached out with the bottle for a top-up and poured himself another. He felt the rum starting to work its magic, pushing the troubles of the day away until tomorrow. "What do you want out of life, Jacob?" he asked.

"Getting' kind 'a personal there," said Jacob. "I just take life day by day and try not to screw up too bad."

"You must want something. Everybody has a goal in life."

Jacob's face flushed and his eyes acquired a sudden hardness. "Like I said, that's personal. Tell you what. Throw your big plan out where I can make fun of it. Show me yours and I'll show you mine."

Why is he so upset? Didn't we already do our fighting for the evening?

Greg said, "Sure, I'll tell you mine. No big deal. All I want is to find a good job, make lots of money so I can get my wife and daughter back." He saw a look of amazement come across Jacob's face.

Jacob started to laugh. "Hell, man, that ain't a goal, it's a life sentence. A goal has to be something in the future. You're talking about going back and fixing the past. Can't be done. All that goal does is blind you to the future."

Greg felt blood start to pound in his temples. The hair on the back of his neck was standing up. He took a sip of rum to calm down. "All right. If mine's so goddamned funny, let's hear yours."

Jacob shook his head. "We both got impossible goals, man. We're both screwed."

"I still want to hear it, Jacob. Fess up."

For a moment Greg thought he saw fear on Jacob's face, which suddenly appeared younger and surprisingly vulnerable. After a long silence, he murmured, "I'd like to see my little cousin again."

"I didn't know you had a cousin."

Jacob's expression changed again, this time becoming defiant and frightened at the same time. "Of course you don't know. And she isn't really my cousin. I just call her that."

It looked to Greg like Jacob had eaten too much and was on the verge of bringing it up. "What was her name?"

"Miigwan." Jacob fell silent again.

After a couple of minutes with no further words Greg said, "It sounds like there's a story there that you want to tell. If you want to talk, I'm all ears. Or we can just drink, up to you."

Jacob held out his cup, took a sip of the fresh rum. "I told you I was adopted, right?"

Greg nodded, vaguely remembering yesterday's conversation.

"When I graduated from high school I decided to find my roots. I figured out where I had come from and went back to the reservation. Worst mistake I ever made." He paused for a longer sip. Jacob's words were starting to slur. He seemed to be staring back through time. "The only good thing about that trip was meeting Miigwan. She was ten years old, happiest, kindest little girl I ever met. I claimed her for my cousin cuz I loved her so much."

"Hell, Jacob, go back and visit her. Hitch if you have to. It seems to be important."

"Can't man. I fucked it all up. I can never go back there. Past is the past. That's why I'm so hard on you. I know the past is set in stone."

Greg's lips felt fat and strange to him, the rum coming on hard now. "I'm sure we could find some way to get you back home. When I get back on my feet I'd be glad to buy you a ticket."

"Just drop it, man." Jacob's tone was very quiet and completely serious. "I showed you my ass. Leave it at that. Let's see how far we get with that bottle before we fall asleep or puke."

SIX
Busted

Greg's eyes opened and it was morning, late actually but it was still dark out. He found that he was lying on the bedcovers but had no recollection of lying down. He swung his feet onto the floor and sat on the edge of the bed, assessing how he felt. Still sore. After a beating like that he would probably be sore for a week. At least there were no cuts, no broken bones.

Jacob had departed during the night. Greg started to take an inventory of his belongings, then changed his mind. Any petty theft Jacob might have committed seemed minor in the big scheme of things.

The cup of complementary instant coffee tasted like floor sweepings. Time to find a place for breakfast.

When he opened the door he found two guys waiting outside. One of them seemed as wide as he was tall, about three hundred pounds, blue parka, shaved head and red toque. His buddy was about six feet but slender, almost skinny. He was wearing an army great coat and a peaked cap. The big guy had his hand raised as if he had been about to knock on the door. "You Greg?"

"Who's asking?"

"We have a couple of things to discuss with you. Can we come inside?"

Greg wasn't feeling particularly co-operative or social this morning. "I'm heading out for breakfast."

"We'll tag along then. Closest place is the Silver Creek Cookhouse. Let's go there. Jump in the van."

Greg didn't want company and it must have shown on his face.

"Sorry to horn in on your breakfast, but we have something to discuss with you. If it makes it easier, we'll even pay for your breakfast. I know the cook. She'll take good care of us."

The words were an offer but the tone a command. Greg couldn't muster the energy to argue. He climbed into the van and they headed off.

They found an empty booth in the Silver Creek, away from the door. The big guy sat across from Greg. His partner sat beside Greg, blocking any exit.

"I'm Franklin," the big man said. "My partner is Felix. Whenever we're together people call us F-squared."

Introductions but no handshake. Maintaining dominance.

"So, you know me. What's up?"

"That's a pretty nice shiner, and there's dried blood in your hair. Have you been messing with the bad kids, Mister Security Guard?"

"Got in a scuffle last night."

"What's the other guy look like?"

"It was *guys* and I'm sure they look better than me."

The waitress brought the first round of coffee, pulled out her pad and waited for their orders. F-squared told her they would just have the coffee.

When Greg made a grunt of protest, she turned

her attention toward him. He ordered ham, pancakes, eggs and toast. Spending other people's money was easy.

He expected F-squared to get down to business now. Instead they went through a ritual of small talk. Differences in the weather between here and the coast, and the like. It turned out that the coast was wet and the north was cold. Who knew? The simple talk continued until the food arrived.

Franklin watched him butter and syrup his pancakes. Just as Greg cut into them Franklin asked, "So what happened last night?"

"I got into a fight at the lookout. Bunch of punks robbed me."

Franklin squinted at him. Didn't say anything for a moment. Greg managed to get a fork full of pancake into his mouth. "I didn't see a vehicle in front of your motel room," Franklin observed.

"Like I said. They robbed me. Took my phone , wallet and the truck. Left my coat and boots, though. That's a bonus."

F-squared exchanged glances. Greg saw Felix nod to Franklin. Maybe the big guy wasn't the one in charge.

Franklin looked out the window. There seemed to be something fascinating going on at the gas bar across the road. He finally turned back and looked serious. "So, what happened to the package?"

Greg's stomach clenched and he started to sweat a bit. Somehow he knew just where this was going. "What package?"

"You had a small package in your truck. It was coming to us. Where is it?"

Damn you Jimmy. What did you set me up for?

"That's news to me. I loaded the truck myself and I didn't see anything I didn't recognize."

"Cute. It was in the door on the passenger's side. Least it was supposed to be."

"Well, I didn't know about it. I don't know you two. Why should I believe you?"

"Why don't you give ol' Jimmy a call? Oh, right. No phone. Breakfast is over. Let's go."

Franklin and Felix stood up and waited for him. When he got up, Felix held his arm and they lock-stepped out the door. Franklin didn't pay, and the waitress just waved goodbye.

The van was parked behind the cafe. Felix pushed Greg up against it. Franklin drove his big fist into Greg's stomach. Greg bent over, retching. Franklin pulled him upright, hit him again in the same spot, then held him pressed against the van.

Greg saw the big hand coming towards him again, tried to flinch away, but Franklin just patted him on the shoulder. "Hurts like a sonofabitch, doesn't it? I bet that's right where they put the boots to you. Have I got your attention now?"

Nod from Greg. Franklin was holding him up against the van. Felix opened the passenger door and Franklin deposited Greg in the shotgun seat.

Greg's belly really hurt. He tasted bile and now had a sudden headache.

They just sat for a few minutes, then Franklin started the truck and drove back to the Motel.

"Can you walk?"

"I think so."

"Good. I wouldn't want to take you to the hospital. Get yourself some painkillers. You're going to need them for the next couple of days."

"Why do you care?"

Franklin shook his head. "Don't be that way, Greg. We're buddies now. Well, not quite, but you're working for me now. Your mission in life for the foreseeable future is tracking down my package, or raising twenty-thousand dollars."

"How in the hell do you expect me to do that? I know nothing about this place. I don't know the players. I'm a complete alien."

Franklin grinned. "Educate yourself and do it fast. One of the reasons I'm so successful is that I don't micromanage. I hand out the tasks. How they get done is up to the people I give them to. You just got yours."

This is what it feels like when your best friend fucks you over.

Franklin opened the center console and took a phone out. He passed it to Greg. It was an old iPhone 5. A charger followed. "The phone's all paid up. You have unlimited everything. I'm on speed dial. I expect a report every day. If two days go by and I don't hear from you that little beauty will ring and you'd better take the call."

"Is this where the threat comes? You'll kill me if I don't?"

"Nope. You go along. You can't help yourself. You'll want to know what happened. Now you know there's more going on than you thought, you'll start to dig. We have mutual interests. We're more partners than anything, for now at least. So we'll help each other.

"How are you helping me?"

"I told you the truth. I gave you the phone. That's all you need."

Greg realized he was being dismissed. Standing in the lot, he watched the van pull away.

He went inside and sat at his desk; turned on the computer out of habit.

The iPhone chimed. He picked it up and answered. "What did you forget, Franklin?"

"Wrong F. This is Felix. We got the motel to store your stuff, but you have to go somewhere else. Don't ask where. Figure it out. As far as we're concerned there are no wrong answers. Just put one foot in front of the other. You'll get there in the end."

"Is this your version of a pep talk?"

"I guess it is. Get busy. Like Franklin said, educate yourself."

SEVEN
Entering the Shelter

After making his police report about the truck, which was a brief, perfunctory event, Greg saw no reason to put off the inevitable.

He got to the shelter about ten in the morning. The person who processed his entry was Child of God Brown. Child of God sounded like some affected name, but it was the actual name his parents had given him in Ethiopia where he was born.

Child of God was not a member of the Salvation Army, though he did attend church there. Ethiopia is one of the oldest Christian countries in the world, going back to 333 A.D. and Child of God was actually a member of the Ethiopian Orthodox Church.

Child of God liked his job a lot. He enjoyed dealing with people in dire straits. He enjoyed it because it made him feel superior. He never let any trace of his feelings show, of course, but he felt himself to be godly and superior. The fact his job was to provide shelter and food to people less fortunate than himself was simply proof of his stature. He liked dealing with the natives, but coming across a white man who was down on his luck made him feel especially elevated. Greg's arrival and request for shelter made his day. Child of God was very sympathetic and coaxed every detail of Greg's predicament out of him. He made the appropriate noises at all the right times in the story. In the end, he asked Greg if he should call the Captain to provide spiritual guidance. Greg said he would consider it, but he wanted to get settled in first.

Child of God finished Greg's paperwork, then led him through the big double doors to the back of the building. The doors were always locked and could only be opened by employees from their offices or by swipe cards at the door. He handed Greg off to a heavy-set guy, around six feet tall. This guy's head was shaved and he had a fleur-de-lis neck tattoo. This was Alfred, the attendant. He had been a criminal most of his life. When he was released from prison the last time, a Captain in the Salvation Army had taken him on as a shelter attendant. The Captain had wisely realized that riding herd on a bunch of street people required somebody with the same instincts they had, the same way of looking at life. Alfred kept order because he was tough enough that nobody wanted to mess with him. He was also able to see through most of the excuses and outright lies that came his way.

The actual shelter was built around a large central open space. This was the common area where clients could watch TV or play games. On the west side was a large room with a fridge, sinks, and a couple of industrial washing machines.

The sleeping area was a series of small rooms arranged around the outside of the common space. The little rooms each contained a bunkbed made of two by fours. Each bunk had a pillow and a hard rubber mattress. Alfred gave Greg a pillowcase, two sheets and a thin blanket. The room he was assigned wasn't in use, so Greg had his choice of bunks. For now he chose the lower.

Alfred also gave Greg a key to a locker. The

locker was small, but large enough to hold clothing and a few casual items. "If you're smart you'll keep this locked at all times. Any time you leave the shelter you have to turn in your key to the attendant in charge. We can search the locker at any time. If we find any contraband you go to the front."

Greg had presumed the time he spent with Child of God in the front office was all the processing that was needed. Not so. Alfred called him into the small office in the front and announced that they had to come up with a treatment plan.

A treatment plan?

Sure enough, Alfred had a long form full of questions about substance abuse, work history, criminal history. He had trouble believing that Greg didn't have any major substance abuse issues. Greg was getting the feeling he was the square peg in the round hole once again.

Alfred eventually came up with a plan that Greg would visit the Captain for counseling. Next he would find employment, hopefully by the end of the week. Once he had employment, he could start the process of finding a place to live.

None of this plan seemed to fit Greg at all. In truth, he didn't want to work any program. All he wanted was to find some way to beat feet South as soon as humanly possible and trade the snow for nice soft rain that didn't need to be shoveled. Still, he signed the plan because it was obvious it was the only way this was going to work. He certainly didn't want to be black listed as uncooperative.

After Greg signed the plan, Alfred gave him a list of rules to be followed in the shelter.

The maximum length of stay was six weeks in any twelve month period.

Bedtime was eleven PM. Lights out; no

exceptions.

Wake up was at seven. This was easily accomplished. All the attendant had to do was turn on the bright overhead lights at seven and everyone would be roused from their slumber.

From seven till nine, wash up and breakfast on whatever was laid out for them. No raiding the fridge.

Hit the streets at nine AM and stay away until three. Lunch was provided in the front and the common area was open during the day , but no access to the shelter in back until three.

Supper was at six. If you were going to be late you had to tell the attendant in advance and they would keep a supper for you.

All residents had to be back in the shelter by eight PM unless special arrangements were made.

Any failure to follow these rules would result in the resident being 'sent to the front'. This didn't sound like much of a punishment. Then he learned what that really meant. Every night at nine, the common area in the front of the building had folding cots set up. Anybody could come in off the street and claim a cot before eleven PM. Having a cot in the front gave you a place to lie down. That's all. There wasn't much protection and the cots in the front are where the addicts, drunks and permanently bewildered spent the nights. There were often fights, crying, people talking to themselves. There was an attendant, but he didn't interfere with what went on unless it went right off the charts. Understandable. They didn't get paid enough to risk life and limb going up against a violent addict.

Now that the treatment plan had been agreed on and the rules explained, Alfred went back to work. He had to do several loads of laundry. He told Greg to make up his bed and then go out front if he wanted lunch. No matter what he wanted to do, as soon as the bed was made Greg had to leave the shelter and not come back until after three.

After making his bed, Greg went out the back door of the shelter. It was the back door of the building but the main entrance for the shelter. A couple of video cameras covered every angle of the entrance area. The snow was dirty and littered with dead cigarette butts. Since this was obviously the smoking area, Greg pulled out his smokes and burned one. He had just got his smoke going when the door opened behind him. Alfred came out, pulling on a sweater. "Hi Greg. I saw you lighting up on the video. Let me have a butt?"

This was Greg's initiation into the etiquette of smoking. Never expose cigarettes unless you were prepared to share. It turned out other residents weren't the only ones to watch out for. Almost all the staff smoked and they were just as reluctant as the clients to burn their own. A couple of the staff were famous for mooching smokes with their own cigarette packages plainly visible in their shirt pockets. Greg decided it had something to do with status. Extorted smokes were like a low-key tax owed by the residents to the staff. Greg wondered what non-smokers had to cough up.

It was actually a nice experience, hanging with Alfred behind the shelter. Now that the treatment plan was signed, Alfred was a different guy, as if he had left his official persona at his desk. Now he was free to chat, tell jokes, tease and generally just be a fun guy. Greg soon found himself relaxing.

When they tossed their butts, Alfred went back inside. Greg tried to follow but Alfred reminded him that he couldn't go back in until after three. He did want lunch, so he walked halfway around the block to reenter through the front. Lunch tables were set up and already the seats were mostly taken. Lunch wouldn't be served for another twenty minutes but it looked like it was going to be standing room only.

Greg found a seat in the corner where he could watch the interactions of the clients. He quickly realized not all the people waiting to be fed were hardcore street people. Many were just ordinary people taking advantage of a free meal. Nobody was dressed for the office, but they were obviously working class and could have afforded to eat at MacDonald's or some other fast food place.

The Captain walked to the front of the room to say grace, and everybody lined up at the pass-through to get their soup and sandwich. The soup turned out to be some kind of hamburger gumbo with lots of fresh vegetables. It was obviously homemade, the recipe entirely controlled by what foods were contributed. Most restaurants in town put their good leftover food to one side for the Sally-Ann instead of tossing it. Some even donated individually wrapped portions that went to feed the people in the shelter.

It was interesting to observe the various types of interactions. Some people just kept themselves to themselves and ate in silence with their heads down. There were a couple of groups that were loud and boisterous and were obviously used to hanging out together. Greg was one of those who just wanted to keep to himself. He caught sight of Jacob across the room, but neither of them made the effort to say hello. It looked like Jacob had found someone to do a better patch up job on his face. His nose seemed straighter and Greg's butterfly band aids had been replaced by three neat black stitches across Jacob's cheekbone.

Greg went back for a second helping of soup. When he'd eaten that, he pulled his coat on and walked outside. He wasn't feeling sociable. Those people weren't the kind he was comfortable with. He realized he would have to stop looking down on them. Like it or not, he was one of them now, and he needed to get used to it.

He had no place to go, so he wandered down 100th Avenue toward the intersection with 100th street. Every shop window he passed got an inspection because he was just killing time.

That thought pulled him up short. Killing time? This wasn't his style. He was a striver and a fighter. He always found some way to win. At least, he always had. This situation was as low as he'd ever been and he couldn't see any way out. What's more, even the effort of trying to find a solution didn't seem worthwhile. If there's no way out anyway, why knock himself out?

He made it down to the 100 Ave. and 100 St. intersection and ran out of gas. He found himself standing on the corner watching the vehicles churning through the snow and just stopped thinking entirely. He did have the presence of mind to stand back from the curb far enough the passing traffic didn't splash him, but that was the extent of his competency.

He'd been standing there for some time when someone tapped him on the shoulder. "What are you doing, man?"

Greg recognized Jacob's voice and came back to himself. "Just standing here staring, Jacob. Hanging out."

"You're lucky it stopped snowing, or you'd be a popsicle. Come on over to the library and get warm."

Greg allowed Jacob to lead him across the street into the warmth and soon found himself sitting at a table against the wall with Jacob seated opposite him. Jacob said, "We aren't supposed to sit here without buying. Want a coffee or something?"

Greg rummaged through his pockets and came up with four loonies. He pushed them across the table without a word and stared off into space.

How can I find the truck? It's my only way out.

When Jacob returned, he was carrying a couple of coffees and a bag. The bag contained two Cinnamon buns. "You got all that for four bucks?"

"Buns are stale, so two for a buck. Lady said they were a day old, but I figure more like three. They aren't hard enough to break your teeth, so dig in."

"How can you eat when you just had lunch?"

"Never pass up food, man. There's always a spot down in your guts where you can stick it. If you don't want yours, give it to me."

They sat in silence, breaking off hard pieces of bun. Finally Jacob said, "I figured it out, man. You're in shock. You never believed anything like this could ever happen to you. Now it has and you're having an ... an *ex* something."

"Existential crisis. That's it. A refusal to accept reality when it's staring me in the face. "

"You always thought you were too good for this life. Now suddenly you're just like me. 'Cept you aren't just like me. I know my way around and you just fell off the turnip truck."

"So, are you going to instruct me and prove your superiority or just gloat?"

"I haven't decided yet. The gloating feels pretty good."

"What do you do when you feel lonely, confused and hopeless, Jacob?"

"Same thing I do when I find twenty bucks on the street and I'm happy—I drink."

"Well, hell. Let's get to it. I have some money. Let's get some wine or something, whatever it is you drink."

Jacob stared back at him. "You can't do that, man. You just checked in to the Sally. You show up for supper drunk and they'll kick your ass out in the snow. Didn't Alfred give the rules to you? Show up loaded and you'll wind up in front. Sure you can have a couple of drinks but you can't get loaded."

"My uncle Charlie always said half-drunk is wasted money."

"He was right, but, if you want to keep your warm place to sleep for the next month and a half, you gotta keep your nose clean. Got it?"

"Yes Obi-wan." The truth was, Greg found the fact he would not be allowed to drink quite dismaying. "What am I going to do, Jacob?"

"How should I know? And why are you asking me? An hour ago you wouldn't even say hello."

"You weren't exactly burning across the floor to shake my hand either. My life turned to crap right around the time I met you. It feels like the two are connected."

"My science teacher in high school used to say something about not confusing coincidence with causality. That's what you're doing. How could meeting me have anything to do with you losing your contract?"

"I guess it couldn't. Sorry Jacob, I'm not thinking straight."

"Kay, you want instruction? Let's go. One crash apprenticeship in how to get by in Macintosh coming up."

For the next few hours Greg tried to be a sponge. Jacob walked him around town, pointing out features of different places they passed. He seemed to have a file on each place and that file had information about who worked there, what their attitudes were. He listed which businesses had customer appreciation events where food was available. The network of back-alleys in town was also a subject for instruction. Which ones were plowed in winter. Which ones had bushes a guy could make a nest in if he wanted to sleep out in the summer. He also pointed out where the prime dumpsters were and explained the convention of leaving the lid open after rummaging through one, so other people would know it was already picked over. Greg had always thought life on the street was aimless and simple. Now it seemed to be complicated and subject to calculation at every turn.

At three o'clock, they wound up at the shelter again with a couple of hours to kill until supper. Jacob went to his bunk to lie down; Greg dug around in the library for something to read. He came up with a copy of “I am Legend” and settled in for a good time with Neville hunting down vampires.

Enjoying a simple story was Greg’s way of turning off his conscious mind and letting his subconscious organize what he had learned. Trying to make deliberate sense of everything just made his head hurt.

Supper turned out to be fish and chips. The portions were big enough for Greg but he could see that some of the heavier fellows would feel deprived. Maybe they could market this experience for weight loss.

"I lost fifteen pounds on the new shelter diet and you can too!"

The time after supper was social time. A lot of the residents knew each other and clustered together. Greg found a chess set, put the pieces on the board and waited for an opponent to appear. It was one of the ways he had of creating acquaintances in these kind of situations. He had used the same trick in logging camps and other places where he didn't know anyone.

There were no takers for a while, then a short fellow with an energetic manner and a gift for the gab sat down opposite him. The new opponent turned out to be a speed chess wizard and by the time they had played three games Greg's ass was sore from being kicked so hard. His opponent was named Lincoln. He had been a lieutenant in the army. Now he was hoping to make his fortune in the oil patch. If there was any money to be made hustling chess he could do well for himself, Greg thought.

Three games was more than enough. They put the board away and spent the rest of the time until lights out talking politics.

At eleven everybody who smoked grabbed a last butt out back then climbed into their bunks. It didn't take long for the snoring to start. After thirty minutes it seemed like all fifteen guys were sawing wood, sometimes in harmony, sometimes in conflict. The sheer volume of the snoring was so much that Greg tossed and turned until three in the morning. He decided to try chatting up the night attendant. He had seen her when she came on shift after supper, but didn't know her name. It turned out to be Belinda. Greg asked if he could go out back for a smoke. This turned out to be against the rules, but like everything else, there were the rules and then there was actual practice. Greg offered to share smokes but Belinda turned out to be free of the filthy habit. After a few more minutes of conversation, she announced she would step out for a breath of fresh air. Greg could join her if he wanted to. She could use the company. They stood around outside in the chill talking long enough for Greg to consume a couple of cigarettes before going back inside. He was finally able to fall asleep despite the noise of the snoring.

EIGHT
The Beating of Blue Dog

It was suppertime, and Greg's second day in the shelter. Everybody had gotten their supper and settled into a spot on one of the long wooden tables. Grace had been said. Some guys hadn't waited for grace, their jaws already working, their forks scooping food into their mouths like draglines.

Jacob stood up and rang his fork against his cup to get the groups attention. "Hold it, guys; got somethin' to tell you."

Almost everybody put their forks down and listened. Only the dragline boys didn't pay attention.

"Blue Dog got beat up last night. He was sleeping behind the old hospital. A couple guys pulled him out of his hole and put the boots to him. Broke his arm. Broke his jaw. Stove in a couple ribs. He said it was a couple 'a white guys. They weren't after his wine or dope, didn't even look at his stuff. They just wanted to thump someone for shits and giggles.

"Be on the lookout for those white boys. Prolly we don't find 'em, but town ain't that big. You find 'em, you let me know. l tune 'em good. Even if I have to go back to jail, be worth it.

"Blue Dog's everybody's friend and he couldn'a done anything to bring this down on him. These just mean buggers. Find 'em for me. I take care of business."

Jacob sat down and the guys set about getting outside of their suppers. Greg chewed slowly and watched Jacob. This was the first time he had seen Jacob acting like a leader. He'd never heard Jacob talk like this, either. His voice was low and guttural and his way of speaking was unlike anything Greg had ever heard. It was like Jacob had never been to school, as if he had just grown up on the street like a weed erupting out of a crack in the pavement, refusing to die.

Greg finished his fried chicken, decided against the dessert of Jell-O or last week's donuts, and went out the back door to smoke. Nobody else was out there as he pulled the pack of camels out of his pocket. The door swung open just as he was lighting up and Jacob joined him.

"You still smoking those damned things?" he asked. Can't 'cha at least get the ones with filters?"

"Lucky for me you don't like my cigarettes, isn't it?"

"I really don't, man. I don't know what they smell like. Burning camel hair is the most polite thing I can say. Give me a couple anyway. I'm feeling self-destructive."

Greg passed over the pack and Jacob helped himself. "You talk different to me than you do to everybody else," said Greg.

"Yeah man, there's different idioms. I talk whichever way is going to make the person I'm talking to comfortable."

"Which one's real?"

"Damned if I know. I don't think the question really makes sense. The way you talk doesn't define who you are."

"Didn't you see My Fair Lady?"

"That was musical comedy man; doesn't have anything to do with life down here."

The snow was falling pretty hard. The security cameras stared down at them from the wall and the lamp standard. It was one of those nights that should have been cold but the snow seemed to warm things up.

"We might find the guys that cleaned Blue Dog's clock," Jacob said. "There's a chance, and I meant what I said in there. What will you do if we find them?"

"Why would I do anything?"

"You got 'a help, man. Safer World Security—that's you, right? We find those boys, by the time I'm done, it'll be a safer world for the people we had supper with tonight."

"That's what they always say."

"There's another thing. Nobody really trusts you. They figure you might be a narc. If you get your hands dirty on this, it goes a long way to fitting in."

"I'm not sure I want to fit in. I'll think about it, though."

Jacob laughed, "Yeah, you think about it. Just remember, this, where you are right now, might not be a temporary condition. Sometimes when you fall into a hole they take the ladder away and leave you to rot." He pinched the coal off his cigarette and stashed the butt in his coat packet.

After Jacob had gone back inside, Greg stayed out and slipped in his F-square call before stowing the phone away into the folds of his jacket quickly. They were applying pressure now, 'disappointed' he hadn't come up with anything yet. F-you he wanted to reply, but didn't. They knew where he lived.

He tried hard to shake away the tension, to simply connect with his surroundings. It was nice and quiet out here, just the whisper of the falling snow and a far off police siren. Instead, he found himself thinking about what Jacob had said and he was surprised to find that he might actually take part in the retaliation.

There was a part of him that was angry and

wanted to lash out, given any justification. He recognized that part, but he'd buried it years ago. Changing from a short-tempered violent punk to a plodding, polite, hardworking guy was what made his present life possible. He'd transformed when he'd discovered Kali, a Philippine martial art involving combat with sticks or knives as well as bare hands, when he was fifteen. He'd spent two years studying with Professor Marcaida and the experience had changed him into a thoughtful, responsible guy. It had been twenty years since his Kali training and now he could barely remember the moves.

There was still a violent side to him. It was just buried. There was still a part of him that wanted to confront and smash. Right now, that part was licking it's lips and looking forward to the feel of fist meeting face.

It was finally starting to get chilly. Greg rang the entry bell and stared up into the security camera so Alfred would see who it was and let him in.

Jacob and Greg were sitting in the hallway outside the library. They hadn't bought anything, but nobody had hassled them so far. Jamie Tompkins shuffled in from the street and plopped down beside Greg. "I think I seen 'em, Jacob," he announced.

"Tell me," said Jacob.

"I was panhandling outside Humpty's. You know, can't stay too long or they put the run on ya. A couple 'a guys come out, climbed in a blue ford explorer and took off."

"Why you think it's the guys beat Blue Dog?"

"One guy had a red ski jacket."

"Lots 'a red ski jackets in town."

"Not like this one. Remember, Blue Dog caught his sleeve on a nail and the feathers started comin' out?"

"Yeah, I thought he was going to cry. He just got that jacket."

"He put a piece of duct-tape over the rip so the down stayed put. This guy had the same duct-tape on the same sleeve."

Jacob nodded. "I figured they was local guys. Somebody from out ‘a town wouldn't know about the old hospital. You done good, Jamie. Give him a couple ‘a smokes, Greg."

"How many is a couple?"

"Five."

"Shit, you're generous with my tobacco, aren't you?"

"You have to pay for good information. You wanna run with the big dogs, you got ‘a act the part."

Greg handed over the cigarettes. There were four little soldiers left in his pack now. Jamie stuck one smoke behind his ear and put the others in his shirt pocket. "What now?" he asked Jacob.

"Now you say thank you to Greg, asshole. He just gave you five smokes. Then get back out on the street and keep your eyes open. More info; better prizes. Got it?"

"I got it, Jacob. Thanks, Greg."

Jamie pulled on his hat and headed back outside.

Jacob said, "We got ‘em. Just a matter of time now."

"You knew about the jacket all along, didn't you?"

"Yeah, but Blue Dog's still in the hospital so I figured nobody else would know. Gave me a way of telling what was true and what was bullshit when I started hearing stuff."

"Do I have to buy a carton of smokes, now?"

"You're too poor to buy a carton. You only got enough for two maybe three packs, then you're flat."

Jacob said this with certainty and Greg accepted it. He had gotten used to Jacob's insights.

"The guys could still disappear," Greg said.

"Yeah, they might, but we got two pieces of information. We know what they're driving and that asshole's wearing the Dog's jacket. In a couple of hours there'll be sixty pairs of eyes all over town watching for them. Biggest problem now is going to be picking the good info out of the bull."

Jacob paused and it looked to Greg like he was reconsidering something. Finally he said "You know, I like the guy I'm talkin' to now better than the guy that bought me lunch a few days ago. You're calmer, with just a trace of crazy bastard around the edges. I like that."

In the end, it took another three days to track down the guys they were looking for. There were three of them, all between twenty and thirty. One was blond, the other two were dark haired. They had formed a nice little pack and went everywhere together. They all worked at Canadian Tire. They shared an apartment on 102nd Avenue. When they weren't at work they worked out at Gator's gym and drank at the Condill. Just a bunch of muscle bound kids trying to be tough guys. They had gotten into fights with a couple of other guys from the Sally, but hadn't ever done anything like the beating they gave Blue Dog.

"We know where they live, let's go get them. We can sort them out at home." This was Jamie's suggestion.

"That would be the stupidest thing to do. That's home invasion and an automatic five year sentence. Also, can you imagine a bunch of drunks all getting in each other's way, pretending to be fighters? Just keep tabs on them. Sometime soon they're gonna have a terrible accident."

The showdown happened Friday night. Word came to Jacob that the targets were drinking in the Condill. He said to Greg, "This is it. We take ‘em now. Let's go."

"Count me out."

"Course you’re coming. You just want me to convince you. Okay. I might not be able to do three. Probably can, but maybe not. And what happens if somebody else mixes in? I need backup. Anyway, you want to. That crazy bastard I can see inside you wants to kick the living shit out of something to make up for all that's happened to him. This is your chance."

Jacob wasn’t wrong.

Jacob, Greg and Jamie headed for the Condill. Jacob had a couple of words with the bouncer, got his assurance that he'd look the other way. Greg and Jacob went around back. Jamie went in the front and staggered up to the targets. He stood there wobbling back and forth until one of the kids said, "What's your problem, bum?"

"Thash my buddy's jacket on the back of the chair. You should give it back. He needsh it."

The kid stood up and pushed Jamie in the chest. He went reeling back, knocking over a table behind him. Beer and curses flew. The bouncer came over before the wolf pack could descend on Jamie. "Take that shit out back," he said. "We already had two fights tonight and that's the limit." He held up a sawed off pool cue for emphasis.

"Get out back, bum,” the kid sneered. “We'll be right out and we'll feed you our boots."

Jacob was no sportsman. He took up a position against the wall by the door. Greg waited in the shadow of the dumpster. He was carrying a small bat somebody had donated this afternoon. Jacob had a piece of two by four, about three feet long. Jamie came through the door, saw Jacob at the ready and took off running. Zero hour.

The young thugs came through the door single file. Jacob waited until the door had closed, then rapped the last guy in line on the head with his two-by-four. The board had a bent-over nail close to the end that ripped into the target's scalp. A big flap of it came loose and flopped down over his face. He let out a howl. When his buddies turned to see what was up, Greg darted out from behind the dumpster and took the legs out from under the blond one with his bat.

That left one guy standing between his two downed buddies confronting two bums with clubs. The odds didn't look good. He tried to run. Jacob cut him off, poked him in the gut with his board and he went to his knees vomiting up the beer and pickled eggs he had sucked down earlier.

After that it was bats and boots, simply move from one fallen hero to another, kicking and hitting. It felt good to Greg. All those years without a scrap; what a waste.

He came out of the blood lust and looked around at what they had accomplished. Those boys wouldn't be showing up in the gym anytime soon. He grabbed Jacob's arm and stopped him from caving one guy's face in. "Enough, man. They got the message. We need to book before the cops show up. Somebody'll call them for sure."

They were late getting back to the shelter, but Alfred let them in anyway. Jamie had given him the heads up when he went back and Alfred was on board. If somebody messed with Alfred's chicks, they definitely needed a come-uppance.

The two avengers hit the showers and cleaned off the blood. When they came out of the shower they found cocoa waiting for them and a shelter full of men wanting a blow-by-blow report of the action.

The RCMP didn't show up until suppertime the next day. There hadn't been any witnesses, but it was too much to expect that none of the guys who heard the story would blab. That was expected.

The cops turned out to be mostly unconcerned. Alfred lied for them, said Greg and Jacob had spent the evening playing crib and had only been out of sight long enough to have a quick smoke.

Sometime after the police finished their interviews, the constable in charge called Greg and Jacob outside.

"I know you guys did the beating, even if Alfred gives you an alibi. We aren't going to do anything this time. The guys you tuned up have been on our radar for a while now. Bum bashing is getting to be a big sport. Go on YouTube and you'll see street people getting beat just about to death. These guys were headed down the same path. Blue Dog was the first time they really stepped out and did something. Nobody filmed it. Probably too dark."

He paused and glared at them. "So, you guys walk. This time. You solved a problem for us and we'll look the other way. But I know you, Jacob Running Feather, and this is a one-time deal. Greg, you're in my book now, too. A guy like you should have better taste in friends. Watch your back when you hang out with this guy."

He settled his hat on his head and pulled on his gloves. "That's all I have to say. Get back inside before I change my mind. Remember, this isn't a free pass."

Greg watched the constable climb into his SUV and drive off, then turned to Jacob, incredulous. "I can't believe nothing is going to come from what we did."

"Believe it. Cops don't have time to worry about every fistfight that happens, especially in this town. Besides, the fight happened at the Condill—nobody pays much attention to what goes on at the Condill. Cops don't roll unless somebody dies."

"He said they knew about those three guys. Why didn't they do something before now?"

"They can't do anything unless they catch 'em in the act. Unless the punks are dumb enough to post what they did on Facebook or something."

"He seemed to have chapter and verse on you, Jacob."

"Well, he thinks he does. Simple fact is, they aren't interested in us. As long as we don't do anything they have to pay attention to, they leave us alone. The only time they do anything is if some townspeople get offended by seeing us around and complain. When that happens, they'll make a show of pushing us around until the heat's off.

"It's the same with the dope dealers. Police know all the players, but it's better to leave them in place. Sometimes a real crime happens around them and the cops move in. Otherwise, it's not worth their time and trouble to get involved."

"Huh. They weren't very interested in what happened to me when I reported it," said Greg. "And no encouragement at all about getting my truck back."

"They only got so many guys, and they spend a lot of time in court, taking them away from the streets. Anyway, there's only one of two ways it can go with your truck. If it left town, they'll never hear anything about it, so they don't have to worry. If it's in town it'll show up sooner or later, so they don't have to worry about that, either.

"Point is, we're invisible to them. Well, not invisible, they see us, but we're beneath notice unless we cross a line or do something that offends a real citizen."

"I never thought about it that way."

"Sure you did. You just didn't reason it out. If you saw a bunch of us hanging out in the bank lobby at night to stay warm, you'd probably crossed the street or hurried on by. It wouldn't be important enough to call the cops about, though, would it? Same thing."

When Greg was first getting to know the other residents that shared the shelter with him he was struck by the stories he heard about how they had wound up in the shelter. A lot of the stories were truly heart-breaking. Substance abuse, relationship meltdown, terrible accidents that took loved ones. When you took those stories into account, it made perfect sense these people were beaten down.

Later on he realized that many of these stories weren't true, or they had taken place ten years or more in the past. It was as if the people involved were fossils, frozen in amber when the tragedies took place, unchanged ever since.

There seemed to be three types of people represented. One group was made up of workers in from the patch who used the shelter as a hotel on their days off. Maybe because they were used to working in camp, they believed they shouldn't have to pay for food and shelter, whether they could afford the price or not.

The second group were the true tragedies. These were the people with serious mental problems or addictions, just barely able to function. They were lost souls who wandered the streets, barely conscious. Members of this group generally stayed in the front because they were unable to follow the simple rules for admittance to the back.

The last group seemed functional and intelligent. Some couldn't hold a job for very long because they couldn't accept authority or got bored too easily. Others believed they had life wired and played the system. They always knew where the free food was, which store was having a customer appreciation barbecue. People were allowed in the shelter for six weeks per year and these guys always knew to the day when they would be eligible again.

To this last group, the struggles of working people were just a sign of stupidity to them. They had figured out a way to survive without working. All they needed to do was scuffle a bit to come up with money for tobacco and a bit of wine. Everything else was available for free.

This was what they projected, anyway. Deep down inside they had to know they only existed as long as the powers that be allowed them.

NINE
Pull Back the Curtain

Greg was having coffee in the MacDonald's in Dawson Creek. Things were finally turning around for him and he'd hitch-hiked to Dawson just to check it out—after his usual "Haven't found it yet" call to F-square, of course. When he'd driven through the town on his way to Macintosh a lifetime ago, he hadn't really paid any attention to the place. For some reason, now he wanted a closer look at the town before he left the Peace Country for good.

Jenna had sent him a hundred dollars, so he bought himself a large coffee and a sausage-n-egg MacMuffin. He was sitting in the back, about to dig in when a tall, well-muscled older man walked up to the counter to order.

Something about him. What is it?

Do I know him?

Then it fell into place. It was Constable Chalmers, the cop who had taken his original report about the theft of his stuff at the lookout. He was in civvies now, obviously off duty.

What the hell, I'll do it. Nothing to lose.

Chalmers sat down at a booth by himself. Greg gave him time to pop his coffee and unwrap his sandwich, then wandered over. He was careful to keep both hands empty and in sight. "Can I talk to you?"

Chalmers looked him over. "I'm not on duty. Catch me at the station."

"I'm not on duty either. I'm going to sit down now. Not trying to cause any trouble, it's just that nobody will talk to me. Don't shoot, okay? Not a confrontation."

"I'll decide whether it's a confrontation or not. What do you want?"

"Do you know who I am?"

Chalmers twitched a quick smile. "Of course I do. You're the security guy who had his truck stolen at the lookout. Now you've fallen into some bad ways and you're hanging around with Running Feather. Keep company like that and nobody'll talk to you ."

"Can I ask you, with all respect, have there been any leads in solving what happened to me? Are you any closer to figuring out what happened?"

Chalmers pulled out his phone and called up the photo manager. He swiped the screen a couple of times, then held the phone out to Greg. "Recognize him?"

Taking the phone, Greg's hope soared. "Sure, he's the one I ran into at the lookout. He was the ring leader who kept me talkin' while somebody cold-cocked me."

"The ring leader, eh? Why do you think that?"

"He was the first one I met, he put himself out in front. I just presumed."

Chalmers held out his hand for the phone. "I'm going to step outside and make a couple of calls. If I'm not back in ten, I'm not coming. In that case, feel free to eat my food. And don't leave. You've started something now that you have to finish."

Chalmers walked out with his phone pressed to his ear. He seemed to be gone a long time, but the hands of the clock above the counter barely moved before he returned. He was carrying an iPad.

"I was just checking with my corporal. He's allowing me to share some surveillance photos with you. We might have gotten back to you eventually, but your obvious friendship with Jacob made us suspicious. Now that you've come forward this way, the corporal says you may just be the lamb Jacob's shearing and not a bad guy yourself."

"Jacob's not like that. He's actually a pretty good guy."

Chalmers said, "Baaaaaa! Look at the pictures."

There were around twenty pictures in the set. All of them were of Jacob and the guy that Greg had described as the ringleader. Several of them were of other guys that Greg vaguely remembered from the attack. He murmured, "What the hell?"

"The timestamps on some of these photos predate the attack on you. Others are later. The guy you just defended, Running Feather, is the real ringleader. The guys that took you are his posse. Sort of. They aren't tightly organized. Let's just say that when these guys do anything, Running Feather benefits in some way. Does that make sense to you?"

Greg started to say no, but something stopped him. He remembered his first meeting with Jacob at the Mondo.

"A really good scam is one where you never catch on and defend the guy that's hustling you. You keep coming back for more."

"Son of a motherless goat. The first time I met him, he told me what he was going to do and I didn't believe him."

"I know. It's his damned smile and *'Ah shucks'* manner. You can't believe anything bad about the guy."

"It sounds like you've fallen for his charm a time or two."

"I haven't had a lot of interactions with Running Feather, but I'd say the score is pretty even since he's managed to con me at least half the time. Once, I even bought him supper and gave him a ride to Pouce Coupe afterward. I was shaking him down on suspicion of petty theft. He started crying and said he was just stealing because his girlfriend had had a miscarriage and he had to go see her. I swallowed that story and gave him a drive. He won that one for sure."

"I guess I shouldn't feel bad about what happened to me, then."

"No, he's a professional hustler, among other things."

"This started with me asking for news about my truck. Anything come up?"

"No, and it's at the bottom of our list. There's nobody rushing to do you favors since you started running with Jacob."

"Gee, thanks a bunch, constable. I guess I'll be on my way, then. Any advice about how I can deal with Jacob?"

"He's a vicious bastard, but you know that. If I was going up against him, I'd want at least two other officers along. Otherwise I'd just have to shoot him."

"He's tough, I know that."

"On the other hand, you're a pretty mean bugger yourself. The performance at the Condill proved that. You might take him, but you need an edge. You can't fight him straight up and you'd have to do something so you don't wind up fighting six guys instead of one."

"Nothing there I didn't already know. Thanks, though."

Greg wandered off into the Mall and left the constable to his coffee.

TEN
The Scrap

It was supper time. Everybody was seated at the long table pushing down food. Tonight it was corned beef and beans, with cornbread on the side.

Jacob was seated at the end of the table near the kitchen. He was entertaining two new guys with moose hunting stories. Jacob had never hunted moose, but he had stories and the new fish wouldn't know the difference.

Greg walked up to the kitchen pass through and filled his cup from the big silver urn. He looked around to see where Alfred was.

Alfred was coming down from his office. He had a small baseball bat hanging down against his leg. It was the same bat that Greg had used at the Condill. He nodded at Greg, crossed his massive arms, and leaned against the door frame of the kitchen.

Greg put down his coffee cup.

There was a heavy serving platter with a bunch of pastries on it. Greg dumped the pastries and walked up behind Jacob. The new guys Jacob was entertaining saw him swing the platter up, their expressions registering horror. The platter swung down in a vicious arc and broke across Jacob's skull.

The impact opened up a cut in Jacob's scalp and drove his head down into his beans. Greg waited until he raised his head. Jacob's face was covered with bean juice and his nose gushed blood.

Several guys who were friendly with Jacob pushed their chairs back, ready to mix in.

"You all stand fast!" roared Alfred, brandishing his bat. "This'll be a private scrap, so keep your asses in your chairs."

The guys eased back down.

Alfred said, "Cops are on their way. You've got maybe five minutes to take care of business."

Greg expected Jacob to come at him with his boots. Instead, he threw his cup at Greg's head, broke his plate as he stood up and rushed at Greg swinging the broken plate like a scythe.

It was amazing to Greg how quickly he was able to back pedal. Jacob didn't seem to be hurting at all, though his face was covered in blood from his nose and scalp. And he was actually smiling in anticipation as he followed Greg around the room.

Greg knew he'd have to let Jacob hit him at some point. He circled around to the old couch opposite the TV. He pulled one of the big cushions loose and threw it at Jacob who batted it away. Greg rummaged in the spot where the cushion had been. The hammer handle he had stashed the night before was still there. Now that he was armed with something, there was a chance to win this.

He circled away from Jacob, holding the hammer handle up in front of him, feeling clumsy and ridiculous, hearing Jacob jeer about shoving the hammer handle up his ass. When Jacob came in swinging the broken plate, Greg slipped sideways and tried to hit Jacob's wrist. He missed the wrist but managed to tag the plate. He saw it break in half, watched Jacob wipe the blood out of his eyes.

Greg felt his wrist flex and the handle started moving. The movement was hesitant and a bit clumsy at first, then settled into a graceful series of swings, loops and circular motions. His muscles still remembered the Kali training. A sense of calm descended on him and he was back on the training floor with professor Marcaida knowing exactly what to do.

Get in close. He'll expect me to evade. Move in.

He saw Jacob had seen the change come over him and didn't know what it meant. For the first time, Jacob looked unsure of the outcome of this fight. When in doubt attack. Jacob came in fast, swinging the plate in a downward diagonal slice.

Instead of retreating, Greg took a step forward, pushed the swinging arm farther in the direction it was going. He held Jacob's arm just above the elbow for a moment and cracked him between the eyes with the hammer handle.

Jacob dropped the plate shard and tried to grapple. That got him a stab in the solar plexus from the handle.

The little hickory club seemed to have acquired a life of its own. It swept down and cracked into Jacob's kneecap and he couldn't help bending forward. The handle cracked smartly against his collar bone, stopping just short of a bone-snapping blow. Greg moved behind Jacob and put him on the floor with a foot sweep.

Jacob landed on his back. He rolled onto his stomach and tried to push himself to his feet, but the arm he was pushing with was the one attached to the freshly tapped collar bone and couldn't take the weight. Greg reached down, grabbed a fistful of Jacob's hair, pulled his head back and swung the hammer handle down toward the base of Jacob's skull.

He stopped the strike in mid-swing. "That's it. We're done. Stay the hell away from me, Jacob."

"It ain't over," Jacob gasped. "Not till one of us is dead."

"I don't feel like dying, and you aren't worth killing. If you want to die that bad, jump in front of a bus or try beating up a cop. Leave me out of it. I'm not that guy anymore."

Jacob started to get up to continue the fight. Alfred raised the bat and made a 'sit' gesture with his left hand. Jacob settled back down. One of the guys he had been telling hunting stories to passed him a handful of paper towels and he made a start at cleaning up the blood on his face.

Greg turned his back on the scene and headed for the back door.

In the alley behind the shelter, Greg stared up at the falling snow forming a halo around the security light, nauseous after the adrenaline rush. He couldn't believe he had gone up against Jacob without being seriously injured.

He shook a cigarette out of the pack with shaking hands and lit up. For some reason, it was as if he was tasting the smoke for the first time. God, it was awful. Jacob had been right all along, his smokes did taste like camel shit. The cigarette went flying into the snow. He was tempted to throw the package away but put them back in his pocket. One of the guys would be glad to have them.

The thing Greg was most surprised by was that he wasn't angry, frightened or anything else. He was just filled with a sense of something being over and wondering why things had seemed so important.

What's the point of standing around outside if I'm

not smoking? Feels kind of stupid.

The fresh air was good, though. He stayed out in the snow and let the aftermath of the fight fall away. He was just about to ring the entry buzzer when a police SUV ghosted up nearly silent in the soft, clean snow cover.

Greg recognized the cop when he got out. Constable Chalmers.

"Is it over?" Chalmers asked, approaching with his hands loose at his sides.

Greg nodded.

"I'm sorry I missed it," Chalmers said. "I guess you won. Here you are with barely a mark on you. Any dead bodies in there?"

"No. Jacob's pretty banged up but I'm sure there'll be no charges."

"I'm sure of that. If nobody needs arresting, I'll be on my way." Chalmers walked around to the driver's side of the SUV. Just before climbing back in, he said, "We found what's left of your truck burned out on a back road near Taylor. It'll be towed in tomorrow. You can come to the station in the afternoon, see if there's anything worth salvaging."

"Are you sure it's mine?"

"The VIN matches. Also the fact that it was burned. That's the common fate for stolen vehicles around here. For some reason they always seem to do it around Taylor. Like I said, come by tomorrow and tell us how you want to dispose of it."

This may be my way out. With any luck I'm free. God, let it be mine!

The cop car slid away down the alley.

Greg rang the entry bell. The door didn't buzz and unlock. He pushed the button a couple more times. Eventually the door opened and Alfred came out, pulling on his coat. "Spare me a smoke?" he asked.

Greg passed him the pack of camels he'd stuffed in his coat pocket. "You can keep 'em."

Alfred lit one and put the pack in his pocket. "You should think about staying somewhere else tonight," he said. "Jacob's licking his wounds now, but he'll probably cut your throat while you sleep if you stay here."

"What am I supposed to do, sleep in front of the ATM at the Bank of Montreal?"

"Not your best idea. You'll just get rousted by the security boys when they make their rounds."

"What then?"

"You can stay at my place tonight. I'm off shift in half an hour. Walk up to the Qwik Mart and wait there for me. All I have is a couch, but it's yours if you want it."

"Thanks."

Alfred nodded. "If you want to stay healthy, you have to find a way to get out of this town. Jacob runs the streets and there'll always be someone letting him know where you are, or willing to thump you to make him happy. You're okay for now but no longer. You know that, don't you?"

"I'd already figured that, just didn't know what to do about it. Anyway, I just got some news. With any luck I'll be out of here tomorrow."

"The sooner the better. What will you do about Jacob?"

"I thought I just did it."

"You know better than that. He'll hunt you down no matter where you go."

"Yeah, I know, and he can find me too. All he needs is a computer. He can track me through our company website. I just hoped he'd let it be."

"He won't. Don't be such a Pollyanna. All he has

is his rep. If he just takes the beating you gave him, he loses everything. You need a more permanent solution."

"Maybe I'll think of something on the walk to your place. Right now I don't have a clue."

Greg watched Alfred go back inside, took a long careful look around and started walking North toward the Qwik Mart.

ELEVEN
Last Day

It was light when Greg opened his eyes. His eyes were sticky, his mouth tasted terrible and he had a kink in his back from curling to fit Alfred's couch. The couch had turned out to be a love seat. It was stained and stank of spilled beer and God knew what else. When his mind kicked in, he remembered all the details of his situation. Today was the first day in a long time that he had a real sense of hope. He made his way to the kitchen, hunted around for the instant coffee.

I'm sure Alfred won't mind if I make myself a cup. If he was paranoid, he wouldn't have let me crash here.

The coffee tasted foul, but the caffeine rush got his mind working at full speed. He looked out the window. It was just a couple of blocks to the cop shop.

And not snowing. Cool. Let's do this.

Greg got to the police station around ten. Constable Chalmers was out on a call, so Greg had to wait fifteen minutes before the mountie was back in the station. Greg signed the report. The thieves had stripped the license plates before setting fire to the truck, making it harder to trace.

"What'll happen with the truck now?" Greg asked.

"You won't be fixing it, that's for sure. You have

to do something with it though. Now that you've claimed it, disposal is your responsibility. The good news is, Raven Recycle will pay you $350 for it if you release it directly to them from the impound yard. It's a good deal. They'll crush it into a cube and eventually it will wind up in China as raw material."

The phone rang. Chalmers held up one finger in a 'Just a minute" gesture. Greg saw his eyes widen as he listened. Chalmers didn't say anything, just made a couple of notes before saying thanks and hanging up the phone.

Chalmers looked like he couldn't believe what he'd just heard. "That's probably good news for you," he said at last. "One of our rookies is at the shelter." He stared at Greg, considering. "Running Feather's dead."

Greg felt a curious mixture of elation, relief and sorrow all at the same time. "What happened?"

"Looks like suicide. He was found at the shelter this morning sitting in the shower. His femoral artery was slashed."

Greg was silent for a long moment, struggling to take it in, to understand what it meant. Finally he said, "I was afraid you were going to say he died because of me. Last night's fight. Jacob said it happened to him once and he went to prison."

Greg could see he'd caught Chalmers' interest. The officer pecked away on his computer, then said, "Yes. He was sentenced to two years in 2007. Apparently a friend and he got liquored up and went fisticuffs over a girl. They shook hands afterward and continued with their drinking. In the morning when Jacob came to, he discovered his buddy was dead. He had a bleed in his brain from the fight and died in his sleep."

"That's what Jacob said. I was never sure if it was

true or he just wanted to look tough. Anyway, you can see my concern because of the parallels."

"Indeed. Listen, I have to head down to the shelter and oversee things, take statements and such. It's going to be a busy day. I'll give you a receipt releasing the truck. It'll be enough for you to make you claim with your insurance provider. Just talk to Clive at the impound. He'll help you with the next steps in the disposal. At some point I'll need a statement from you about the fight last night."

"I'm here now. Let's do it."

"No time. And no hurry, either. We'll build a timeline of the last couple of days of Jacob's life but I don't expect we'll find any surprises. Go deal with your truck now. Come back later today and give a statement. Fair enough?"

"I guess that works. It's hard to believe Jacob's dead."

Greg arrived at the impound lot an hour later. He'd stopped at Timmy's for a breakfast bagel and coffee. Not that he was hungry, he needed time to think, to put space between the events of the day.

At the impound, Clive checked the vehicle receipt and went over the steps in the disposal process with Greg.

"Can I check her out? There might be something I can salvage."

"Good luck with that, but yeah, knock yourself out. Just go through that door to the lot. In case you have trouble recognizing her, yours is the one with the melted tires."

"Har, har. I'll go see what I can find."

"Sure. I'll call Raven and get them to schedule a pick up. This time of year they shouldn't be too busy."

Greg grabbed a screwdriver from the bench on his way out. Clive was right, Greg's Ram 2500 was the only vehicle in the lot with melted tires. It was sad to see his home on the road reduced to a chunk of scorched metal.

Okay, let's see how lucky we are.

He crawled under the back of the truck.

Please be there.

Yes!

The safe was welded to the frame above the rear axle. Greg had gotten the idea from the magnetic key holders that people used so they wouldn't get locked out of their vehicles. He jimmied the safe with the screwdriver and pulled out the contents of the box: Ziploc bags, a credit card, a passport and some duplicate identification. The prize was the Ziploc bags. Each one contained thirty fifty dollar bills.

I am so out of here. First class, in the air and gone baby gone.

He wiggled backwards until he was clear of the truck and stood up. Looking back toward the office, he saw Clive was still at his desk and facing the street.

Might as well check the passenger door and see what Santa brought.

The door panel on the passenger side was scorched but looked to be intact. When he levered the top edge with the screwdriver, it crumbled. Pulling his flashlight from his backpack, he flipped it on and shone its beam down into the door cavity. Surprised and yet not surprised, he could see two small bricks wrapped in foil and plastic, sealed with heavy tape. They should have melted.

He pulled the bricks free, and after another quick glance at Clive, jammed them into his backpack and climbed down from the cab. He patted the hood of the truck one last time, then headed back into the office to return the screwdriver, collect his three hundred and fifty bucks and make a graceful exit. Time to see what was happening at the shelter.

Lunch was just wrapping up when Greg got to the shelter. He looked up the alley that ran behind the shelter. There were a couple of cop cars parked across from the entrance. An ambulance was just leaving, headed towards 100th Street. With no siren, it was probably Jacob being moved to the next stage in the process.

Greg sat down in the front and looked around for somebody who could bring him up to speed on the events of the night. There didn't seem to be anybody around.

Huh, maybe the cops have kept everyone in the back until they're done processing.

There probably wasn't much point talking to anybody else. All he'd get would be rumors and outright lies. If they hadn't been there, most people would just make stuff up to seem in the know.

He saw a flash of red near the entrance. It was Blue Dog, late for lunch. Greg waved him over. The Dog saw the wave, nodded and headed for the big coffee urn on the side table. When he sat down, Greg could see he'd been crying. His eyes were red and there were salt tracks down his cheeks where tears had frozen.

"I guess you heard 'bout Jacob, eh?"

Greg nodded. "Just the bare bones. What have you heard?"

"He killed himself in the shower last night. Sliced his leg open and bled out. Shitty way to go, man."

"Anybody know why?"

"That's the strange thing. Usually everybody acts like they know stuff, even if they wasn't there. None of that now. Nobody seen this one coming."

"Anybody blaming me?"

"Nah, man. Jacob was a big boy, lost fights

before. Everybody was wondering how he'd pay you back once he got healed up. It's a soap opera."

There wasn't much to say after that. They didn't know each other real well anyway. After a couple of minutes of silence, Blue Dog said he was going out for a butt. Greg could see his eyes filling with tears again.

Nobody else came over to talk. It was the same way as when he'd first showed up, they didn't know what to make of him so kept their distance. He guessed most people would pretend to be sad about Jacob, but it would be hard to say how many actually would be. Jacob had inspired as much fear and resentment as he had friendship.

Greg found every time he had a positive feeling about Jacob, a picture flashed into his mind of the look in Jacob's eyes when he swung the broken plate at Greg's face.

"Chalmers will be glad to see you." Alfred was looming overhead, bald head gleaming. "It'll save him chasing you all over town. Come on in the back. They're taking statements and they've done everybody but you."

"No use putting it off, I guess. I was going to clear out my locker as soon as you opened up. Now I don't have to wait."

Constable Chalmers had taken over Alfred's office for the interviews. That way Alfred could continue with his chores. The floor had just been mopped and was already being sullied by boot tracks. There weren't supposed to be any street shoes allowed in the back, but you couldn't tell cops to take their boots off. And as long as the cops were stomping around, why worry about anyone else.?

Chalmers was busy with Mealy Pete, so Greg put his backpack in his locker and talked to a couple of the guys. Pretty soon Alfred beckoned him toward the office.

Chalmers was ticking off the names of the shelter denizens as they were interviewed. "Ah, Greg. Best for last, eh? Did you get your truck straightened out?"

"Yeah. She'll soon be a big cube headed for China."

"Did you manage to salvage anything?"

"There was a safe welded to the bottom of the truck bed. I had a credit card and duplicate ID in there. The safe survived the fire. So I'm a registered citizen again and I can fly out of here."

"Life turns on a dime, doesn't it? The safe was a good idea. That way if you get mugged you can get back in business."

"Unless they steal the truck."

"I'm not surprised the safe survived. These guys usually throw gas in the cab and douse the outside. The only part that gets really hot is the cab."

Chalmers dropped an evidence bag onto the desk. Greg recognized Jacob's knife—a Mora—under the plastic. "Do you recognize that?"

"Sure, it's Jacob's. He had it sewn inside his coat."

"Illegal to carry a knife this size concealed."

"Lots of things are illegal. He just used it as a tool. It isn't useful as a weapon. With that little handle and no guard, a guy would slice his hand open if he stabbed someone."

"That's true. I'm just dotting the i's."

Greg couldn't see any blood on the blade of the Mora. "Is that what he killed himself with?"

"No, that would be this box cutter here." Chalmers pushed another evidence bag across the desk. No shortage of blood on this one. Greg shuddered.

"Why'd he used the box cutter?"

"Simple. He could always have a sharp edge. Did

you know he was a cutter?"

This was a surprise.

"No, I didn't. You found lots of scars?"

"The insides of his thighs were a maze of scars, some were fresh, some were years old. It was a long standing habit."

"That's a dangerous place to cut. So what's the thinking? He was doing his ritual and just decided to bear down a bit harder? What the hell?"

Chalmers nodded. "We'll probably never know the answer. Do you recognize this?" Another evidence bag. This one had a small photo in it, the middle size that you get in a bundle of school pictures. It was of a chubby little Indian girl about ten years old. Her shiny black hair hung down in two braids. Her skin was nut-brown and gleaming. She was smiling as if she had just found a pony under the Christmas tree.

"Yeah, it's Jacob's. I've seen him take it out and look at it sometimes when he thought nobody would see. He never actually showed it to me, always put it away when anybody noticed it."

"There's a word on the back: Miigwan. I googled it. It's Ojibway for feather. Apparently it's a popular girl's name."

"Jacob called her his cousin."

"Jacob is pretty much a mystery. Do you know anything about where he came from?"

"The night I was robbed he told me he went back to the reserve after he finished high school and it was the worst mistake he ever made. The day we met, he told me he was adopted, raised white in North Bay."

"No name, I suppose?"

"Sorry. Pretty sure it wasn't Running Feather, though. Is there any chance of finding his parents?"

"That will be up to the brass. There's a good chance they won't think it worth the resources. Given enough time and manpower we could probably track him back but there's no big reason to make the investment. Are you taking right off?"

"I might stay one more day, fly out tomorrow. Why, do you need me to stick around?"

The Constable shook his head. "No, I don't think so. If something comes up we can contact you through your office, can't we?"

"Sure, they'll always know where I am."

Not bloody likely. I'm never going back there again. If I ever run into Jimmy, I'll beat the shit out of him.

Greg signed a statement saying that everything he'd said was voluntary . He shook Chalmers' hand, cleaned out his locker and walked out of the shelter for the last time.

He walked down the street and checked into the Lakeview. He had the money now so why not?

The biggest thing on his mind was where to go next. When he'd turned his truck north and this all began, he'd been sure he loved the lower mainland more than anyplace else on earth. Now he didn't care if he ever saw the place again.

What about Jenna? Well, she was obviously done with him. Maybe it was time he was done with her.

What else—the house? Let the bank have it. It didn't mean anything to him anymore.

And I'm done with the security business. That was mostly something Jimmy and I did on a lark anyway. If the clients can screw you over the way Hydro had, and it was legal, what's the point?

For the first time in years, Greg felt completely free. He was light and in control. He could go anywhere and do anything. After what he'd been through in the last little while, a whole different set of things seemed to be important.

For now, he didn't need to make any decisions.

Instead he headed across the alley to the Roustabout for a brew and a burger.

Just before he went out the door he pulled out his phone, and made the usual daily call to F-squared first, then broke tradition and made a second call.

"Marlin Travel. This is Janet. How can I help you?"

"Hi Janet. I wonder if you can tell me how to get to North Bay, Ontario from here."

Greg had a buffalo burger with the big, wedge-shaped fries and gravy. He sat with his back to the wall, watching the door. F-squared arrived just as he was sopping up the last of his chips and gravy. One F sat on each side of the table, hemming him in. The view of the door remained intact. They both ordered coffee, just to have something in front of them.

“So. Greg,” Franklin said. “You’ve located our parcels.”

“Yeah. The truck was burnt out but somehow the packages survived in the door.”

“So, where are they?” This from Felix.

“I have a room here. The packages is up there. I didn’t figure you’d want them handed off in the middle the Roustabout.”

Franklin nodded. “You’re turning them over to us, then?”

Greg laughed. “Yes, seals and original wrappings are intact. I did think briefly about sticking them in my duffel and heading for the plane, but I decided that wouldn’t be wise.”

“Smart thinking,” said Felix.

“Truth to tell, it was very tempting, until I realized that I didn’t have a clue how to move items like that and there was a good chance of being caught by the security screeners.”

Both F’s nodded. Made sense.

"There was another reason as well," said Greg. "I want to get on your good side. This whole experience has made me realize how bored I am with my straight little security life. I'd like something with a bit more excitement and I figured you could help me find it."

Franklin's eyes widened. "Did you now? What did you have in mind?"

"I don't know and I don't expect you to know either at this point. Tomorrow I'm heading for Ontario. If there's anything that needs to be picked up and transported back here, or if there should be a car that needs to be driven out here, I'm your boy. I've proved my loyalty. Now it's up to you to figure out how to use me."

Greg could almost hear the gears grinding in Franklin's head. When he looked at his partner, Felix made the palms up, 'I don't know' gesture, then nodded.

"Very well," said Franklin. "Keep the phone with you. We'll be in touch when we come up with something. Shouldn't take long. Just have to make some calls to Toronto and check in. Does that suit?"

Greg nodded, "Sure. I figured you probably had some possibilities I could help with." He passed his room key across to Felix. "The number's on the key. Your packages are on the closet shelf in the back on the left hand side. I'll wait another ten minutes, then come up. Leave the key under the doormat."

When F-squared had gone off in search of their packages, Greg ordered a cognac. He could see his reflection in the window by the front door. He raised the brandy snifter to himself in salute and toasted his new life.

The End

Glenn Palmer is a retired computer nerd from SFU. He's always lived in a fantasy world. For the last five years he's been writing down what he sees.

100th Avenue Urchin (Finding Peace Trilogy)

By Katy Clarke

Her mind subsisting on a continuum
Between obligation and choice or isolation and intimacy.
Ghostly arms squeezing the last
Drops from a branchless soul,
Like ribs too small,
Surrounding her dehydrated heart.
Smoke floating from the breath
Of her lost intentions,
Faded petals once brilliantly inked,
Now worn, lacklustre on her spine
Lips cracked, left wanting, whispering
Lies to cover her inebriation, floating
In between the surface and the bottom,
Accepting her impaired peace.

Katy Gray Clark invented enthusiasm and proves it when she rides her bikes, works with kids and especially when writing poems about our cool Peace Country as a 'boomerang' resident.

South Peace Sanctuary (Finding Peace Trilogy)

By Katy Clarke

Knobby fingers grasping
For the last newspaper,
Padding frail bones from the
Howling, wicked winds that bite the night.
Pulling closer and closer to the cold
Brick wall, scribed with illiterate literature,
Mocking those finding
Shelter beneath it.
Deadened stars fill his sky.
Meaningless hope no longer
Being sent.
Only a meagre memory of money,
That found solace in a
Herd of human dust.
Perhaps this is his truth,
His South Peace sanctuary

Katy Gray Clark invented enthusiasm and proves it when she rides her bikes, works with kids and especially when writing poems about our cool Peace Country as a 'boomerang' resident.

Gold Claim

By Kathy Murphy

Life moves at a different pace here. Time expands and contracts so you lose track of the days. "Today must be Tuesday, no Thursday." There are no phones, no internet, no TV, no dishwashers, not even running water. You get up in the morning, run to the biffy, wash in the icy cold basin and head in for breakfast.

It's a leisurely affair with everyone lingering over coffee and visiting. No need to check the time; you start working when you decide to go. We boil water over a propane flame when it's time to do the dishes or it might be hot enough from the kettle on what we call our "microwave" — a flat metal plate on top of the wood burning barrel that heats the cabin.

By the time the dishes are finished you start thinking about what to put out for coffee break. I joke that we eat like Hobbits here: breakfast, followed by coffee, then lunch, afternoon tea and/or "happy hour" with a drink and snack, then dinner. Everything takes longer to prepare but it doesn't matter because there's nothing else fighting for your attention. It's a zen-like state. When you wash, you wash, when you cook, you cook; there is no multitasking and no interruptions. The days seem endless and they all blend together. Kathryn marks an X over each completed day on her calendar. Otherwise, it's very possible we would overstay our return to the real world of alarm clocks, work and a myriad of obligations.

When it rains, we huddle in the cabin with the fire burning but when the sun shines, sometimes five minutes later, we sit outside to catch its warmth. It is cold in the mountains at night and feels like Fall in August so we hoard the last moments of Summer. Last night everything froze and there was a layer of ice on the water buckets this morning. Now the sun is out, the bugs have returned and it's as warm as a Hawaiian beach. The weather is a constant surprise with the only surety being change at a moment's notice.

We travel through the surrounding area by quads, truck or walking. Talulah, Ron's dog, runs beside the quads when he and John go exploring and in her joyful oblivion runs right past the meadow with the bear in it.

This is fortunate because she has been known to chase a bear and bring it back to her people when it decided to return the favor. So far we've seen a variety of animals including Stellar jays, chipmunks, a porcupine, a bobcat, a bear, a moose, and a mouse that took up residence in the insulation in the hood of our truck. The poor thing popped out near the windshield wiper and started running back and forth as we bumped along a very rough road.

You know the roads are bad when a mouse wants to bail out.

On our trip in, I was amazed at how quickly nature takes over when you leave it alone for a year. The road in had three to four foot saplings growing in the middle of it and the branches of the larger trees on the side were doing their share to impede our progress. It seems like we just arrived but tomorrow we make the trip home. It's a place I yearned for the other night as I shivered under three layers of blankets—central heating is a wonderful thing. Returning home always makes me happy when I'm back with family, friends, and pets, but I'll miss this place. For me, going to the Gold Claim isn't about finding riches; it's about finding peace and I hope to carry a bit of it in my soul when I return.

Kathy lives in Taylor B.C. where she is lucky enough to be surrounded by people and pets she loves. She is especially fond of firemen, but her favorite is her husband John. Once dubbed "The Volunteer Queen" by her friends, and known to "ride off in all directions" at once, she is finally learning the value of prioritizing. Her family, which includes three amazing children, and her friends are always first in her heart but she is now making room in her life for the fun stuff, like reading and writing.

i. making peace with my mother

by r. d. adair

i feel as though i must first apologize for how i entered; half-breath and whole-fisted, twisted and silent. a bundle of burdens taken away on steel wings. oh, how you worried, writhed and wept. went to a world of neon cages and man-made suns to see the thing you had created, kept company by contraptions and doubt. to see the fruits of your labour laid out, signing papers and putting your flesh and blood in the slick hands of strangers. you ate uncertainty for breakfast and anguish for lunch.

i spent the early years of my career commanding questions, marching them from my belly to my tongue, appetite unconquered. a dominating soul, five years old and ancient to my peers all my answers were demanded from you. you caught them fearlessly, fighting to find if i could find an equilibrium in the seesaw motion of my madness. we both realized i would not.

alas, you cannot compete with the dead parent. the immortal morality of the man made into memory as momentous, an unflawed faceted aquamarine. i would spend the rest of my life throwing blame like shrapnel. in the chaos, neither of us left unscarred. today, we are far from unfaulted. the cracks between us barely mended before we falter once more. picking glass from our wounds and scratching back our skin,

hoping to peel the other's eyelids back and be seen.
howling our hopes in silence, refusing to stare back.

tripping tardy, we will always tumble a touch too late for each other's embrace.

ii. making peace with my brother

by r. d. adair

while i was born to be beheld by behemoth machines, you were cast into the shadow of the baby unborn, the supposed sister that never was. the little brother born after the storm, i held you close and caught myself tasting undying devotion for the first time.

i sought so sincerely to shield you from the unseaming of our mother, the taste of death as our father slipped past in your 6-year-old arms, heart hollowed out with the scraping of the ambulance on the front curb. i wanted in vain to keep you in your child's heart, denied your existence to the tormentors and torturers that would seek you if they could hear that steady beat.

i owe you acres of apologies, in my anger at my failure to find you safety, i lashed with lascivious tongue and languishing limbs at you. you understood the pain as ours, and for that, i rejected you.

as age grew into wisdom, i found you always at departures, darting on to the depths of something daring. i gazed on as you outgrew our beginnings and found your appetite for all things adult. i'm learning pride without resentment as you realize realities only once dreamed.

arms stretched tired, i will always be straining for the strength to surrender.

R.D. Adair is an occasional poet and always over-thinker, who lives with her South African nomad, Jaryd, and over enthusiastic dog, Corki. This is her first print publication.

Mary

By Wade Kelly

In 1951, with only 10 months of Normal School in Victoria and a brief stint in a one room school at Budd Lake (near Prince George), Mary packed her suitcase and hit the road to teach in one of Canada's more rural locations. She had chosen the Peace River area for practical reasons—they paid the most. The plan was to make good money for a stint and move on. But something happened. The water of the mighty Peace got into her blood, and over the next half century she raised a family, ran a farm, and made a life in the place she soon called home, the Peace Country.

Mary was born in 1930, to a Welsh immigrant mother and a father who had abandoned any other heritage, identifying simply as Canadian. Mary's mother came from Wales at the tender age of 21, but she had wanted to come earlier. At age 16 she had an offer from a family she worked for to relocate to Canada, but her family refused. The embers of a Canadian adventure stayed glowing, and as soon as she was able, as an emancipated adult, she made her way to Canada. She found work at a boy's orphanage in Winnipeg prior to meeting Mary's father. Years later a few of 'her boys' would end up relocating to Prince George where she was able to line up work for them. Once a surrogate mother, always a mother. A deep caring for the less fortunate, the down on their luck, and the displaced, was a theme written in the family's DNA.

Mary's story, in many ways, typifies the frontier experience of a young Canada and an often unexplored northwest. Growing up her family moved a number of times before settling in Prince George; father Charles Howard, mother Elizabeth, brother Art, and Mary. A modest family size for the time, but not short on love. Her father found work at a sawmill in Giscome, a community 40km north of Prince George. Work was not easy with long days, poor pay, and generally unsafe working conditions. Workplace accidents were commonplace and even fatalities were not uncommon, but a job was a job and the young family needed to eat. The echo of socialist thought reverberated throughout young Mary's household. Communism was barely a generation old and still a largely untested experiment. The rights of the worker, of the common man, of equality for all, were common themes around the family dinner table. Her father believed in the labour movement, he saw firsthand how workers were treated: the caustic work environments, the unsafe conditions, the disregard for human life. This new country deserved better. Living in a remote community was not an excuse to take advantage of workers and violate what he believed were human rights.

In 1945, the International Woodworkers of America (IWA) set up shop in Prince George. In short order Mary's father was involved with the worker's movement at the Giscome mill. There Charles helped establish a workers' union and, in time, segued from working at the mill to running the union. By 1949 he was the business manager for the IWA's Prince George office. Throughout WWII, the community banded together to support the soldiers. From the Red Cross to selling war bonds, Mary remembers how the community, a world away from the war, worked together to do what they could. Now in a post-war Canada, Charles continued his work in the community on the march for freedom and equality; the very things young soldiers from the close-by base had fought for. He became deeply involved in the labour movement from the ground floor, first with the CCF (Co-operative Commonwealth Federation) and eventually helped establish a new political party, the New Democratic Party. This was the world of Mary's formative years.

Mary scrimped and saved until she had accumulated enough money; her parents paid for half, she paid for the other half, of a piano. On paper it was a great idea—certainly a fashion of the time—but try as she might, Mary did not have a musical bone in her body. Aside from the occasional visitor, the piano she bought as a teenager quickly fell into a state of disuse. When Mary completed high school, the piano's sale was the ticket to her first grand adventure as a liberated adult. Mary looked to education as a way to shape the minds of the next generation. The funds from the piano furnished her tuition for teacher's college at the Victoria Normal School. After ten months of normal school, Mary assumed a position in Budd Lake, a one-room school where she'd arrive each morning to start the fire prior to students arriving. She lived on the teacherage. Her parents, or occasionally Art who'd just got his license, would drop her off on Monday morning and pick her up on Friday evening. The contract lasted a year. With her toes wet, it was time to truly go out on her own.

On a Sunday night in late August Mary flew into Fort St. John, British Columbia, a burgeoning oil, gas, forestry, and agriculture boomtown far north in the province. The dirt roads were lined with wooden sidewalks. Mary recalls it being dusty. There were two hotels, the Fort, and the Condill. She was told the Condill (built in 1942 and, though it has seen better days, still stands today) was the nicer of the two, and she checked in. After making a few inquiries around town, she discovered that she would have to wait at the Condill until the mailman had enough mail to merit a trip to Cecil Lake. On Thursday, four days after arriving, the mailman fetched her to deliver her to her final destination. Barely out of college, there she would take the reins of a classroom at Transpine school, a two-room school house, grades one through four.

The mailman walked her into the Cecil Lake General Store, dropped off his deliveries, said good luck, and bid her farewell. To her surprise and consternation, no accommodations had been arranged and there was no teacherage established. The ministry had not even alerted the community a teacher would be arriving or had, in fact, been appointed. At the tender age of 21 she forged on. One woman, a pillar of the community, emphatically stated "I can't possibly take the teacher." That woman recommended someone else, who in turn recommended someone else. They milled about the store working their way down the small list of possibilities, taking full advantage of the party lines that connected the dispersed community. A gracious woman named Greta finally relented with, "Oh, I guess I can." And that, was that. Mary would walk a mile to the school each day, teach, and walk back at the end of each day. Her supplies, a blackboard and chalk. In rain, snow, and forty below, she would teach.

Mary met Harry at a dance in the old Cecil Lake community hall. A courtship began and they quickly fell in love. Over the next ten years they would live in Saskatchewan and Prince George, producing four children (the fifth came in '67) along the way. Mary would teach on and off through the children and moves—sometimes her own class, sometimes substitute teaching. But something in the air brought them back to the Peace. They scrimped and saved, eventually putting enough away to buy a property in Cecil Lake. There was a small cabin on the land but not much more. Over the years they would clear land, build a house, raise animals, raise children, grow vegetables, volunteer in the community, help build a new hall, a curling rink, an arena, a school, and the list goes on and on. They did the things you see in movies. While Harry worked the land, Mary shaped the minds of children. Always teaching.

Throughout her life she instilled the same values that her parents held so firmly. Values of equality and fairness: hard work deserved a decent wage and no one should ever go hungry. Those values are in her students, her children, her children's children, and her children's children's children. Mary is unassuming but Mary is fierce. Mary is my Grandmother. Her daughter Bernice puts it perfectly, "what a pioneer and champion of equality and strength my Mom is." She is indeed a pioneer of the Peace Country who left an indelible mark on the community of Cecil Lake and the hundreds of children she taught over the years. She is now 86; we still have much to learn from Mary.

Wade Kelly currently teaches at Charles Sturt University in Wagga Wagga, Australia. For the first 17 years of his life he lived on an acreage near Fish Creek, where his family still resides. While always excited to explore new places, the Peace Country holds a special place in his heart; no matter where he is, the Peace is home.

L.O.A. (Living Out Allowance)

By Kevin Buchholz

It's your bonus they said.
Bonus for what?
Well for working so far from home.
It's what I got paid just for being reliable and loyal.
It's what I got just to stay where I worked.
And it's all gone.
I could not tell you where or when exactly.
But it has all been spent.
What did I buy with all that free money?
It paid for someone else to be with my family.
Every day, every night, every birthday and hug.
I was never there for any of that.
And in the end it was all paid for and gone.
One hundred and fifty dollars a day.
That's the most I could get paid.
And it paid for it all.
It paid for my loyalty, my abilities and something so
precious that nothing else compares.
It also paid for all my memories.
Memories I couldn't make.
Memories I can't erase.
Memories I will never have.
And ones I'll never get to make.
For one hundred and fifty dollars, I sold my life away.

Life in the Patch

By Kevin Buchholz

I'm doing it I said.
Look at all I'm accomplishing.
Everything I'm asked for and tasked with.
All of it comes so easy.
If only I knew, if only I saw.
It happened so fast it was as if time had stopped.
I'm winning I remember thinking.
Like it was all that mattered.
I never watched, I never saw.
Never asked; just believed.
Winning, winning in the patch.
Like it ever existed.
Then I asked. And small the question was.
Yet none of it mattered.
It had amounted to nothing.
No matter what I said or did.
I was nothing at all.

Kevin Buchholz was not born nor raised in Fort St. John, but he has been happily living here for a few years now.

The Manners of Potted Chrysanthemums

By Patricia M. Emery

I'm noticing people of my "sixties" generation utilizing Facebook to convey their "Thanks" to hosts of dinners, parties, and barbecues via their social media. All the Facebook community sees their "thank you posts" and "likes", including the larger audience of those of us who weren't invited to the party or barbecue.

I wonder if people still take the time to write a thank you note, bring the host or hostess a "Bread and Butter" gift, or phone to genuinely convey their thanks; or is it somehow more genuine to have the large audience of social media?

I think back to a time before social media.

The simpler times of potted chrysanthemums.

I'm a young child riding in my parents '55 Chevy Bel-Air across town to our annual New Year's Day family dinner on the west side of Victoria. It's always very damp and chilly so I snuggle under an old grey army blanket to warm up. No seat-belts back then. The Bel-Air's fans and defrosters were blasting some heat, but never quite enough to keep the large windows from fogging up.

We often stop at 'Joe's Market', the Green Grocer, at Quadra and Hillside, so my Mom and I can run in and purchase a potted Chrysanthemum. Joe's Market is open 24/7, and the shelves out front are loaded with colourful potted plants, large bunches of cut flowers, and wooden boxes laden with fresh vegetables and fruits protected from the drizzle of rain by a large blue and grey striped awning.

My mother always explains as we go into Joe's, that it's very important to take our hostess a potted chrysanthemum to thank her and show our appreciation. What makes the potted chrysanthemum an appropriate "Bread and Butter" gift is it is pretty, practical, and long-lasting, and therefore a thoughtful gift. My education in manners includes learning from mom that "cut flowers" really aren't an appropriate "Bread and Butter" gift as a busy hostess will be preparing for guests and does not appreciate the fuss of locating a vase, trimming the stems, and trying to arrange flowers amidst the turkey or roast carvings, pots and pans, and an over-loaded counter top of bowls of salads, trifles, and pies.

I also learn that potted Chrysanthemums are appreciated as pretty and practical gifts for birthdays, visiting the elderly or ill, or for special occasions, such as Thanksgiving.

There is a manner and art to selecting the appropriate colour. One could purchase a pretty pastel coloured chrysanthemum for a visit to an elderly great-aunt, but would never pick that colour for a great uncle. Your selection for an elderly great uncle should be yellow or deep purple. Pastels are for spring events such as Easter and golds are for autumn events such as Thanksgiving.

My mom and aunts are such green thumbs they replant them outside in the spring, and the plants would flower again in late summer. As children of the depression they appreciated the value of the chrysanthemum.

I remember New Year's Day in 1960, when I got to pick-out, for the first time, a potted chrysanthemum as a thank you gift. There were over fifty chrysanthemums to choose from, in a wide variety of pastels, golds, purples, yellows; all in brightly foiled pots.

I spot that one special potted Chrysanthemum that would convey not only my family's appreciation to our hostess, my aunt, but also my maturity in selecting appropriately and wisely. I chose the most beautiful chrysanthemum with twelve pompoms of three-inch diameter formed by rows of glistening snow white florets. The plastic plant pot is covered in shiny bright green tin foil and a tall red plastic pick saying, "Happy New Year". Joe carefully wraps the plant in crisp cellophane and wishes us a most Happy New Year.

I am so excited when we arrive at my aunt and uncle's home. I run up the stairs carrying my perfect chrysanthemum, dashing quickly past my extended family who are all visiting in the living room, to find my aunt in the kitchen. Aunt Clara is preparing dinner among steaming pots and pans and simmering gravy on the stove-top. The aroma of turkey and dressing wafts in the air as my Uncle precisely carves the turkey.

She stops her busy dinner preparation to receive the chrysanthemum. She gives me a huge hug, and I notice her patterned red poinsettia Christmas apron is damp and there are beads of sweat on her brow from the day spent chopping and peeling vegetables, preparing dressing, baking pies, and cooking a huge turkey.

She carefully places the chrysanthemum in the place of honour in the center of her dining table on the white lace table cloth also adorned with the best Royal Albert china, silverware, and crystal.

Throughout dinner my relatives compliment me on my selection of the chrysanthemum.

After enjoying a fabulous dinner with much laughter and stories, we pitch in and help with dishes and clean-up.

My beloved chrysanthemum then receives a new place of honour on a white lace doily in the middle of my aunt's large walnut coffee table in the center of the living room, as our family regathers to play dominoes and canasta.

Joe's Market Corner Green Grocer still exists after all these years, and surprisingly, is largely as I remember it, with Joe's grandchildren carrying on the tradition. Yes, the chrysanthemums there are still a delightful variety of types and colours outside on the sidewalk shelves. It always takes me back to some happy childhood memories.

I moved to the Peace almost forty years ago and have always missed having a corner green grocer. I find on my grocery trips to Save-On Foods, the first area of the store I go to is the flower section, hoping to find a lovely potted chrysanthemum.

I often purchase one for a friend or neighbor who could use some cheer, or as a hostess "Bread and Butter" gift, remembering my manners as I learned as a child in Victoria. Sometimes I buy one for myself, just because, and then I feel a little tug in my heart and I smile.

Social media or not, how could you ever go wrong with a potted chrysanthemum?

Patricia Emery moved to the wide skies of the Peace over forty years ago, following her heart for both adventure and employment. She recently retired after an extensive career in public health nursing and community program development. Patricia attended a creative non-fiction writing course last year and is thrilled to have her first piece of creative non-fiction published.

Everything He Wanted

By Shea Cummings

As far as Charlie was concerned, tonight was a good night to end it all.

He folded the brown paper bag down the neck of the bottle and took a swig, and then fought back a gag. The whiskey burned his throat, but if he had any chance of going through with this, he needed it. His stepdad Joe was right–he was a coward.

Charlie wished Joe would have just hit him. At least the bruises would have healed. Instead, the bastard hid behind his Bible every Sunday morning, shaking hands and smiling at his fellow Bible Thumpers. It was all love and peace until they were home—or at least in the car—then the insults and belittling would start. And all the time, Charlie's mom acted like she didn't hear anything.

Joe's favorite saying rang in Charlie's head. "If you were any stupider, I don't think the love I have for your momma and the good Lord could keep me from beating you silly."

In time, Charlie realized his mom wasn't going to do anything. He gave up pleading with her to make it stop. She'd always say, "Joe's doing the best he can, trying to make a proper man out 'a you, since your daddy walked out." That just made Charlie angrier because his dad only left because Charlie's mom was sharing her love around town too freely. If Charlie had been old enough to decide for himself, he would have left with his dad.

A dribble of whiskey found its way down his chin as Charlie polished off the last of the bottle. With an unsteady hand, he fumbled in his pocket and gripped the cold handle of the handgun. Joe probably hadn't even noticed the gun was missing.

He took a slow breath in and held it for a moment before letting it out. "I'll show you a damn coward, Joe." Tears burned his eyes as he raised the gun. The cool steel pressed up underneath his chin.

Eyes shut tight, he squeezed the trigger.

***

"Hello. Do you mind if I sit with you, friend?"

The gun fell from Charlie's hands to the stone steps of the church with an echoing clatter. He stared at the man taking a seat beside him. He stammered, trying to answer, but couldn't.

"It is kind of chilly tonight," the man continued, turning to face forward, a strong smell of weeks without showering coming off him. "Do you come here often?"

Charlie managed to find his tongue. "Not really."

"I do," the man said. "It feels like home." The man's clothes were filthy and tattered, and Charlie noticed a toe sticking out of his left shoe. Charlie guessed he was homeless. The man turned to face him. "Can I ask you something?"

"I guess so."

"Why did you come here tonight?"

"Why do you think, old man?" Charlie waved the gun in the air, the dim street lights bouncing off its deadly curves. "Are you blind?"

The man smiled warmly, unimpressed. "I see the gun, but that does not answer my question. Why did you come here? Why tonight?"

Charlie shrugged his shoulders trying for nonchalant and came up short. "Seemed like a good night to die." He expected rejection and judgment; that's how Joe would have reacted. This man was different though, he didn't seem surprised or shocked. Instead, he continued to gaze at him. This guy was actually listening to him, and… there was kindness in his eyes.

He felt a rush of hot tears flood his face. He rubbed them brusquely in a futile attempt to hold them back. A few escaped, leaving darkened spots on the stones at his feet.

"Still not an answer, my friend."

"Well, there is this girl at school—Alyssa I think—and she was talking about God, and what she said was different. So I asked her some questions. Unlike my stepdad and the rest of them Thumpers, she was nice. But then I told her she was crazy. That didn't seem to bother her, though. So I asked her why it didn't bother her to be called crazy. She just laughed and told me to talk to God and He would give me peace and I would find answers to all my questions. It was all pretty weird. I mean, even if God was there, you couldn't just talk to him, right? But here I am, right in front of …" he raised his hands and formed quotation marks in the damp night air, the gun in his right hand leaning drunkenly at the action. "'God's House', seeing if maybe he would answer me if I showed him how serious I was."

The man nodded thoughtfully. "That is a better answer. Why do you think you cannot talk to God?"

"Is why the only damn question you know?" Charlie waved the gun around some more, exasperated. "God never answered a single prayer of mine. Why would he start listening now?"

"What if I told you he has always heard your prayers?"

"I'd call you a liar," Charlie spat.

"What if I told you that tonight is the answer to every prayer you have ever prayed? That this is the moment your entire life has led to." His gaze was piercing, but then it softened. "I am here to save you, Charlie."

Charlie's laugh echoed off the stone walls of the church. "No offense old man, but I'm kind of way past the point of no return here. You ain't stopping nothing. I think it's time for you to go. I wouldn't wanna hurt you."

"I never said anything about stopping you, Charlie, but I am here to save you. You just do not see it yet... but you will."

"You off your meds or something? You ain't saving sh—" Charlie stopped, locked eyes with the man and shifted away from him. "I never told you my name. Who the hell are you?"

"My name is Michael. I am an angel of the Lord, Charlie."

Charlie stared at Michael for a moment, expecting more, like "I'm joking" or something. "You're not kidding?" When the man calling himself Michael's gaze remained steady, that was it. All the emotion of the evening, all the whiskey, hit him, and Charlie lost it. He wheezed between laughter and braying sobs, tears streaming down his face.

Michael sat there patiently waiting, unsmiling.

"Okay, okay, good one. Who are you, really?" Charlie asked, running his fingers through his hair, when he managed to gain some composure.

Michael just stared at him. This made Charlie uncomfortable; he felt like the man was looking right into him. If someone had asked him if he actually thought God or angels were real, he'd have answered, "no", but now, he was not so sure. Could this man really be an angel? Could there be a God?

"How do I know you are who you say you are? If you say faith, I swear to God— " He caught himself and shook his head before going on, "Or whatever—it's all over and I'm taking you with me." Charlie held up the gun.

"Your uncle made you do things when you were young. Things that hurt your little mind and soul." Michael's eyes were piercing but kind.

Anybody could know that. Uncle Jeff is still in prison from me telling on him.

"But instead of healing over time, you grew bitter. There was no peace for you, only justice." Michael's voice softened. "I know about the missing cats and dogs in your neighborhood."

Charlie's eyes grew wide. No one knew about that but him!

"And the plans you made to kill your mom and stepdad."

Tears of shame burned Charlie's eyes, and he was crying again. "Stop! How do you know this stuff?" His chest heaving, he moaned, "Where was God when I needed him? I asked him over and over to take away the pain."

Michael rested his hand on Charlie's shoulder, spreading a warmth through Charlie, like a fire burning from his belly. "It is time Charlie."

"Time for what?" Charlie choked out.

"To let peace consume you and heal you. This is what you have been searching for. You have suffered more than any young man ever should. Your suffering did not go unnoticed by my Father."

"How come he waited so long to let me know he was real?"

"Your heart was hard. You were not ready."

"And I am now?"

"That is up to you, Charlie. Though you must know, this is your last chance. Redemption will not knock on the door again after tonight."

Charlie didn't know what to do. On one hand, he wanted the peace and healing this man was offering, but he could not bring himself to trust the words Michael was saying. If God was real and had been listening to Charlie like Michael was saying, why show up now? Why not before?

"I don't think I can, Michael." Charlie hung his head. "I can't trust anyone but myself."

"That brings me a sadness that is greater than you could ever imagine. All of heaven weeps for the choice you are making tonight, Charlie. Goodbye, my friend." Michael's hand slipped from Charlie's shoulder. He stood up, and with a regretful look, turned and hobbled away.

Everything Michael had just told him played through Charlie's mind in an instant. His whole life flashed before his eyes in scenes, the good things and the bad. Memories of his real dad playing with him at the park when he was a little boy. Then his uncle's face was there and his stepdad's. The last image was that of his mother on her knees beside her bed, crying.

"Michael, wait!" Charlie sprang up and ran towards him. "How does this work? Do I say some stupid prayer, or what?"

A smile, like a thousand suns, lit up Michael's face. "Do you want to experience a peace that will surpass all human understanding? Is it redemption and love that you desire?"

Charlie took a breath. "Yes. Yes—to all of it."

"Then it's time to go home."

Betrayed, Charlie's hurt, then anger, flared.

"Then what's all this crap about God, and peace, and redemption? I say I want it, and you tell me it's time to go home."

Michael grasped Charlie's shoulders and gently turned him around to face the steps they had only moments ago been sitting on together.

Two people were blocking Charlie's view of something on the steps. A man and a woman; the man on a cell phone talking frantically.

"Hey, that's my bag," Charlie called out and ran back to the steps, but the man and woman paid him no mind. He darted between them. His blood ran cold at seeing his own lifeless body, arms splayed across the church steps, his dead fingers still clutching the gun. The top of his head was gone, blood and brain now spread in a wide crimson fan across the cold grey stone.

The sight before him was surreal. He was broken. Pathetic. He wondered if he ever had a chance. It was okay, though. In that moment, the past didn't matter anymore.

He averted his eyes, unable to look any longer. Michael had come closer, though he too was unnoticed by the crowd now gathering around Charlie's body. "How…?"

"You accepted the free gift of peace and redemption, Charlie. It is time to go home."

Home.

Charlie left the crowd and walked with Michael. He understood now, and for the first time he could remember, there was peace inside of him. At last, the war was over.

He was going home.

THE END

Shea is a follower of Jesus, a family man, and an indulger of coffee and espresso… at the same time preferably. He is a spinner of stories and a writer of words. To call him an avid reader would be an understatement to the amount of words he consumes in a week.

The Peace Region has been home to Shea his whole life. He was born in Fort St. John, grew up in Dawson Creek, and now currently resides back in Fort St. John with his wife and son. He is a small town kind of guy, but he dreams about city lights, and hopes to one day trade his stories for money.

There is a lifetime of stories floating around in Shea's head, some short and others long. His preferred genre to write (and read) is fantasy, but thrillers and horror are high on the list as well. It is not uncommon to find Shea talking to his characters – or to himself, depends on your perspective. He tries to let them write their own stories, stepping in only to make introductions.

Throughout school, Shea had a few poems published in various anthologies, but into his late teens he shoved his passion for writing into a dusty chest in the attic in his head. He never planned to open it again. If there is one thing life has taught him, it is that things rarely go as planned, and so it is with the stories that he writes.

"Try not to be offended when your characters change the story.
It's their story, not yours."

– S. Cummings

Sunday Devotions-As They See It

By Ronnie Roberts

Anna kept her head down when she entered Peace Church, but it was clear to anyone who noticed her she was still wearing the same glasses she had broken over two weeks ago. A half-moon piece of glass was missing from her left lens, cut out as neatly as if by design. Rain clung to her short, iron gray hair and worn coat; and she tried hard not to hobble too clumsily in her now very wet shoes. Oh how her feet hurt in the cold. The driving rain had made the walk especially hard.

She slipped out of her coat and hung it over the back of the oak bench. Sinking into her usual seat she smiled at Gary Holland, who hastily moved himself and his overcoat further along the bench. Gary was an odd duck she had to say—always holding himself apart from everyone.

But who's to say what goes on inside people's heads? Maybe what some people viewed as Gary's snobbishness was actually shyness.

She opened the clasp of her purse. Inside was the vivid pink envelope her granddaughter had used to send her a Happy Thanksgiving card. Anna had scratched out the writing, and placed her tithe into it. When the collection bowl was passed along her row, she proudly placed her contribution in along with everyone else's, and with a smile, opened her hymnbook to 'In His Grace'.

Father Lars caught her eye and winked at her. He was such a character and she loved him for it. She wondered if he knew that some days, it seemed to her, it was his Sunday sermon and her time with her fellow parishioners alone that kept her head up through the week. Yes, she was eighty-six years old and her body protested her every move, but she was here amongst friends, and it was another wonderful day to be alive.

***

Gary Holland frowned at the collection plate as it made its way toward him. Jesus, he couldn't go anywhere without someone's hand out; just exactly when had he become the local bank? He sent his wife Dorothy a dark look, which, as usual, she pretended not to see, then stood to remove his damp wool overcoat, carefully smoothed and folded it on the seat beside him so it wouldn't wrinkle.

No sense fighting it. Dorothy liked to see and be seen, and she would insist they glad-hand with Father Lars before their usual Sunday brunch with the Frasers. He looked up in time to catch Dick Fraser's wave.

Gary lifted his arm and pointed silently at his watch then held up two fingers. Dick nodded. Gary unbuttoned his suit jacket and sat down.

The collection plate appeared before him like magic—yeah, like he didn't see that coming. He tossed in a hundred-dollar bill. There. That should keep them off his back for a while.

***

Father Lars kept glancing up at the door. It wasn't like Anna to miss Sunday's service. Perhaps her fall two weeks ago had been more serious than she'd let on.

Oh, there she was, dripping wet, but here, nevertheless. He knew from experience she would be horribly embarrassed if he asked Mavis to go help her with her wet coat. Anna was a feisty old girl, he'd give her that.

He watched her hobble to her usual seat, her shoes leaving a wet trail on the carpet. She slipped out of her coat. She wore her blue dress today, with the lace collar her grand-daughter had made her. He remembered how delighted she'd been when she'd received it.

Uh-oh. Gary Holland was sitting beside her, holding his cashmere coat away as if it would somehow be tainted if it touched Anna's.

Dorothy Holland was making the usual rounds amongst the parishioners and Gary did not look happy about the arrangement, acting out a strange pantomime with Dick Fraser before sinking down to sit with Anna.

Father Lars had to bite down on his lip to keep from smiling at the odd pair. He watched Gary toss a bill into the collection plate, and look up to see that Father Lars took note.

Father Lars bowed his head in silent acknowledgement. Every penny would be used wisely; but it was Anna's hot-pink contribution that made him smile. She had so little, yet gave so much.

Before beginning his sermon, he said a quiet prayer for Gary Holland, the poorest man here today.

Ronnie Roberts is the tireless, talented leader of the Writers of the Peace, the literary glue that holds us together, showing us the way to better writing while having fun doing it." Okay – so Pat made me say that.

Glue, huh? I can be sticky, especially after eating caramel popcorn, (which I hardly ever do!), and writing is fun (and maddening, and rewarding and sometimes reduces me to tears of frustration), and I did write a book for fiction writers entitled Complete Boot Camp for Fiction Writers.

Besides that, I've published six novels – The Wedding Dress Promise Series and the Poet Oregon Series and numerous short stories in magazines and anthologies. What I'm super excited about now is the three book Sci Fi series I'm currently writing, Earth Survives: Lost Sentinel, Cursed Apprentice and Deadly Messenger. What's not to like? Time travel, a post-apocalyptic world, a telepathic heroine, a battle between good and evil? Yup, Pat is right, writing is so much fun!!

Oh – and my family came to Fort St John 'temporarily' in search of work ten years ago. We fell in love with the people and seasons of the Peace and stayed.

A Peacenik Searching

By Carolyn Robe

There's a wildness to God's mercy.
There's a wildness to God's love.
Tsunamis, terrorist warnings,
What are we thinking of?
A felon from New Orleans
War resister for a cause
Holed up six years in Canada
Evading unjust laws.
Praying to the fetishes
Bear, Mountain Lion, Snake
Leaving under amnesty
Deciding what to take
Teaching English there in Yemen
In Cairo, Istanbul,
Teaching English in Malaysia,
Living to the full--
There's a quiet, gentler life
Far from the writhings of all war--
With faint pulsating rumours--
Choose to study war no more.
There's a freedom in God's mercy.
There's a freedom in God's grace.
Continually searching
To find a finer place.

Carolyn Robe has a BA - English from the University of Oregon and a MA - Ed from Western Carolina University – and has a deep appreciation for the opportunity to attend "Writers of the Peace" at the Ft St John library. A long-time member, Carolyn was recently inspired at a meeting to make a solemn declaration on September 20, 2016: "I will create poetry for five minutes every day for 365 consecutive days..." (I would like to think that this allotment of time will increase daily as I move into 2017!)

On Writing "ITCHY SPOT"

By John Adam Kelderman

I'll tell you. This was not fun to write.

Fair warning.

Introductions first. My name is Tom Barnabas. You are about to read how at twenty-one years of age I decided to sit down and write my first short story. Titled "Itchy Spot" it is a semi-true account of an incident that happened between a girlfriend and I in '97. I workshopped the hell out of this story in university and tried to anthologize it for a book in 2016. My peers and old university professors commended me on the authenticity and the dialogue, the pace, the characters. I cleaned it up a bit for you, so here it is, number one. I only like the first line, "They have just finished making love." It holds weight throughout the rest of the piece. Although juvenile, it is collected here in the endnotes. "Itchy Spot" was not a fun story to write. I used to pass it off as fiction. When I try to remember it now at nearly forty, the actual details—all of the hard facts—crowd around me and push in my heart.

This is how I will begin. "Tom's Journey from NS to BC". Maybe that's what the story should be titled. Or perhaps "How I Learned to Stop Worrying and Love the Peace". Maybe I won't get to explain how I came to live in Fort St. John, British Columbia, but I'll try to keep up with the competing settings, themes and racing voices, and as best I can, try to define them for you as I go along. If you don't want to know how in a very jumbled and streaming way "Itchy Spot" came into being, then just skip to the story in the endnotes.

Usually at sixteen or seventeen, high school kids plan or predetermine a path or a goal for after graduation. Mostly they apply to universities or have some sort of job lined up. In fall of 1997, after graduating in the spring I moved to the city and took a job as a travel agent at a place called Royal Tours. I built itineraries for wealthy Americans to come see little old Nova Scotia: Peggy's Cove, the Cabot Trail, Louisburg, Lunenburg, etc.

I was well suited for work at the travel agency and found myself liking it. I enjoyed the writing aspect. I spoke with people from all over the United States and Canada and then built agendas to accommodate their personal tastes. I held meet-and-greets with clients at the airport and took product knowledge tours all around the Maritimes and Eastern United States. The perks: the travel, and a company credit card to write off the expenses. Other than my father's print shop I'd never been exposed to such a new and well-oiled business and I found myself a part of it, helping, contributing.

But here I've gone and forgotten to mention something important. There had been a ceaseless voice starting to sing in my heart during my last years of high school— "I want! I want! Strike!" At first it was just a whisper. I'd read about the same thing happening to a fellow in a book once. It wasn't so bad at this point that I wanted to jump out a window or anything. But over the years it got there or near there, anyway.

Back to Royal Tours. My mother and her future husband started the company together in 1997 under the guidance of a wrinkled, British émigré named

April Blucher. She was old and smart, but irascible and mean. She owned a B&B compound in Fall River and an Inn at La Havre, a beach house in Risser's. We considered her lake house in Fall River our head office. My mother worked the books so her job was at the B&B. I worked in the company's retail space on the fringes of the city in a newly developed industrial park called Bear's Lake. Wedged between a Chinese buffet and a vacant storefront, the outlet became my second home. The neighbouring unoccupied space later became our expansion but in the meantime it served as Royal Tours' smoke shack. Just a heap of stones, old wood, beams and raw materials, nothing else. It is a Titleist Golf Pro shop now and next door there is a shuttered Danier Leather Ladies store. We were all just brands in our death throes.

But back then it was Royal Tours International. Run by one Frank Comer and the British woman April Blucher and managed by the development firm SBD. They were hawkish men who owned the mini-mall in Bear's Lake—the buffet, the empty lots, all of it—Greek brothers who had gotten rich building a downtown hotel in the eighties. Stavros Brothers Development. George Stavros, Xandros Stavros and Apollo. Apollo Stavros managed Royal Tours alongside Frank Comer.

We had our individual workstations. No walk-in traffic. We fancied ourselves tour-operators. We used an archaic social chat program called ICQ to network the office. Counter person, itinerary-writer and phone catcher. I worked alongside Mikey Minto, Frank's nephew. Frank is my stepfather now. I don't know what that makes Mikey.

One day, I'm not sure when, but during the time somewhere between September 1997 and April '98, I sat down and wrote "Itchy Spot".

I moved to the city when I was seventeen, like I said, in late summer 1997. I lived in Downie Hill with my mother on the third floor of a newly constructed apartment building. The Hill was isolated from the city. Nearby Charcoal Lake and Bear's Lake provided some hiking spots, but I don't remember hiking or swimming that year. Before I knew it I had wintered over in the apartment—I was a shut-in with nothing but the distant glow of the city in my window. And with it returned the voice—"strike!"

I started an emotional affair with a woman over ICQ during that time when I first moved to the city. She—this young woman I sort of fell in love with—lived in Ontario. My high-school sweetheart Sara didn't know at the time that I'd been chatting with this other one, I forget her name.

Sara was a freshman at one of the universities in the city. She lived in the residential dorms but sometimes stayed with me at my mother's apartment, a half-hour city bus ride away. Or sometimes I snuck in there for the night by dodging hall monitors and chaperones. The nights and weeks we didn't stay together I busied myself playing guitar, smoking weed, grocery shopping with mother, chatting on ICQ. I was still a kid.

Here it is years later and I forget the girl's name. I want to say Lynn or Amber-Lynn, something like that. Rae Lynn. But while those may be close guesses, they aren't right. Her name is locked away in my head somewhere. Maybe by writing this story it'll come out.

After my folks divorced in 1996, my family broke apart. I doubt we'll all ever be in the same room together again, save for a funeral or something. My brother and sister already lived outside the house so I had to pack their bedrooms into boxes when my mother moved to the city. I packed my father's room, too. My mother couldn't handle that. The youngest at seventeen, I didn't know what would become of me. We lived in rural Nova Scotia. I had yet to complete a year of high school and I didn't have a plan for after that, much to my Dad's chagrin. Little did I know, he had his own plans to worry about.

When I was younger I'd heard that some of my friends had to stand in court to tell a judge which parent he or she would rather live with. I didn't want to stand before any judge. But I'd thought about it. I knew I was old enough to make my own decisions. Wasn't I? And I knew that in the greater, deeper scheme of things, indecision was also a decision. Could I simply float between my Dad and his new girlfriend and my mother and her tears? Was I capable of such cruelty of the heart?

Immediately after the divorce my mother and I packed up the house and she moved to the city and shortly after my high school graduation I did the same. In between, during a period of six months or so, I stayed in my father's love nest, a secret apartment he'd rented for trysts with his girlfriend. He moved in to her house, outside of town. At that time I worked as a lifeguard at the Community Aquatics Center. I finished my high school year living in that place. I remember little, other than when my brother's college year expired, he stayed the summer of 1997 with me. We drank, smoked pot and fooled around with our girlfriends in that place. Miranda Avenue, I think.

Not that any of this really matters. I don't think this piece will be one of those stories where you'll see me or any other character change or come of age. Maybe I just lack a certain level of clarity regarding the person I once was and the person I am today. I don't know how comfortable I'd feel talking to him now if I were to meet this old version of myself on the street. I think of it more like an overdue journal entry maybe. A jumbled diary, a botched confessional. Or maybe it's a rushed piece of autobiography. A snippet without many questions. "The Germination of Itchy Spot" I'll name it.

I find that when I write a story I bring up more questions than answers. I am apprehensive about this and I really shouldn't be. I am afraid. I think: maybe by writing a story something from memory, something true will attempt to bubble out and provide more answers than questions. Sometimes you meet a person and it seems like they are the answers to all of your questions.

Linny. Let's just call her Linny.

Just one thing to note before I begin in earnest: I know you are thinking that I should write more about how "Itchy Spot" came about. You know, the technical aspects of how I plotted and planned all the elements of the tale. I won't be touching on any of the craftsmanship per se, but I assure you that all the background exposition you'll need to contextualize the story is going to be in here. I reassure you now. Read along and you'll see, maybe it'll make sense by the end. Maybe I did change. Maybe change is the only thing that is constant.

My friend Richie Haight introduced us. He was a large kid with yellow teeth and a pimply face. He wore rough bleached white-boy dreads. Sometimes he'd come by my place and we'd play guitar together. Virtuosos of many things. We shared an interest in music and computers; he loved to talk politics, too. He was quiet, with small eyes behind his wireless round-frame glasses. In a way I was glad to have a friend like him. His humble nature grounded me and taught me how to be quiet and listen.

In high school tech class he showed me some rooms on mIRC and ICQ and gave me access. I remember two. One called #Citylocals, and the other, I forget the name, was a general chat room for writers and favoured authors. It's here I first read about the dirty realists Richard Ford, Raymond Carver and Toby Wolf.

These chat-rooms, however early in their infancy, required new terms to learn and introduced an entirely new vocabulary of acronyms and words and phrases. A new language emerged: pings and pongs and lag reports, 1337, A/S/L, BBS, TEOTWAWKI, "ease of use". I think we believed then, in some weird and paranoid way, that Y2K spelled doomsday. Maybe not for everyone, but for me it was. In those days you could see all the members of the chat room on one side of the screen and you could see the administrators names in a different color. Then the general chat happened in the center of the screen. Richard introduced me to some of his friends. They came equipped with all kinds of strangely styled names, The_D3v1L, RayOfFyre, and ~Ch1tz~. Linny's screen name was AnG3LBl00D.

RepeaterRepeater. That was me. It was also my first Hotmail account, repeaterrepeater@hotmail.com. I think I coded the password with some kind of literary reference—the name of a character from a Hemingway story or something. Maybe Faulkner. I liked to read these classic modern authors in my youth. As a child I hoarded many volumes and magazines. I inherited from a dead uncle a Reader's Book Club set of Hemingways: A Farewell to Arms, For Whom the Bell Tolls, and The Sun Also Rises. I acquired used copies of Reader's Digest and found a full set of Funk and Wagnall's Encyclopaedias in a cardboard box with some early 80's National

Geographic Magazines and Archie Double Digests for four dollars at a garage sale in 1992. I was twelve years old when at a bookmobile used-book-drive I found a DH Lawrence poetry collection. It was my favourite. "When I Went to the Circus" and "The Rainbow" stand out. And I owned a nearly destroyed original chapbook of TS Eliot's The Wasteland, published by Hogarth Press in September 1923. I read later in life that this was one of only a few hundred copies made that had the type handset by Virginia Woolf. I didn't know much about Modern literature then. The Lost Generation sounded like a good fit for me. And that copy with the splotchy blue faded cover was probably worth something. What I don't know. Worth nothing compared to what it gave me as a young man new on words. An artist in the making.

At fourteen-fifteen I listened to jazz music and Herbie Hancock. I tried to skateboard and tried to play bass guitar in a band and tried to join the online community phenomenon. I had Richie come to my house and install the proper programs so that I had mIRC and ICQ downloaded to my rebuilt Compaq Presario. I loved chatting and meeting new people online. Why Linny, who was from Ontario, was ever on a city locals chat room I'll never know. Richie invited her I guess.

The rooms were basic chat rooms. ICQ annoyingly had perfected some of the blips and MSN later developed a chat service that bumped them all out in the end. Not to mention the advent of Facebook. Anyway, this was before all that. Although if you wanted you could probably find ICQ and working mIRC chat rooms still operating in today's hyper-futuristic capital 'I' Internet.

It went something like this. It's the best I can do to represent the feel of the actual room. On paper or in this writing program it's kind of hard come to find out:

#Citylocals [+nst]: City PUNK ROCK bands, etc--------

ANG3LBl00D

The_D3V1L

RayOfFyre

EvanFlow

~Ch1tz~

RepeaterRepeat

@HelloKitten

FYMboy

~riotGrrl~

***Now talking in #Citylocals
****Topic is now City PUNK ROCK bands, etc
*** Set by `RockFISH Fri. Nov. 97 22.21.29

<EvanFlow> Welcome to #Citylocals, RepeaterRepeater
<ANG3LBl00D> hello RepeaterRepeater, the chatroom is invite only. The administrators are myself and @HelloKitten. If u want to create a private chatroom with any of the ppl in the room, feel free to msg them. This is pretty chill.

<FYMboy> hello ppl :D
<~Ch1tz~> LOL u n00b got lagged out. U got PWNd
*** ~riotGrrl has joined #Citylocals
<EVanFlow> anyone else see The Dickheads show last Friday?
<ANG3LB00D> it's not easy being the only girl in the room
<~Ch1tz~> nobody asked me
**** ~Raymo_1982 has left the room [Ping timeout 268 seconds]
*** The_D3ViL has joined #Citylocals
<ANG3LB100D> My man Repeater is coming in, soon. Behave urself @FYMboy. He's nice, not like u :P

And so it went something like that. In the early days of fairly accessible online chatting, things seemed friendlier and less dangerous than they are now. No Tinder or Grindr, no Lovematch.com or eHarmony. That was years away.

It was in this simple way that I met Linny.

We listened to each other. We both liked music so we chatted about Nine Inch Nails, Marilyn Manson and Fear Factory. We exchanged pictures. I sent a picture of me I'd tinted blue in the Paint application on my Windows '95. I looked skinny and fresh-faced, clean-shaved and handsome. Black boat-necked long sleeve, hair crazy, staring off into the middle distance. I still remember that image. I saved it on a 3-1/2" floppy disk for the longest time. I looked like Robert Smith from The Cure. I think I threw it out, finally, last summer when I cleared storage boxes out of my father's crawlspace.

Stories have conflict and characters go through change. Do you see my desires moving me, giving my life definition and meaning—not meaning in a spiritual sense, but in the narrative sense? If you are reading this story of mine that is because for whatever reason you have designed a desire to read it and that spirit motivated you to do it. Desire—that voice. Who we fall for or lust after in my experience seems mostly out of our control. A single desire can lay waste to the smartest man's life's work. How genuine is that? Cheaply done, Tom? No, it is much more complicated. Besides, I thought this story was about me cheating on my high school girlfriend Sara with some out of focus and near-nameless Internet girl we'd named Linny. Or was it about how I wrote "Itchy Spot"?

Damn it all my mother used to say.

But remember, I did mention before that it would come around didn't I? All the pieces will sort of fit, no?

Catfishing wasn't a thing back then. Actually it probably was come to think of it, but I wasn't worried about that with Linny. Live-streaming did not yet exist and downloading was minimal. YouTube hadn't come of age. The Internet was just a screaming baby back then, best personified by the 3D rendered Cha-Cha Baby, dancing in primitive time-rates and key-frames, proliferated through emails, on all the geocities websites, on the show Ally McBeal (1997-2002). No motion capture. These were the last days of art. Blue Swede's version of "Hooked on a Feeling" beat along from way back in time, a track released on their 1973 album of the same name alongside other classic cover songs—Allen Tousaint's "Working in a Coal Mine" being the most standout other than the cover of the BJ Thomas song. So the track provided accompaniment to a nonexistent and immortal baby as it danced into a restless and uncertain future.

The filename was sk_baby.max (1996)

Besides all this slop I've brought up, there is Linny floating timelessly in my mind, at the limits of my distraction—no, she was more powerful than a distraction: Linny was an escape.

This is what we talked about: I don't think Sara wanted to have any discourse about my broken home in the engaging way Linny did. Linny had interest. So we started a friendship. I could tell her how stupid I felt or how lonely I'd gotten in my relationship with Sara. We spoke on the phone and ran up phone bills. I used phone cards. I smoked menthols in the small spare room beside my mother's and chatted on mIRC and ICQ for hours into the night. I looked forward to waking and getting to work at Royal Tours International in the mornings because I could chat with her on ICQ from my desk.

"Just make sure you wrap your cigarette butts in paper towel and squirt the wad in the sink," my mother would say before turning in for the night. My teenage addiction to cigarettes had graduated into a pack a day habit and I had turned into a shut-in, a pothead and a nighthawk.

"Mom!" I'd say. "You said, 'squirt the wad'; what the ...!"

Yeah, I was that guy. Still am today. Maybe that's why I can't seem to stay married.

My mother, after their separation. I still remember watching her from the upstairs window of my childhood home, watching her pull into the driveway. I'd just smoked a cigarette. I rushed to wash my hands in the sink when I saw her arrive. She drove a white Dodge Intrepid. It was when she was separated. Within the first days or weeks at least. I watched her through the window as she cried in the parked car. I tried to cover my smoky odour (idiotic because my mother had no olfactory senses, had burned it out from years of inadvertently inhaling ink and solvents in her and my Dad's printing franchise).

She sat in the car with the engine off and the windows turned down. She smoked a Matinee Slim as she cried. I went out there for her to touch and hold.

I felt like some unassuming enlightened person. How had I gained this saintly and humble demeanour? I didn't cry. I just held her and listened. I said comforting words like "I know" and "It's okay" and "It will get better" and I found myself promising like I knew what I was talking about. I tried to be strong where she was weak. Confront her vulnerability. Mine too. Maintain the yin and the yang.

I didn't need the details, I told her. I was feeling them out with my heart next to hers. I held her close. My mother. The woman who birthed me and brought me up.

Later that night we smoked cigs on the back porch, our faces puffy with exhaustion. We didn't even acknowledge the fact that we'd both picked up the bad habit. We drank wine and cried when we needed to.

I still don't know the details of my parent's divorce and I never will truly know. Anyway, those particulars don't matter. That's another story.

Linny helped me deal with these new things. Besides music, besides empty relationships, lives. From boredom blooms desire. We'd both experienced the broken home. Nothing is new under the sun. Sara had also come from a divorced family. Had a single mother, three brothers. Daddy issues. In her life as well as mine there were points of connection but I just couldn't grasp them. I struggled. She had just arrived at that point of reference before I did and probably didn't want to go back. Linny was different. We had our own language apart from the parenthesis and colons we used to make happy faces in the days before emojis. I wrote freestyle poetry for her. We exchanged pictures like I said before, and we spoke on the phone more and more.

Sooner or later we talked about a meet up. She had enough money to take the train from Ontario—Markham, I believe—all the way to the east coast. I had this image in my head, an image of Linny stepping off the train in my hometown. I pictured her and I staying in some hotel somewhere, Dartmouth maybe, at the Marriot Harborview where they had a $365 per night penthouse.

We spoke excitedly about these ideas and fantasies. She told me things about her. Sexual things I'd never heard of before. She wanted to be tied down, humiliated. Wanted me to walk into the room and say, "What? You're already wet. How could you get so excited so quickly?" and then leave the bedroom and watch TV for a half hour. Come back and take it slow, make it last forever. Fun role-play, friendly and consensual. She yearned for something different and I did too. Otherwise I do not think I would have begun an emotional affair with this young woman from across the country. People always told me to follow my heart.

I cheated on Sara, sure. In high school before all this. It was with a younger girl, a cute, round-eyed girl with a shy smile named Shannon Raymond. She was new to my group of friends. One of her girlfriends, Karen, dated one of my pals, Jerome, etc. We were kids. Fifteen or sixteen, that's all.

Sara and I were counsellors at her Venture Christian Church group. She attended the camp for a month at a time; on her insistence I acquired a boy's counsellor position, so I had only two two-week residencies two weeks apart. Sara stayed the entire summer as a head-counsellor. In those two weeks without her my social life amped up and I put my moves on Shannon Raymond.

Young, intoxicatingly beautiful. Tight wiry hair, athletic and tall. One night at a party we had sex, semi-consciously. We were drunk. This is the paragraph where I describe two naked high-school kids in a dark bedroom on the floor, holding each other up, poking and pulling and rolling around on the outdated carpet with a party raging above and the muted hoots and hollers of rowdy drunken skater kids in our ears. It was in my house, to my bed she'd led me, come to think of it. But I always felt that it was my intrusion into her body.

These paragraphs also describe in detail, my silly desires which by the way didn't stop after this incident with Shannon Raymond, or after Sara, Linny, Ricki. The list never stops and maybe never will. Maybe I'll never learn.

At another party, at my house again.

These were in the days when my father was far, far away with his girlfriend and my mother was in and out of the house for various reasons; she had regained a social life, visited friends, consumed boxes of wine, cried and laughed and healed herself ceaselessly. I wish I'd taken her example. Too obsessed with girls and partying, drinking, drugs. I guess I was confused and didn't know how to deal with my dad's cheating, let alone my own. Was he really the ultimate model for my behaviour? An example? Had I become him so soon? We were two people; I had to remember. Of the same blood. Had he heard what I heard? The voice? "Want! Want!"

Now I hear Jeannine Riley, from the 1973 motorcycle movie Electra Glide in Blue in character as Jolene. She says, "Well, well, well. My two knights in shining armour, Mr. Tall and Mr. Small."

I felt like Mr. Small.

The whole thing came apart rather quickly after that second party. Sara was back from her stint at the Christian camp. My friend Steve told her all about my affair with Shannon Raymond. I was downstairs in the basement of my house playing an old beach-worn guitar, sitting deep in the furniture, sipping beer with a couple of others. Petra, Kimmy, Jerome, Will. Steve rushed in suddenly. He looked concerned.

"Tom, I just told her everything," he said.

"What? About what?"

"We were talking and it came out. I'm sorry. About you and Shannon."

"Oh no," I said. I said it but didn't really feel it until later.

Damage control? I rushed outside. Sara was nowhere to be seen. I smoked a nervous cigarette in the light of the back porch, scanned the slow partiers in the yard. Some did handstands on the roof of the gazebo or congregated in small groups to smoke grass in the driveway. Others played basketball naked by the toolshed. Many summers ago my brother and I built a one-room shack about thirty meters into the trees. Our camp. Insulated windows, screen, a bunk bed, a ladder, a table. A beanbag chair if I remember correctly. The roof slanted so rainwater drained away from the building. I followed our flagstone path past anthills and many ferns and alders and big poplars, past the compost heap my dad had used for grass clippings.

In this little shack I found Sara, and she beat me. She pounded her fists into my face, my stomach, my back. She cried, bawled and said, "How could you, how could you?" And I began crying too. I cried because I still felt trapped between my sympathy for Sara and my love of being free to do anything I wanted, to seemingly build myself out of nothing. Ex nihilo. It felt like I should be able to do it if I wanted. And I wanted. That night Sara became an obstacle. Sara stood in my way, and she fought me. The problem was mine. Mine to fix, mine to either repair or abandon. Was it abandonment? We stayed together for another two years after that, even moved across country together. It wasn't right or wrong. Right and wrong were just words to me.

But it was in Downie Hill, back around the time I'd written "Itchy Spot", when I was having an emotional affair with Linny and trying not to spend as much time with Sara and I was a confused man, and I didn't know what I wanted but I just kept hearing that voice "I want! I want!", but knowing nothing of what it was I wanted. I ultimately fell apart and broke down with shame and guilt in the vacant space beside Royal Tours. Was it Linny? Later that night I smoked pot on the balcony of my mother's apartment and really thought about my life. You choose what you leave behind but you decide what to take on in the future. This is the epiphany.

As we approached the date of our meet-up I became nervous. She was going to meet Richie, too. But Richie, she explained to me, was just a friend. She wanted to fuck my brains out. She'd sent me pictures of herself, posed on her bed. Images of her in black camiknickers with dark lips and eye makeup. Fat legs bent. One arm held out and up to take the picture, I'm sure, on some oversized and expensive digital webcam. A lip-ring. Hair dyed black. She was kind of a goth girl. Not a bullshit mall goth girl, either. I think a bit of me really wanted to fall in love with her. I'd lined up a car. I think I even told my mother what I was doing—planning a weekend away with another girl. Maybe we'd go to Oak Island Inn down the shore, walk the beach. I'd get her back to Richie's in a couple of days, after we'd fully fallen in love and had reluctantly untied our bodies as passionate young lovers often do.

I was excited for this. I yearned for it.

I said before that Sara visited me from her dorm a couple nights a week. We played card games like Crazy Eight Countdown and Cribbage. We talked a bit about the old days when Jerome and I were in a band with Steve. We talked about when we'd played the converted church. In those days, before I left for Fort St. John, we talked a lot about the good times we'd had. It was like a slow and silent goodbye was happening. She just wanted me to be happy. I wanted her to be happy as well.

I knew it wasn't right. What I was doing behind Sara's back with Linny. It was in some ways worse than the physical cheating I'd done with Shannon Raymond. Worse even than the other times, the times I didn't tell her about, the times I'm omitting now from this story. Because what did it matter if I cheated on her before? What was I trying to prove now? I was convinced I wanted not Sara, but the whole world and the freedom and abandon and potential energy in it. Was it selfish of me to think that I deserved that much? If that was what made me happy, did she want that for me?

So I didn't go through with it. I called it off.

I found Linny on mIRC, in the #Citylocals room and asked her to a private chat. It was there in those sterile and insulated digital confines that I told her: all plans and fantasies were cancelled. No rain checks were given. No excuses.

In my mind she remains "a flat personality on a flat screen, best seen in two dimensions… imponderable and touchless."

Thank you DH Lawrence.

In fact, I never spoke to Linny again after that. Not once. I moved to Fort St. John about three weeks later. Royal Tours International went belly up and my mother moved to Ontario to be nearer my sister. The family was busted apart again. Shows you how shallow love can be when it's up against real-world complications. And shame on me. I stayed with Sara for another six months—a half a year, when she moved to Fort St. John. She lived with my brother and Jerome and I. In 2000 we made the official break. We should never have lived together. Summer of 1999 to spring of 2000. That's how long it took to make the decision.

When I returned home from Fort St. John for Christmas '99 and New Year's 2000 I cheated on Sara again. The final time. And this proved itself to be the last straw in our relationship.

My psychologist tells me that life is nothing but a constant flow of desires, replacing each other as they are fulfilled. This is what gives our life meaning.

I met Ricki at a Christmas reunion party. Some high school friends threw the bash. We had casual sex in her apartment in the city a few days later. I spent New Year's Day 2000 on an Acadian Lines Greyhound bus. I retreated back across the country as I tried to forget my bad life and the horrible choices I'd made and the decisions that simply got me out of one situation and into the next. Ricki seemed different. But she looked physically identical to Sara. Ricki the rebound. Hate to say it but she was an escape hatch and stand-in with a more proper and educated demeanour. I fell in love with that professionalism. We kept in contact through email and phone cards. I talked to her during work hours once I was back out west in Fort St. John. For six months we spoke, engaged, connected. She encouraged me to apply to university.

I think I denied the cheating the whole time. Poor Sara. I lied to her. She loved me. I knew this. I had too much of my father in me and I guess I didn't love her back, not enough anyway. The only true analogy I could take away from what had happened to my parents and what was happening to me was that I'd hurt my partner, badly, and the only thing I could do to make it up to her was continue in a strange and awkward way to be her friend. We're still friends to this day. She was married recently. I emailed her, wishing her luck. The sad, misogynistic and anti-chivalric side of me used to think that the Shannon Raymonds and Linnys and Rickis had been deployed out into the world simply so they would fade into the background fuzz of life and memory. But I knew Sara would remain present, firm, fixed, fucked-up, whatever she was, whenever she was, she inspired "Itchy Spot".

We broke up in Fort St. John on good terms. Jerome moved out and began living with a girlfriend he'd met, Bridgette something. Sara and a friend had gotten their faces pierced, wore shabby clothes, changed their lifestyles. They started drinking expensive coffee and attending protests. They did knitting projects together. They partied constantly. They dreadlocked their hair. We lived in the same apartment for a couple months on 86th Street. I slept on the floor of a storage closet down the hall from her. In a matter of days Sara had become my first ex-girlfriend.

I left on the bus. Sara and Jerome came to see me off. My brother and I were already on bad terms by then. There was a lot to that and I think maybe the situation with Sara and I in his face arguing all the time drove him bonkers. I understood. We still don't talk much to this day, though. That's another story.

I packed my guitar, a box of possessions and a knapsack of day-gear for the 72-hour ride. In the parking lot I met some Quebeckers with a bunch of weed to smoke. I disembarked at Montreal with them three days later. It was late April or early May. I met Ricki and we spent a week at her sister's walk-up flat in the Plateau. We attended Russian restaurants. I think we went to the movies as well. We took in Sophia Coppola's The Virgin Suicides with a soundtrack by Air, the French Band.

Ricki and I went to the movies, fooled around on her sister's hide-a-bed, ate at new places every day, attended strip clubs and bars at night. We checked out Habitat 67 on the banks of the St. Lawrence, and she took me to see the botanical gardens in Rosemont-La Petite-Patrie. We drank at bars with posters on the walls for upcoming shows. Big names like The Cure and Dinosaur Jr. She knew the city. She took me to all the hot spots: the underground mall and the art galleries, the museums. It couldn't have been any other city but Montreal. I felt the city move beneath me with a new lover, a new friend. We went to McGill and checked out the campus. We went to Isle Notre Dame. We had a romantic time. For a moment I was at peace, the voice was silent. We travelled to the city by train, in our own berth, and we snuggled up to watch the May showers whizz by outside. And the trees of Quebec and New Brunswick passed in a quick blur as we made love through the night, covered in those rough grey, itchy wool blankets Via Rail provided. We smoked cigarettes in the berth, naked, with the windows down.

She wasn't the inspiration for the "Itchy Spot" short story I'd written, the first story I wrote when I was twenty-one as a student in Brian Baker's first year Creative Writing course at one of the universities in the city. Ricki may have in some way inspired me to write, but Sara was the inspiration. I sent the first draft to my high-school English and Canadian Literature teacher.

I told Ricki I'd written a true account of an incident that happened between Sara and I. I fictionalized some of it and jazzed it up for the sake of it—I was always told to never let the truth get in the way of a good story. But I'd figured it out by then and I was excited and wanted to share my newfound talent with her. We lived together as roommates for a short time on Inglis Street in the city, but I found that I could not fall in love with her. I was broken.

She did eventually read "Itchy Spot". After that she never spoke to me about story-writing again. So unsure, so self-conscious. Jealous, too. What I've learned, painfully, is that the little voice saying, "I want! I want! Strike!" will never completely go away.

Years after, when all of this was behind me, I'd gotten a BA in English Literature and I was blinded by student debt and faced with the desperate need to provide for myself and my wife so I returned to the Peace River Valley, to Fort St. John, where the old boys say that once you drink from the waters of the **Peace you'll always return, which is a funny story. I've never drunk from the Peace River and yet I've been here again and again. Funny how you live your whole life wondering where you'll end up, but when it comes down to it, to the nitty-gritty, to the base materials, you're always here, it's always now.**

This isn't a story about that. It's not really a story at all. I'm reading it now, back to myself, and I've decided that ultimately it's just a journal exercise. Could I call it a story? I don't know. I'll let you decide.

Had anything changed from beginning to end? Or was I just explaining the context of another story? The story of how a story was created. That's what I should call it. But you wouldn't like that, would you? It'd be clever but it would also be cheap.

I read it back now and I think, did I reveal too much? Did it come out of me as easy or as hard as I let it in? I suppose a bit of me likes that it came out this way, like I had something invested, like it was my job to write this story. No one said I had to stick with fiction. They only told me to break the rules. I could be brutally honest and call it a confessional. I could call it "The Confessions of Tom Barnabas" like HP Lovecraft's "The Statement of Randolph Carter" (1920)—maybe it's more like that tale than any others: just me, calling a dead man on the telephone. I don't know. I wanted to subtitle it "Barnabas the Rain King" because of that voice—a voice I share with Bellow's Henderson, but that's an awful obtuse allusion. I'm no Henderson

It seems like I've gotten to the end of the story. All that needed to come out came out, I think. It is my calling to be a writer. And I wouldn't have found this calling if not for these strange moments with girls in my youth.

With a degree of juvenile pride, I call it my first story and enjoy reading it almost twenty years later. Whereas most authors would have buried their early works, become ashamed of them, I hold this piece up to the rest of my stories as one of the best. Haruki Marukami said in the introduction to one of his first novels that the early stuff is like an old friend you come back to every once in a while, a familiar friend who you admire and respect. I guess I respect this story. I respect "Itchy Spot". But this one is a different kind of story for me because all my moral failings and misgivings are on display for you to read about. I stand by my assertion that this is a story about how I came to write "Itchy Spot". Maybe the conditions and things that happened will someday inform the story, maybe the story will inform readers about me, at least a little. I don't know. Even though I'm a cheating asshole throughout this one there's a little kindness in here. Like I said before it could be about my parent's divorce or my almost-tryst with Linny. Maybe it's about how to fall in love with the idea of someone. I didn't know Linny, I just wanted someone to soothe that eternal voice somehow. I really thought she could. Linny ignited my ash heaps into flames and I'll never forget that. But it's the insatiable voice in my head that made me run, made me cancel with Linny in 1998, and ultimately I have to accept that it's the same voice that shaped who I am today.

"My Complacency: How I wrote 'Itchy Spot'."

I guess that because some things in this story are about Linny or my affair with Ricki I should change their names, but I see it more as a companion piece to "Itchy Spot." And then I think, maybe I shouldn't change the names. Maybe it's about honesty. But then I remembered I'd already changed Sara's name in "Itchy Spot" to Morgan.

I've written stories about change and I've written about people growing. These are the best ones. I've come to find out that staying on a set course, surprisingly, will never fulfill me. When I read back the manuscript you can see a little bit of me has changed, grown up throughout the years. I suppose I was changing the whole time.

I guess I am always looking for what I am always sure of. I tell myself that I am going to be a writer. I am presumptuous enough to think I'll enjoy some degree of success in doing this. I think I knew this just by the first story. But it's no good. It's melancholy and derived. Lovers smoking in the dark. Arguments between young people. Present tense. Symbols. Typical shit.

Someone once told me that desire is measured by the distance between two things. When the gap draws close, desire fades. So is the gap what love is? I always wanted to know. Could one extend that space and live there blissfully in between, or would desire destroy desire? Obsessive, relentless, never fading desire. Is there such a thing—is there any true love that isn't unrequited? Isn't true love and true desire the act of not having, as opposed to attainment, fulfillment? What is love, then? I have many desires yet I have no fulfillment. But I do have desires. The want keeps me happy. It keeps me up at night sometimes. The want. I wake up sweaty, slick like a seal. I leave my bed and leave the house and sit out in the grassy back lawn, naked, confused. For some reason I always end up crying. But I convince myself that it's ok. This is love. You are in love, I say to myself. You should be happy.

You can't fake these feelings. Why do they arrive when they do? Why is the object of desire always so far away? They say separation makes the heart grow fonder but it doesn't.

"I want! I want! Strike!" The voice is familiar; it is almost my own voice but it's steeped in such desperation that it's almost unrecognizable. Maybe Hobbes said it best, "All human action is fundamentally motivated by the desire for pleasure."

I prefer Lacan's word for desire: jouissance: the lost object, or feeling of absence.

Maybe I depicted desire as a poison for the soul. And although that may have some merit, the longing and the craving and the thirst is what ultimately dissatisfied me. The naked truth is that there are things we desire but cannot have. We place boxes around our selfish longings like invisible little barriers accessible only by choice, by will, and fuelled only by immaterial and immature urges that fade so quickly and never reappear in the same form twice.

So the other part of this story is more complicated and it requires an understanding of desire and what the human heart is capable of once that voice inside is sparked. It's about truth and consequence. There's something else, however, something magic in "Itchy Spot", in the first one. It's like my V-card of fiction. I knew. I knew, as young as I was, that I'd write all this down.

Adam Kelderman is a short story writer from Nova Scotia; now a resident of the Peace. This is his first published work.

Liard to Peace Country in July

By Carolyn Robe

Silken water envelops us at 40 degrees centigrade
Gravel bites our feet
We rest on underwater concrete benches
Laughing children play with buoyant logs
Babies float in cooler downstream waters
Gravity pulls as I climb steep steps out
I rest by the side
Only to return to the water again and again

I try not to stare at numerous tattoos
Or gawk at a beefy fellow,
His long blond dreadlocks trailing
Matted in the water

Children thrilled by adventure
Pay no attention to parent's
Issued warnings

Councillor Davies
Regales us
Liard at New Year's stories
Frost around the hot springs
Bathers spiky frozen hair
minus 30 degrees...

We climb the ramp
Gender-neutral washrooms
And beyond—Mary K.
Studies information
Mineralized hanging gardens
Not available to the public
Why?
Yellow sign; locked gate
Caution: Problem Bears
Sign's four-year posting
Quite the "Bear Problem"

Back at the Northern Rockies Lodge at Muncho
Our only option—$41.00 Entree
Permission for soup and salad?
Permission grudgingly granted—$21.50
(With bargain scoop of sorbet)
Gas available at Muncho
$1.98 per litre.

Kathy Mc highly experienced
Two lane highway driving
Takes us south a few hundred kilometers
In one day…

Jade Lakes, a folded mountain
"As scenic as Banff," says Mary K.
We see Wood bison; Wild chicken
Caribou; Wild sheep
A solitary black bear
All share the roadway with us

We reach Peace Country
Fuchsia seas of fireweed
Ripple because of the
Conflagrations last May

Yes, go ahead—travel North
"As scenic as Banff"
But—maybe
Take along food
And money for gasoline!

Carolyn Robe has a BA in English from the University of Oregon and a MA in Education from Western Carolina University – and has a deep appreciation for the opportunity to attend "Writers of the Peace" at the Ft St John library. A long-time member, Carolyn was recently inspired at a meeting to make a solemn declaration on September 20, 2016: "I will create poetry for five minutes every day for 365 consecutive days..." (I would like to think that this allotment of time will increase daily as I move into 2017!)

iii. making peace with my body

by r. d. adair

i thought i loved my bones best, the bare spaces between breaths beautified me beyond the slip of skin i wore. i wanted to keep myself translucent, trepid and torn. i penciled myself a skeleton over fragile wrists and the wrath of my waistline. i focused on the frailty of figures, diagrams and detailed dossiers of days that stretched seven long years.

i fed myself the addiction of emptiness.

i still cannot recall if i gave my body to him or if he stole it. sometimes, the semblance of remembrance reminds me i do not care to uncover what lies beneath. alas, i have learned it is not easier to endure the echo no matter which way the waves travel.

there are days, now, with knees known to fail and a heart that hammers a hint too hasty that i ache for the touch of nothing. it is then, that i pick my bones up from the earth and plant them into a skeleton, now tall with cognizance beyond the scaffolding and skin. i have learned of full breath and freedom from foreign fingers, finding solace in the pace of my lungs when all is still.

i've learned to love the taste of vitality.

iv. making peace with my heart

by r. d. adair

i spent the earliest awakening of my youth yawning in yearning, arms stretched to fingertips, reaching just a hair's breadth away from that unidentifiable something settled in my psyche as significant. i needn't find the nerve for knowledge with a heart that hastened without question; i thought myself hardened by the failings of my father's own heart, the missteps of my mother fading on my mind's horizon a lesson learned for me.

time taught me that the firsts have a finality that will quake your shores. the wave receding reached to my bedrock and scraped me dry with debris; i was schooled in the power of preconceived poetry, the potency of immortalization without researched reason. the habit of humanity to harmonize loss and love in a misguided marriage a lecture i must have missed.

i owe myself an apology i have been apoplectic about since i first found myself faulted. the fissures i found in my foundations will always be my failing, but only because i was so sincerely intent on seeking them. perhaps it is part of my person to perch on the cracks and seek their depth with the sharp lens only one's own eyes can muster, but it is a lesson i must unlearn.

today, i am remembering how to unfurl my fingers.

R.D. Adair is an occasional poet and always over-thinker, who lives with her South African nomad, Jaryd, and over enthusiastic dog, Corki. This is her first print publication.

Ripples

By Kathy Murphy

Hannah watched the concentric circles ripple out and sighed. She knew she could do it, if she could just find the right rock. She walked closer to the bank of the river and there at her feet was the perfect one: flat, uniform and just the right size. She flipped her wrist and... success. It skipped three times. She jumped up and down and laughed, but didn't bother turning around. There was no one there; there never was.

She sat down under her special tree and was perfectly happy in that moment. This was her place. The fence kept out vehicles, but not a determined ten-year-old. The wind whipped bright yellow leaves around her with a bite that made her shiver. She reached into her pocket and pulled out the apple, just to look at it. She had decided to give it to Aiden but the temptation was too much; one crisp taste and sweet juice trickled down her throat.

"I'm sorry Aiden," she said aloud when she looked at her empty hands. She stood up slowly, looked around and wondered if this would be her last visit before winter came. 'I better hurry,' she thought, 'before Aiden's babysitter drops him off and he's left alone with Mike.'

Eating the whole apple made her burn with guilt. She got one every school day from Amy but usually gave Aiden half. 'It's funny,' she thought, 'Amy gave me an apple and an apple Amy gave me an apple and an apple gave me Amy.' One lunch hour she'd looked up from her book and saw Amy about to throw her apple away. Something about her face made Amy ask, "What?" So she stammered something about apples being her favorite.

Amy said, "I don't like them but my Mom thinks she can make me eat them by putting them in my lunch. You can have them." After that they were friends and Amy gave her an apple every school day. They really were Hannah's favorite now.

If she was lucky she might be able to sneak change from Mom's tip jar. If Mike hadn't emptied it first. She would do that today and take Aiden down to the Esso for some candy. It was risky but she had eaten the whole apple and he was such a good little kid. There wasn't anything else to eat and he loved chocolate bars.

At the door she knew she was too late from the sound of crying and swearing.

When she walked in, Mike said, "Where the hell have you been? Make the little bastard shut up or I'll give him something to cry about."

"I'm sorry, Mike. I'm here now Aiden, it's okay." She gathered her little brother in her arms.

"It hurts, Han," Aiden sobbed.

"Shh. It's okay, I'm here now." Hannah tried to soothe him, but the tears still flowed. She really was later than she thought. Her mom should be home soon.

"I'm not the fucking babysitter," Mike yelled. "This is all your fault."

Hannah knew this mood, knew it would have been her instead of Aiden if she had only gotten home in time. She whispered, "I'm sorry", more to Aiden than to Mike.

"I'm outta this shit-hole. Tell your mom to meet me at the bar."

Hannah took Aiden to the couch.

"What's wrong Aido?"

He held out his arm and screamed when Hannah examined it.

"Okay buddy, I won't touch it."

She got Aiden to lay down on the couch while she tried to decide what to do.

***

When Marie walked in five minutes later things just got worse. Hannah had heard it all before: "Her feet hurt, they didn't appreciate her, she put a roof over their heads and all she wanted was a life," and on and on. But this time her mom was in a really bad mood.

"What did you do? If you kids drive Mike away like you did your dad, I'll never forgive you. I deserve some happiness, too. You think I can afford a full-time babysitter on what I make? You're supposed to be here right after school," Marie yelled.

"Mom, I think he hurt Aiden bad this time."

"Don't you bad-mouth him, you little bitch. This is your fault for not being here." She threw her purse at Hannah and the contents flew everywhere. "Pick that up! I'm done with you. Aiden better not be crying when we get home."

Marie grabbed the purse back from Hannah and slammed the door on her way to the bar down the block. Aiden made a whimpering noise, like a wounded animal.

Hanna asked "What happened Aido?"

"I'm supposed to say I fell."

"It's okay buddy. I'm going to make it okay. Just remember that whatever happens, I love you. Okay?"

Aiden nodded. Hannah walked over to where her mom's phone had landed. Her fingers hit the numbers 911 and she heard herself talking while part of her brain screamed, *"NO!"*

"Please send an ambulance. I think my little brother broke his arm. He is four. No, I'm alone with him. I'm ten. Please hurry, it really hurts."

Hannah kept on the line like they said but the voice in her head was saying, *"They'll take Aiden away and you'll never see him again. Mom will hate you and it really is all your fault this time. You're breaking up your family. You're as bad as mom says."*

All of the sudden there were flashing red lights outside the trailer and the room seemed full of big men. One of them had a teddy bear for Aiden and was kneeling next to him speaking gently.

Another one asked Hannah, "Can you tell us what happened?"

"I don't know. I wasn't here," Hannah told him.

An RCMP officer came in. She seemed nice and not scary or mean like Hannah expected. She wasn't mad at Hannah for not watching Aiden.

"How can we reach your mother?" she asked.

Hannah guiltily held out the phone and confessed. "I took her phone."

It didn't matter. Someone going into the bar had seen the flashing lights outside their place and told her mom. Marie came banging through the door, yelling, "What the hell do you think you're doing in my house? That's my son. Get your hands off him."

"Ma'am your son has a broken arm. We're taking him to the hospital. Please calm down."

"Don't you talk to me in that smarmy voice. You get out of here. You've got no right."

While the police and firemen were distracted by her Mom, Hannah crept out the back door. She went to her hiding spot in the neighbour's shrub, waited a minute to see if anyone noticed, then ran down the alley.

She wished she'd grabbed her coat because it was getting really cold now.

It wouldn't matter soon.

When you went into water that felt cold, pretty soon you got numb and it didn't feel cold anymore. Nothing mattered now that Aiden was safe.

She repeated, "Safe, safe, safe", as she made her way down to the river.

Kathy lives in Taylor B.C. where she is lucky enough to be surrounded by people and pets she loves. She is especially fond of firemen, but her favorite is her husband John. Once dubbed "The Volunteer Queen" by her friends, and known to "ride off in all directions" at once, she is finally learning the value of prioritizing. Her family, which includes three amazing children, and her friends are always first in her heart but she is now making room in her life for the fun stuff, like reading and writing.

The Single Woman's Wilderness Survival Guide

By Kirsten Barkved

When I tell people that I moved from Kelowna to be in Fort St. John, their initial reaction is almost always their honest one: Why?

It's a perfectly legitimate reaction and I can understand their incredulity. It seems like a backwards move: people generally want to move *SOUTH* instead of *NORTH*. See: -40 winters. See also: wearing five layers to be five minutes outside. See also: miles away from liberal majorities. See also: abundance of snow.

I moved up north for two reasons and neither of them are good ones. And since I value honesty and can't come up with a good lie for why someone would elect to move from Kelowna (where it has reasonable weather, not -40 winters, has wine, etc.) to Fort St. John (see above), then I'll keep to the real story, which is: I moved north for 1) love, and 2) work.

Both of which, it turns out, failed me. Miserably.

***

wil·der·ness ˈwildərnəs'/noun

1. an uncultivated, uninhabited, and inhospitable region. Derived from wildness, which, in its literal sense, is the quality of being wild or untamed.
2. a wilderness is a place where wild-ness occurs. Synonyms: wilds, bushland, inhospitable region, desert, no man's land.

***

Wilderness Survival Guide

Step 1: Gather Your Bearings

If you find yourself lost, scared, and in trouble while you're out in the wild, don't fret. You can never be 100% prepared for whatever the wild throws at you. All you can do is choose how to react and maintain a will to survive the deep and vast uncertainties that is wildness.

There is no substitute for experience in any uncontrollable situation, and your reaction in a survival situation, especially in the wild, depends on your education and training. Always keep in mind that anything can happen to you. Try to remain calm. Try to keep prepared, no matter how crushing and vast your present situation may be. But above all, plan to survive. The most prepared and resilient person can still succumb to the mental distress of being alone in the vast and unrelenting wild. Nature is unforgiving. Having the skills to survive it is one thing; the will to carry on is another.

***

Two years ago, I wanted a change.

This wasn't like, I want a haircut or a nose ring, kind of change. It was the kind of change I wished I could remove from my body. Like how a snake sheds it skin, I wanted permanent difference. To look around me and be lost. New. A stranger to my surroundings.

There was nothing for me in Kelowna, at the time. I didn't see myself getting any experience in the competitive job climate I was in. It was either stay and work three part-time, minimum wage jobs, asking people if they wanted a bag for their milk or fries with their drink, or go north, like so many other people I knew were doing. To trade my soul for big time money for a year or two, pay off my loans, actually afford to eat name brand Mac and Cheese. You know. The finer things.

It should also be mentioned here that I was one of those "entitled" millennials you always hear the media griping about. Fresh off the "I just graduated with an arts degree and am going to change the world" kind of attitude. Coupled with a summer of binge drinking my fears of never finding a "real" job, trying to figure out what I was going to do with my life, and naively wondering why all the writing companies weren't queuing up outside my door asking me to be their next star writer. I was two shots of tequila away from a 3:00 am sobbing phone home/mental break down waiting to happen.

But instead of facing it head on, instead of staying where I was and unpacking the problems while serving over-privileged white people with too much plastic, surgery and not enough will power, their fries, I moved north. And did so with a man who loved me.

We were just 6 months into a relationship. Fresh, baby green grass of a relationship, we were doe eyed. The I love you's came after heartfelt, late nights of long discussions, unpacking our issues (him: depression, drugs, suicide; me: alcohol, anxiety), both of us testing the waters of one another's crazy, hoping the other wouldn't run, secretly wishing they would so we wouldn't get hurt.

Neither of us did.

But,

I should have.

***

Fight or Flight

1. the instinctive physiological response to a perceived harmful, threatening, or dangerous situation, which readies one either to resist forcibly or to run away in order to maintain survival.

***

"A wilderness, in contrast with those areas where man and his own works dominate the landscape, is hereby recognized as an area where the earth and its community of life are untrammeled by man, where man himself is a visitor who does not remain."

***

It was a five-year plan, we said.

Only, it didn't work. We began to call it home.

We moved north. Moved in together and got jobs relevant to our career goals. I got experience. He got sober. We made a life in a small, northern town above the 56th parallel. We made friends. Grew roots. Sunk deep into this version of us. And slowly, to us, Fort St. John became more than a place on a map. We started making plans.

He proposed. I said yes. I was in. I was twenty-seven and knew nothing else but this person and the life I was weaving with him. We charted our future like lines on graphs. I pined for wedding dresses and our first dance. I bought a book on baby names and we picked out names we liked; one for a boy and three for a girl.

Who was it that came up with the saying "too good to be true"?

My mom used to say something to me growing up that I don't think I appreciated until this year. It was kind of like when your mom tries to give you relevant life advice, and you, as a teenager, let it slip in one ear and float out the other because you obviously knew all the answers to life's most important questions.

She would say that every 27 years, Saturn returns to the same place in the sky, the same place it was when you were born. And when it does, it brings chaos and upheaval. Big changes. Life turmoil. It's supposed to be the time in your life that defines when you leave your youth and enter adulthood.

I used to laugh and say "okay, mom, sure." Because my mom was always saying things like that. She's your typical 70's hippie living in the 21st century, boasting mood rings and wearing tie dye skirts.

But this year…this year I started to believe that maybe my hippie mother knew what she was talking about when she talked about Saturn.

***

Step 2: Find Your Will to Survive

If you find you're suddenly where you shouldn't be, try not to panic. Trust that you will get through the next few days (or however long it takes) as long as you maintain your will to survive. Above everything, this is the most important part of surviving in the wild: your mindset. Maintaining an attitude and determination to succeed, live through and get through anything is what will get you through your trials.

***

Early on a Monday morning in the second week of January, I got ready for work. It had snowed the night before; a light dusting of white blanketed the roads. Morning in the snow is my favourite time in winter; you feel like a ghost, drifting through a sea of white, a sea of frozen water, everything muffled. It's a new world. You can do whatever you like in it.

I got to work before anyone else that morning. I remember because there were no other tracks leading up to the door. Work had been slow, lately, so people were taking their time coming in. Around the office (around town, really) there was always the fear. The fear that this could be your last day. This could be the last time you see your colleagues, sit at your desk. Work was scarce. That's life up north, these days.

An hour into work, I was called into my boss's office. Because I'm a creature of worst case scenario thinking, and because I can do the most basic math (even though I failed it twice in high school), I walked to his office with my heart hammering violently in my chest, my palms a sweaty mess in my lap as I sat across from my boss, and before I could cross my legs or brace myself for what was coming next, I was being let go.

That was the first bad thing.

***

For anyone faced with a wilderness emergency survival situation, fear is a normal reaction. Unless an emergency situation has been anticipated, fear is generally followed by panic then pain, cold, thirst, hunger, fatigue, boredom and loneliness. It is extremely important to calmly assess the situation and not allow these seven enemies to interfere with your survival.

If you find yourself suddenly feeling like you're in danger, if you're afraid of your new physical surroundings, of not being rescued, or even just afraid of the unknown, don't fret.

Try to stay calm. Remind yourself that you can do anything. That you are capable of anything and can and will survive this. Try to remain mindful of your breathing. Maybe sit down. Say your name to yourself. Count your breaths and come up with a plan of action. If possible, make friends with bear. Become part of pack. Become a bear. Turn fear into growling and growling into action.

***

My plan of action the next day was not to sit on the couch and cry about my sudden job loss. I took my shock and buried it beneath a will to carry on and make an enemy of my loss—my stubborn, strong-willed, Aries father would have been proud.

It was hard, at first. I drifted through the next day, whipping my fingers through my hair, wondering what to do with my time. I'd never been let go, before. I cleaned the fridge. I mopped the bathroom floor. I sorted the cupboards and tossed out dry goods—why did I have mustard powder? When did I buy Coconut flour? I walked Ollie. I took myself to a café and wrote. I knew that the shock would come, and that the despair of losing a dream career would bring, in its wake, a swell of sadness, disappointment, and worry, and the important thing for me was to keep moving. Keep going. Keep the pain at bay.

I would write a novel, I said.

I would update my resume and find freelance work online, I said.

I would look into going back to school and finding a new profession, I said. Something outside writing. Something tangible. Certain.

I put on a brave face and told my fiancé when he got home the plans I had made. Wrote them on a list. Put said list on our fridge. Goals for how we would get through this together. How I wouldn't let it impact us.

An hour later, I was throwing the list in the garbage, holding Ollie, my dog, and absently kissing the top of his head through tears. Smiling girls in white dresses from bridal magazine cut-outs sat crumpled atop my list, their painted faces lovely, demure. Finite.

Ollie and I sat there on the kitchen floor, one of us not sure what just happened, the other wondering when the human would stop crying. An hour ago, I was googling how to make floral crowns and DIY centre pieces. Crying, on the kitchen floor, I had no more reason to make either.

***

Step 3: Don't Panic

If you find yourself suddenly stranded, lost, or alone, the number one thing to do is: accept it. Accept that you're stranded, lost, or alone. Don't panic. Panic leads to confusion, confusion to poor judgement. If you panic, you will die.

To survive the wildness, one must be able to think rationally through the pain, fatigue, and emotional stressors of their physical and mental environment. Without the ability to think clearly and problem solve, one's survival rate decreases exponentially.

The will to survive comes from the deep motivation of wanting to live. Without that inherent want, there isn't a need.

It has been well documented that most people, when faced with life or death situations in which there is a very real possibility of great suffering or pain before death, prefer to give up and get it over with.

No one wants to continue to suffer if they believe they are going to die.

Once you have accepted the fact that you are lost, stranded, or alone in the vast wild, your survival rate goes up.

***

heart·break 'härtˌbrāk'/noun

Mental anguish or pain caused by loss or despair: grief, heartache, sorrow.

A broken heart (also known as
a heartbreak or heartache) is a term **metaphor** for the intense emotional—and sometimes physical—stress or pain one feels when grieving.
The physical signs of grieving include:

1. Exhaustion, muscle tightness or weakness, body pains, lack of energy
2. Insomnia, disturbing dreams
3. Headaches, difficulty breathing,
4. racing or pounding heart, trembling or shaking, chest pain

***

To survive heartbreak, you need to transform the chambers of your human heart. Protect it fiercely. Like a bear would. Consider life in isolation. Consider folding inwards. Disappearing entirely. Turn to alcohol. Turn to sex. Bury yourself in work. Avoid and dodge and weave to prevent your open wounds from any more harm. Protect yourself at all costs. If necessary, harden.

***

Step 4: Find Shelter

In order to protect yourself from the extremes of the wild, you will need a small shelter. Nothing is more vital than maintaining your body's core temperature—this helps protect you from the physical signs of fear, which, when confronting the realization that you are lost, can decrease your chances of survival.

Physical signs and symptoms of fear

- Difficulty breathing, followed by exhaustion
- Racing or pounding heart.
- Chest pain or tightness.
- Trembling or shaking.

A shelter is necessary for survival. Having a place to keep warm, safe, and gather yourself while you formulate a plan. A good shelter must protect you from the harsh elements, be comfortable enough for resting, and maintain your core temperature. A shelter will shield you from the temperatures of the wild, especially when you find yourself lost in cold and low temperatures, such as open mountain faces, snow, or the open north.

Remember: cold lowers the ability to think. It numbs the body, and reduces the will to survive. In the vast, open wild, especially in places as harsh and cold as the unyielding north, never allow yourself to stop moving.

***

I escaped the Peace with Ollie and a few of my belongings. Retreated north to family, band aids on my heart; everything about me an open wound that wouldn't close properly. How could I live in the same city as him, be under the same roof as him? Someone who was my home and wasn't anymore.

He wasn't the first one who kissed me but I wanted him to be my last. He wasn't my first love; he wasn't even the first one I pictured the "rest" of my life with. But he was the one I wanted to build a home with, the person I looked at in the morning and thought "I want to keep this. I want you forever."

It was the kind of love that I felt deep. That washed over me like waves at midnight on a hot day, pulling me deeper into something lovely, immersing me until my ears were under water and everything around me was faint, numb. Far away. It felt like I was the only person in the world who knew what love was. And whether it was one morning, suddenly, or over days, weeks, or months, he no longer felt the same. And I was left homeless, jobless, and lost in the north. Miles from places I knew and people I loved and where I wanted to be.

That was the second bad thing.

***

pain pān/noun

- physical suffering or discomfort caused by illness or injury.
- mental or emotional suffering: sadness caused by some emotional or mental problem

1.

"she's in great pain"
synonyms: suffering, agony, torture, torment, discomfort
see also: heartbreak

***

Pain may often be ignored in a panic situation. Remember to deal with injuries immediately before they become even more serious.

***

I made plans. He withdrew. I found colour schemes. He broke his sobriety. I set a date in chalk. He erased it. We sat in a room and I watched the planes in his face rise and fall in despair and I understood then that he wished more than I did that he still loved me. We clung to an idea that was turned to sand, slipping through our fingertips until all that was left between us and our hands, at the end, was space that was as wide and open as a tundra or desert. A wildness that was never meant to be civilized or claimed.

I was a visitor who did not remain.

***

Step 5: How to Get Rescued

In order to get rescued, you need to know the most basic hand signals to alert a vehicle or helicopter or plane you see pass overhead. Curiously, a wave is considered a sign to not land. Instead, if you see a helicopter or plane, form your arms in a "Y".

If you have a signaling tool like a flare, flashlight, or mirror, make use of them the second you see a rescue helicopter. Reflect the sun off the mirror in the direction of the helicopter to attract its attention. If you come across a road, wave down the first car you see using wide gestures.

***

Sometimes you need to rescue yourself. Sometimes you need to flag down a car in the middle of nowhere with your car.

I've done both.

6 weeks into the tundra of my heartbreak, I found myself at the edge of a highway in a smoking car, airbags out, glass shards in my hair, and Ollie in

the back seat who, if he knew what stars were, would be seeing them. I had a cut lip and ringing ears; I would later find bruises up and down my body and would complain of a slight concussion and neck pain. But if you hit a snowbank at 90 km an hour and sustain no real injuries, you basically have actual magical powers.

Three days earlier, I had agreed to a new job in Vancouver. It was my helicopter, my way out. I had searched in vain for a way to climb out of the vast, unyielding torment, and I succeeded. I was on day two of travelling south. I had literally packed everything my small Toyota hatchback could fit. My dashboard was littered with Tim Hortons wrappers, both a testament to my will to survive the 14-hour stretch and my motivation to get south to more coffee options. I had Shania Twain singing her woes about men in the background. There was a rock in my boots and leftover bagel goop in my braces, but I didn't care. I had a way out. This was it. I had a new job, the promise of a new life, and Ollie at my side, who, aside from barking wildly at indignant looking bison on the side of the road, had remained mostly docile.

It was a mostly uneventful trip. Until we hit ice. That was the third bad thing. The departure of Saturn.

***

Step 6: Remain Positive

Survival is a state of mind. It's all about positivity. It may sound silly, but it's just as important as food, water, shelter, and keeping warm. Remaining positive increases your chances for survival because it improves your mental endurance. It doesn't matter if you're physically strong or have read all the wilderness survival guides; if you aren't mentally strong, if you don't practice positivity, or have a will to endure, you will succumb to the wild.

Loneliness is a strong survival enemy that can hit you without warning. It will strike you when you realize you are the only person around who you can depend on while in your situation. Nowadays, modern society barely gives us a chance to test our ability to adapt to silence, loss of support, and separation from others. Don't let loneliness gnaw at your positive attitude. Fight it by keeping busy. Try singing, whistling, daydreaming. Tell yourself how important you are. How you matter. Positivity is key in surviving ~~heartbreak~~ the wild.

***

"It was like the classic scene in the movies where one lover is on the train and one is on the platform and the train starts to pull away, and the lover on the platform begins to trot along and then jog and then sprint and then gives up altogether as the train speeds irrevocably off. Except in this case I was all the parts: I was the lover on the platform, I was the lover on the train. And I was also the train."
— Lorrie Moore, A Gate at the Stairs

***

The northern wild does something to you. It reminds you of death and love and resilience and defeat in every cold inhale you take. Its vast open tells you to go home and also reminds you that you have no home here. You are a visitor.

You have no home here.

The wildness of his heart was a vast, frozen tundra. There were moments we felt we would make it. There were moments of pure joy. But I wandered through it and came out the other side, alone. I was only ever a visitor in that untamed landscape.

***

Step 7: Recovery

Once you've been rescued or have escaped the uncertain wild, take time to process. You need to recover. Dress your wounds and set your broken bones. Sleep and reflect on your time spent lost and wandering.

Heal.

See a therapist. Drink alcohol. Copious amounts of it. Take baby steps back into civilization. You may flinch from time to time when you hear a coyote howl; the trickster who lured you into the wild in the first place. They are reminders of where you once were and who you used to be.

Breathe.

Say yes to trying new things, but only if they don't scare you. Say yes to dates. Go on one and marvel at how easy it can be to un-harden, to release yourself back into the wild.

Watch a harvest moon rise and swell over the tops of buildings. Or trees. Or ocean, or desert, or northern tundra. Wherever you are; it will look the same.

It doesn't matter how many wilds you walked. It always looks the same.

Kirsten Barkved is a writer, dog whisperer, and gold-medal high-fiver who lives, breathes, and writes in Vancouver, BC with her canine counterpart, Ollie.

The Lies We Tell Ourselves

By Kevin Buchholz

The ones we use that allow us to crawl out of bed in the morning
The ones we use to convince ourselves that our lives matter
The ones we believe in the hope we won't get screwed over
For the only reality I know
Is the one I choose to see
For we are nothing more than salesman and storytellers

Kevin Buchholz was not born nor raised in Fort St. John, but he has been happily living here for a few years now.

A Cloak of Black Emotion

By Carolyn Robe

A shape shifting cloak of black emotion
Billows behind me in the steady wind.
I gather this thick and heavy garment unto myself--
With fever and chill, I turn to walk backward.
The cloth takes on my own particular shape.
The wind dies; the cloak hangs lank
Unnecessary with a weather change
Now hot, still and sunny.
This hooded piece is mine, not me.
I remove its weighted presence—
Take it home and fold it away forever.

Carolyn Robe has a BA in English from the University of Oregon and a MA in Education from Western Carolina University—and has a deep appreciation for the opportunity to attend "Writers of the Peace" at the Ft St John library. A long-time member, Carolyn was recently inspired at a meeting to make a solemn declaration on September 20, 2016: "I will create poetry for five minutes every day for 365 consecutive days..." (I would like to think that this allotment of time will increase daily as I move into 2017!)

Just a Regular Friday Night at North Peace Tower

By Ronnie Roberts

I am constructing a gourmet jelly roll. I squish the bread with Mom's marble rolling pin. It's heavy and works great—the bread looks like dough now. I cover it with peanut butter, right to the edges, then add a good thick layer of raspberry jam so the peanut butter doesn't show.

Now raisins. I place them in rows of twelve, in celebration of my twelfth birthday, coming up in just fourteen days. I push each raisin into the goo; that's the secret, pushing them right in. Now when I roll it up, careful not to squeeze too hard, everything stays inside and sticks together. Standing back, I view my masterpiece. Perfect.

A thud from the apartment next door shakes the light overhead and sends Mom's crystal tinkling in the china cabinet. I glance at the clock. Yup, right on schedule. The Thompsons are winding up for their big Friday night fight.

Catching a raisin in my mouth I hum to cover Mrs. Thompson's muffled but high-pitched pleading and head into the living room for the remote control. A little noisy camouflage usually did the trick.

"Don't you know any other songs?" my brother Kevin complains from behind a girly magazine he got from his friend Steve Romaniuk in 32B.

"Nope." I hum louder. This being Mom's Friday at the store and with Dad away at camp, Kevin is hard at work absorbing each page with no worries of getting caught. What a loser. "Hey Kev, it's just not the same without a flashlight, huh?"

He drops the magazine an inch, sending me a sour look. He sees the jelly roll. "Geez, can't you eat normal food?"

I flip on the TV and see Mom's been watching the home and garden channel again. Some woman is busy folding napkins into fancy shapes and yammering away about presentation. I hope when we finally get our own place, Mom doesn't go all decorator on us. Just another year of away jobs for Dad, and we'd have the down payment for a house of our own. When we move, all Kevin cares about is going to the same school with his friends. Personally, I'm holding out for a basketball net in the driveway.

"You know Mom doesn't like you eating that crap in the living room." Yeah, like Kevin cares where I eat. He opens up the magazine and holds it sideways, studying the picture.

I flip to the sports channel. Golf. I say, "This 'crap's' got all four major food groups covered," then take a bite and chew with an exaggerated, open-mouthed motion. I make sure Kevin is watching. "Want some?"

"Geez." He ducks behind the magazine in disgust.

I smile. He's so easy to gross out. Ever since he started junior high, became a jock and started liking Joanie Stoltz, he'd been an easy mark. What can I say? Making my brother crazy gets me through the day.

The phone rings. Kevin turns the page and ignores it. Either it's Mom, in which case Kevin would have nothing to say beyond a series of grunts, or it's a girl, in which case it's uncool to answer right away. I shake my head in wonder. Could the zit cream he's always hogging the bathroom for have turned his brain to mush? He used to be a regular guy.

The phone rings again. I mute the TV and pick it up. "Hi Mom."

Kevin slumps on the couch. No Joanie tonight.

Mom tells me she's bringing pizza home for a late supper. It's been a rough night at the store. I compliment her on her choice, having the four major food groups well represented.

From behind Miss February, Kevin complains he must be adopted. I nod in agreement.

Mom says, "I don't know what's going on tonight. Everyone's in such a miserable mood. The customers are petulant, and this afternoon, when I took the bank deposit over, even the bank teller was in a bad mood. Must be a full moon. Oh, just hang on a minute, Hon. I'll put you on hold."

While I'm waiting I glance out the patio door but it's not quite dark enough yet to see if the moon's full. And petulant? That must mean crabby. What did the moon have to do with it? I know it does something to the tides. Oh, and Werewolves. Yeah. I'd get right on that. I'm laughing when Mom comes back on. "You sound happy. What a relief to hear someone happy. Is your brother nearby?"

"Kevin?" I chew at a ragged nail and eye Miss February. Surely she wasn't born that way. "Oh, he's kind 'a busy reading a magazine—."

Faster than spit, Kevin is off the couch and grabbing at the phone. I'm ready for him, twisting away and laughing soundlessly at his red face. Covering the mouth piece, I whisper, "What a fish."

Boom! An explosion of noise rips through the air. Our window panes move in and out, looking like they could break any second; Mom's crystal's going crazy in the cabinet. Kevin and I both clutch the phone, frozen as another thunderous explosion echoes through the North Peace Towers apartment building.

A deadly, choking silence closes around me.

I jerk when a piercing scream from the hallway rips up my spine. Kevin and I gawk at one another, waiting for an explanation for what we've just heard.

Gunshots at North Peace Towers?

Gradually I become aware of a frantic buzzing noise and realize it's Mom, yelling on the other end of the phone. Before I can command my frozen arm to raise the phone to my head, another scream cuts through the air and my skin goes all goose-bumpy. A woman is screaming in the hallway. Now I can hear her pounding on the doors, pleading for help.

We run to the door, Kevin yanking on the knob and fumbling with the deadbolt at the same time. After an eternity, it opens. No longer muffled, I recognize Mrs. Thompson's crying—don't I hear it every Friday night?

"He's drunk! He's got a shot gun and he's going to kill me!" she shrills from down the hall.

Kevin sticks his head out, then inexplicably, draws back inside our apartment, slams the door and locks it.

My jaw drops in disbelief. "Kevin, you've got to let her in!"

"No, I don't." His face is a white mask I don't recognize.

I go for the door.

Kevin knocks my hand from the deadbolt and pins my arms behind my back. I twist around and try to butt him with my head, but know I won't win. Locked in Kevin's sweaty grip, my chest heaving, we listen to Mrs. Thompson pound on each door in turn and hear that none would open and admit her.

How many of our neighbours are hiding like we are? Good ol' Mr. Mathers, the fitness fanatic? Miss Jenkins the nursery school teacher? How about Sammy, the butcher down at the grocery store? He thinks he's a pretty tough guy. Why isn't he helping?

I twist around to face my brother. "Kevin! No one's helping her!"

"Shit!" With a shove, Kevin releases me and fumbles with the locks, yanking the door open again. "Mrs. Thompson!" he yells in a voice I don't even recognize. Kevin's freaking scared out of his mind.

We search the hallway. It's empty, but we can still hear crying. The only other thing happening is the hum of the elevator at the end of the hall, the numbers going up as it carries Mrs. Thompson's sobbing out of earshot. An eerie quiet returns to the hallway, like there's nobody there, but we all know everyone is there, hiding, holding their breath, waiting.

With shaking hands, Kevin yanks me back inside, locks our door again, then practically lays against it, his breath coming in noisy gasps. Finally, he turns back to look at me. His eyes are wide and dark and it's like he doesn't see me at all. "You can quit looking at me like I'm an axe murderer, Justin."

I tear my eyes away from his, stare at the locked door in disbelief, and whisper, "You slammed the door."

"I know what a shotgun can do." Kevin's voice is dead. "I had no choice."

"You had a choice!" I yell back, feeling sick at seeing what a coward my brother really is. "You could have let her in. We could have helped her."

"Not how you think." Kevin stalks over to the phone, picks it up from the floor and raises it to his ear like it weighs a hundred pounds. He turns away from me and I hear him tell Mom we're both okay and the door is locked. They talk some more, but I'm not listening. Then he hangs up the phone, picks it up again and in measured movements, dials the police. Again he turns his back. That's okay—I don't want to see his stupid face anyway.

I shove past him and slump onto the recliner, scared by this new view of my brother, detesting the sight of him whispering into the phone. Some hero. I look away. I see my jelly roll, lying beside the remote control. All the raisins stayed stuck.

My stomach slams into my mouth. I'm sick and crying all at once, shaking and hot, then suddenly clammy. I feel Kevin pick me up and push me onto the couch. He pulls off my shirt, wipes my face with a cold, wet face cloth, then covers me with Mom's favourite quilt. Clutching it, I wonder if she'll be mad I'm messing it up. Kevin cleans up the floor and the recliner.

"The cops are already here," he tells me, like that's what I'm thinking about, huddled like a stupid baby in my mommy's blanket. "Mom's on her way, too."

Now here was news I could use. Numbly, I watch him move around the room, like everything is normal, only I know nothing will ever be normal again. Kevin picking up stuff, Kevin smoothing pillows—like that lady on HGTV. Finally, he sits down on the other end of the couch.

I move my feet away from him, knowing I hate my brother more than anything or anyone I have ever hated in this world. My throat is on fire from throwing up and my heart is burning with loathing for Kevin. I despise myself for not overpowering him, for not having the strength to help Mrs. Thompson.

I snake my hand out from under the quilt, grab the remote and slide it back under cover beside me. I don't change from the sports channel; I just hold the remote in my hand. It feels good, like I could change the channel if I wanted. Change something.

Kevin reaches for Miss February. His hands begin to shake. Now his whole body is vibrating, rattling the pages of the magazine. Miss February disappears inside Kevin's fist and his mouth is open, but no sound comes out. Forgetting about being mad at him, I grab him and try to stop the shaking. He holds me so hard it hurts, and I'm along for the jerking ride.

"It's okay, Kev." I'm surprised by the squeaky sound my voice makes. "I was scared too."

We just hang onto each other, and the searing hate is gone from my gut. I feel weird and wobbly inside, but relieved at the same time. Hating someone takes a ton of energy.

After a while, Kevin's shaking slows down and we push away from one another, returning to our own end of the couch. I crawl back under the quilt. Kevin lets his head fall back against the cushions and heaves a huge sigh, then pulls up the front of his shirt and rubs his face with it. Some zit cream gets on his shirt, and his face is red and kind of shiny, but I don't have the heart to bug him about it.

I notice it's getting dark in the apartment, but I don't want to turn on the lamp. The flickering light from the TV is enough. Besides, the darkness feels friendly, and kind of safe, where you can't really see each other's eyes. Where you don't have to hide how you feel.

I un-mute the TV.

A loud knock on the apartment door and we both jump out of our skin.

"Shit!" Kevin squeaks.

Is it Mr. Thompson, come to look for his wife?

Would he be knocking at our door if he was?

"Anyone home?" a man's voice calls through the door. "It's the police."

Kevin and I race to the door, bumping and crashing into one another in our eagerness to see a friendly face.

We stop just short of opening the door. "How do we know you're really the police?" Kevin sounds pretty brave.

I give him a thumbs up.

"One of the 911 calls came from your apartment. Open the door, son, I have to make sure you're okay. Are you all right in there?"

Kevin looks at me questioningly. Hey, he wants my opinion. Nice turn of events. I tell him, "He doesn't sound anything like Mr. Thompson. Besides, Mr. Thompson's drunk. This guy isn't."

"You're right. He sounds like a cop." Kevin turns the dead bold and opens the door cautiously.

A tall, uniformed cop looks us over, then peers past us into the apartment. I practically sag with relief seeing him standing big in the hallway, his uniform dark and crisp, his hat shading intelligent eyes, a gun and billy-club strapped to his side. This cop looks like a bad guy's worst nightmare. My stomach does a nervous flip, glad he's on my side.

"Who's in there with you, son?"

I blurt out, "That's just the TV. It's golf," then clam up. Yup, that's exactly what the cop's interested in—what's on your TV, you moron.

With his hand on the hilt of his gun, the cop glides quickly through the apartment, his eyes sweeping each room. Wordlessly we watch him work. This guy's better than the movies. Satisfied we're alone, his sharp gaze returns to us.

Kevin jerks out of his stupor and says, "Oh. Right. Just me and my brother."

I suddenly remember I don't have a shirt on anymore. Can the cop smell that I'd been so scared I'd tossed my jelly roll right here in the living room? I cross my arms over my bare chest and avoid meeting the cop's eyes by looking over at Kevin.

The cop nods. "How old are you?"

"I'm fourteen, my brother Justin's twelve."

I like the promotion; it'll be true enough in two short weeks.

"Your parents out?"

"They're both at work. My Mom's coming home now. I talked to her. She said to call 911."

"Smart lad. Lots of 911 calls, but every call is an important one. It's best you stay here, locked up tight. We can't have people milling around the building right now. Keep your door locked and don't let anyone in, understand?" The cop moves swiftly back out the door into the hallway.

"Yes. But—is Mrs. Thompson okay?"

"Mrs. Thompson's just fine. We have her safe. Mr. Thompson is still somewhere in or around the building. You lock back up, keep your lights off and don't let anyone in unless it's me, alright?"

"But, Mrs. Thompson. We didn't—I mean, she wanted..." Kevin's voice fades and he looks down at where his hand is twisting the door handle. I sneak a peek at the cop and see something flicker in his face. He knows what happened. Mrs. Thompson probably blabbed the whole thing.

"You did the right thing son."

I practically fall on my ass in surprise.

"You called the police, and you called your mom. This is an adult matter. You have your little brother to protect. Just go back in, lock up and wait for me or another uniformed officer to give you the all clear. Got that?"

Kevin nods. The cop reaches in and pulls the door firmly closed. Kevin locks it and we trail back into the living room. Kevin flicks off the TV, leaving us in total darkness. We can hear the cop move on down the hall, checking other apartments, talking with authority. It seems everyone is opening their doors now.

My eyes adjust to the dark pretty quick. I point to a space in the hallway, central to the whole apartment. From there we would be able to see the outline of practically everything, but no one looking in our windows will be able to see us.

Like Mr. Thompson.

"Let's sit over there on the floor."

"Alright." Kevin throws a couple of cushions on the floor and half lays beside me. I can see already he's feeling better. He says, "Are you scared?"

"Nah, not anymore. The cops'll get him."

"Yeah. He's drunk. They'll get him for sure."

Our place is a ground floor apartment, a corner unit, and from where we're huddled, I can see both the patio door at the end of the living room and the kitchen window, each lit up from the street lights outside and casting enough light into the rooms to know I'm home, even if I am crowded against the wall between the oak trunk my Dad built for Mom last year and the coat stand.

I stay quiet, because I know Kevin doesn't want to talk, and run my hand along the satin smooth finish of the trunk, remembering all the hand polishing Dad did to get it this nice. Mom had cried when she'd seen it. I ease the lid up a crack and breathe in deep, inhaling the smell of cedar that always makes me think of Dad. I bet Mrs. Thompson's husband never made her a nice trunk for all her special stuff.

The weird silence is broken when Kevin's stomach suddenly gurgles really loud and long. We both snicker. Kevin rubs his stomach and whispers, "Missing the four major food groups."

I whisper back, "I know where you can find them."

Kevin makes a face. "Not your finest hour."

I nod. It was pretty gross.

Then he asks, "Why do you think she stays with him?"

I shrug my shoulders. I'd heard Mom ask Dad that same question lots of times since the Thompsons' moved in next door. If Mom and Dad didn't get it, how would I?

I reach over and grab a trailing corner of Mom's quilt and drag it across the floor toward us, then wrap it around my cold, bare shoulders. "What I want to know is, why did Mrs. Thompson go up in the elevator instead of running outside? Maybe get into her car and drive away? We're on the ground floor."

"Yeah. It's like those stupid slasher movies where the scared babysitter runs upstairs instead of out the open front door. All the time the whole audience is groaning, 'Why are you going up there, you loser? There's no way out.'"

I feel kind'a mean sitting here bad-mouthing Mrs. Thompson. Her husband's tracking her through the complex with a shotgun and all she ever did was be scared out of her mind. We weren't at our smartest either when we were scared. "Maybe she didn't have her car keys?"

"I guess." Kevin lays right down, and rests his head back on his hands. "I don't think I understand anything grown-ups do."

I look at him in surprise. And I'd thought it was only me, and it turns out my brother's just as mystified as I am. Now he's looking directly at me for the first time since this whole thing started. I know he wants me to understand why he didn't let Mrs. Thompson into our apartment. He wants me to agree with him, and I'm pretty sure I'm not going to, but I don't want to fight with him anymore.

His gaze shifts past me and he stiffens, silently points toward the kitchen. I shift and follow his wide-eyed gaze and together we watch the silhouette of a police officer slide silently past the kitchen window. The cops are only thirty feet away from us, looking for a crazy man with a shotgun.

A shiver goes through me. I need to talk too; I need to fill in the gaping quiet with something. "Okay, why'd you do it?"

Kevin turns onto his side, his eyes shiny in the dark as he looks straight at me. "When I opened the door and saw Mrs. Thompson down the hall, yelling about the shotgun, the first thing I thought of was Dad." His voice fades and I can see he's back in the moment when he slammed the door the first time. Then he brushed back his hair and continued, his voice stronger. "Remember what Dad told us about shotguns?"

"What's that got to do with anything? I'm not just a little kid, you know, waiting around for my brother to rescue me all the time. I do pretty good at school and there's lots of tough guys there. We could have just let her in and locked the door." I slow down to catch a breath. "Kev, I wouldn 'a got hurt."

Kevin looks tired. "I wish it was that simple."

"It is that simple."

"No, it isn't. Remember Dad telling us about that hunting accident back home when he was a kid? He said the shotgun almost cut the man in half, Justin." He sits back up in his eagerness to convince me. "In half. Shotguns aren't stopped by apartment doors."

"But we could have all run out the patio door."

Kevin sighed. "Well, I only thought of that later, didn't I?"

So he would have let her in after he'd thought of a way out for all of us. Just knowing there had been hope makes me feel way better. Even though I live to hassle him, I guess I kind 'a want to be like Kevin. He's strong, and always there for his friends, and for Mom when Dad's away, and even for me, his pain in the neck brother. I'm surprised to find I like Kevin. Who knew?

I can never let him know, though. There'd be no living it down—ever.

I catch sight of a movement with the corner of my eye. I grab Kevin's arm. "Look! Out the kitchen window."

Another crouched figure, outlined as clearly as if in daylight against the white sheer curtains, slips silently by and pauses, a clear shadow, mere steps away from where we're hiding. But this time there's a difference. I whisper, "No hat. Kev, this guy's not wearing a hat. It isn't a cop, they're all wearing hats. This has to be Mr. Thompson!"

Kevin jumps up and yells, "That's him!" He darts to the apartment door, unlocks and wrenches it open, all the time yelling about Mr. Thompson sneaking around outside our kitchen.

Three cops thunder down the hallway, and pour into our tiny apartment. I hear the guy by our window yelp and start running. He sounds as scared as Mrs. Thompson.

The cops knock into and leap over our furniture, yelling into walkie talkies as they fly by. They fumble with the catch on the sliding door then burst out onto the lawn in full pursuit of a lone figure lurching toward the kiddie park. Suddenly the bright reflections of red and blue lights sweep across the apartment walls from outside as cop cars with their lights flashing and sirens wailing pull in from everywhere, spilling out cops, with more cops on foot with guns drawn seeming to fill in the gaps. The swirling coloured lights make the whole yard look like the carnival that comes to town and sets up in the mall every Fall, only this carnival isn't fun. No clowns and candy floss here, just screams and shotgun blasts. The only thing that's the same is the throwing up after the rides.

Mr. Thompson is slammed to the ground, his shotgun wrenched from his grasp. Cops are everywhere, pinning him down, talking on walkie-talkies, talking to each other, running to important places. Mr. Thompson doesn't have a chance.

Kev and I step further out onto the patio and I'm surprised how balmy the night air is—Indian Summer gone wacko. Still, I grip the quilt around me tighter.

Across the lawn, we can just make out Mr. Thompson laying face-down and spread-eagle in front of North Peace Towers, surrounded by police and all his neighbours. A huge white light is trained onto him, changing night into day. Mr. Thompson is crying. He's sobbing, great gulping sobs, saying he's sorry, that he lost his job, that he's sorry and how it isn't his fault, and nobody understands him, and how he loves his wife, and how sorry he is.

Kevin and I look at each other and shake our heads. What the hell?

That guy's a pathetic, crying, wimpy nut-bar—big man with a gun, weasel without one.

Then I see Mrs. Thompson rush across the lawn from out of a police car parked on the street, trying to escape the cops who are holding her back from getting to him. She's crying too. Crying that it's all right, that she loves him and forgives him.

"I don't friggin' believe it," Kevin says incredulously.

I've noticed Kevin seems to have all the best swear words real handy tonight. I don't friggin' believe it either. Grown-ups can be really stupid sometimes, and this sure is one of those times.

As Kevin and I watch the Thompsons and the cops and all the neighbours who'd gathered to watch, the weight of Kevin's decision slowly seeps into my brain. I'd thought my brother, high-school jock, potential boyfriend to Joanie Stoltz, secret girly magazine reader, was a coward, but I'd been wrong.

So he'd been scared and just like in the movies, he'd run up the stairs instead of out the open front door—in the end, he'd done the right thing, for the right reasons.

A strangled cry comes from the parking lot, and my mother flies across the lawn toward us. A cop steps up to stop her. She waves in our direction, and I can just make out some of what she's saying, "...my sons... alone..."

The cop glances our way and nods her through. She closes the gap between us faster than I've ever seen her move before. She slams into us and clutches Kevin and me to her, her heart pounding in her chest so hard I can feel it against my cheek. Man, I never knew Mom was so strong. Her grip is like iron, but good. We don't say anything, just huddle together in a nice tight wad of arms and legs and squished faces.

I have to say, it feels great. Friggin' great!

Ronnie Roberts is the tireless, talented leader of the Writers of the Peace, the literary glue that holds us together, showing us the way to better writing while having fun doing it."

Okay – so Pat made me say that. Glue, huh? I can be sticky, especially after eating caramel popcorn, (which I hardly ever do!), and writing is fun (and maddening, and rewarding and sometimes reduces me to tears of frustration), and I did write a book for fiction writers entitled Complete Boot Camp for Fiction Writers.

Besides that, I've published six novels – The Wedding Dress Promise Series and the Poet Oregon Series and numerous short stories in magazines and anthologies. What I'm super excited about now is the three book Sci Fi series I'm currently writing, Earth Survives: Lost Sentinel, Cursed Apprentice and Deadly Messenger. What's not to like? Time travel, a post-apocalyptic world, a telepathic heroine, a battle between good and evil? Yup, Pat is right, writing is so much fun!!

Oh – and my family came to Fort St John 'temporarily' in search of work ten years ago. We fell in love with the people and seasons of the Peace and stayed.

Hunting in Peace

By Whitney Braun

Wet waders waded
Through the sky high rickety reeds
To beat the dawn that's coming
And the ducks that feed.

The muskeg water chills the hunter's bones,
He rubs his hands together.
Breath billows through the fog,
This fall morning—perfect weather.

Steel shots shift, shake in his pockets,
A shotgun heavy on his shoulder.
Cheeks and nose painted black,
His hands and feet still getting colder.

Luminous light ignites the sky
Dawn creeps above the tree line
Any minute now, he waits
Noise in the distance, a group of nine.

There they come—wings whipping, clipping,
A flock of ducks come in to land.
He sights them quickly down the barrel,
Plants boots, deep breath, calm hand.

Finger lingers on the trigger,
Bang! Reload, lickety-split.

They splinter, spread and panic
Re-sight, Bang! Another hit.

"Retrieve!" he yells into the mist.
Behind him comes an ungraceful tromp,
The lab dives in, careless to cold
On instinct, finds one with a gleeful chomp.

Rinse, repeat until bag limit reached,
Wait, breathe, aim, then shoot.
The team works quick to beat the heat
Then packs up and hikes away with loot.

Whitney Braun is a bit of a dabbler. Born in Fort St John and raised in Rose Prairie, Whitney's interests include (but are never limited to) farming, skiing, baseball, football, painting, reading, writing, and snoozing with her cat, Rascal, by her side. Her novels, 'Worth the Risk' and 'Worth the Chance', can be found on Amazon and in our local Coles bookstore.

First Snow

By Patrick D. Ferris

Larry took his new Caribbean bride, Giselle, out through the old farm-house door and into the middle of the yard, near the deceased apple tree. Here they stood ankle deep in the first virgin snow of the winter season. The cold air charged their nostrils giving them both goose bumps as a Peace country breeze gently made the wind chimes sing.

Larry lovingly put his hand on her shoulder, starting one of his famously lame speeches, "Giselle: We need to talk…about us…and snow. You were here for a couple of weeks last Christmas but you've never experienced a real, full on winter before and it can get on your nerves."

"I never thought about it, Larry. Tell me; how does snow get on yar nerves?" she asked, a bit sarcastically but with her charming Trini accent.

Larry continued to lecture, "Winter can be hard. You wake up sometimes and there is snow all over the place. It has to be swept, shoveled and managed."

She stood for a few moments waiting for more of the story but apparently that was all to be said. "So? Ya farm where large tracts of dirt is plowed, rocks picked, earth smoothed and weeded. Ya fertilize, plant and grow stuff which later has ta be cut, harvested, managed and moved to market. It's what ya do."

"True, but we Canadians are profoundly annoyed about snow. Weather is a personal thing up here," he reasoned.

"The weather is the weather, Larry. In case ya haven't noticed, nobody has come up with a way ta control it and can barely even predict what it will do. It is what it is."

"I know, but we tend to grow up hating the snow because it is around us, all the time," he countered.

"Doesn't it just snow for a few months in the winter? Four or five months, tops? Ya do like to make up stories about how much snow ya never got and how cold it never was," Giselle pointed out, logically.

"I know we like to make it sound harder than it is because we hate it so much. It gnaws at us and eats at our souls. People will leave friends, well-paying jobs, family and everything dearest to them to move away at huge expense and hassle, so they do not have to shovel snow."

"Yar kiddin', right?" she said.

"I kid you not," Larry said grimly.

"So, do they move to the desert or some place that will never see snow?" She asked.

"Well, not usually, because the desert gets too hot in the summer. They just move where it only snows a few times in the winter and mostly rains."

"But it does snow, there, once in a while?"

"Yes, but they do not speak of it. As far as they are concerned it only ever rains which is fully acceptable."

"So… just as long as the rain doesn't freeze it's considered better?"

"Yes."

"So instead of shoveling snow, they rake and shovel leaves, mow grass and deal with a lot of rain instead of snow?"

"Yes."

"But no curlin', skiin', sleddin' and such?"

"No. They do summer stuff when it isn't raining."

"But it rains a lot?"

"Yes."

"Larry; I'm confused. How is this an improvement over snow?"

"It is a huge difference to them."

"So, if I say I moved here because I was sick of beach sand and the heat, they'd understand?"

"No. They think that is better than snow, provided it's not too hot in the summer."

"Let's go back to somethin' ya said earlier, Larry. Ya said they'd hate it if it's too hot."

"Yes, it can't be too hot."

"So ya say it can't be too hot or cold enough ta snow?"

"Yes."

"You Canadians live in heated and air conditioned homes all year around, don't ya, generally? Seventy degrees or whatever ya set on the thermostat?"

"Correct but they still don't like snow, even if they don't live in it, exactly."

"Ah… of course. When do these snow hatin' thoughts occur to Canadians?"

"We usually grow up hating snow or hear we should hate snow. It's a DNA thing."

"So yar sayin' I should not like snow? But last Christmas we came up here and did a lot of winter activities and I liked the snow. Am I weird?"

"No. You are from Trinidad and don't know that you should hate the snow. Maybe later."

She put her arms around him and held him close, looking closely into his eyes, smiling, "Ya aren't kiddin me, are ya? Water falls from the sky, everywhere but when it freezes...."

"...crystallizes, Giselle... Crystallizes."

"Don't interrupt. ...and you Canadians take this crystallizin' transformation as a personal insult and will move away from everything and everyone you hold near and dear at great personal sacrifice to escape it?"

"Pretty much."

"And you think you have got away from a fate worse than death?"

"I'm afraid so."

"I thought this kind'a thing was a cultural, religious or economic immigration due to severe hardship but it's just to get away from snow?" She sighed, rolled her eyes, "And here I thought ya Canadians were a logical people. Ya can imagine my surprise."

"We are not quite perfect just yet, Giselle."

She smiled, pushed him over and washed his face with snow.

Pat Ferris was born in Winnipeg, Manitoba on a chilly January 11, 1954 day. His family eventually moved to Victoria where he spent his formative years but pined away for those sharp, cold winters buried deep in his DNA. In 1975 Pat moved to Fort St. John for six months to experience the burgeoning natural gas industry and feel the cold winters he sorely missed. Forty-one years later he's still there, now turning his hand to writing romance/adventure novels such as; 'Gypsies' and 'A Gypsy Engagement'.

North Peace Blues—Coda

By Glenn Palmer

ONE
Graduation

Paul Tucker went straight home after the graduation ceremony. He shrugged off the pleadings of his friends to join them on a cruise around the lake. "I'll catch up with you tonight," he told them. His girlfriend Tawny was the only one who knew what he was up to. She gave him a quick kiss and whispered, "Good luck, Paul. I'll see you tonight."

When he arrived home there was a government sedan parked in the driveway behind his father's Mustang and his mother's Saturn.

Paul was an Indian who had been adopted when he was around two years old and raised by George and Hazel Tucker. He knew nothing about his roots aside from being Ojibway. His parents had promised that when he finished school they would help him find out about his origins. Today was that day.

The policy of the adoption agency had been complete secrecy for years. In the last couple of years things had changed. The trend now was to allow adoptees to know where they came from and integrate back into their source bands, if they wished.

His parents were waiting for him in the kitchen. The government representative was Mrs. Wilkinson. Paul had had a couple of interviews with her and she'd promised to dig out the information he needed in time for graduation.

"Well, Paul, there really isn't much information available," she began. "I'm not trying to hide anything from you. There simply isn't much in the system. Because the policy in those days was complete secrecy, they didn't bother to record much."

"What did you find out?"

"I found the band and reserve you came from, and your mother's name. That's about all there is."

"Tell me, tell me."

"Your mother was a member of the Raven Lake First Nation. Your birth is documented, so you can probably get first nations status without any trouble. That First Nation has six reserves. Your Mother came from Sabasking Bay 35C Reserve."

"Where's that?"

"All the Raven Lake reserves are on Lake of the Woods."

"Can I go there?"

"You can, although I'm not sure how you get there. A lot of the settlements are only accessible by boat. I imagine if you made some calls to the tourist office in Kenora they could tell you more. That's what I'd do."

"What was my mother's name?"

"Gladys Coldwater. She died the year after you were born. You were placed for adoption by your grandfather, Wallace Grayleg."

"Why do they all have such strange names?"

"Those are their white names. A lot of natives were given arbitrary names by missionaries or government workers. Their white names don't have anything to do with their Indian names. They are just labels assigned to make it easier for the system to keep track of them."

"How do you know my mother's dead?"

"Your grandfather said so. That was the reason for the adoption."

Paul looked through the file Mrs. Wilkins had brought. "There isn't much here, is there?"

"I know you must be disappointed, Paul, but there's enough here to get you started if you want to run down your roots. People have started with a lot less information and been successful. Are you going to visit the reserve?"

"I'll find a way. If my grandfather is still alive when I get there, I'd like to talk to him. Maybe I can find out what my Indian name was. What was the white name on the application?"

"Peter Grayleg."

"Why not Coldwater?"

"I don't know. Maybe they don't pass names the same way we do. Something to ask your grandfather when you see him."

Paul returned to the file.

Mrs. Wilkinson stood up and put her coffee cup in the sink. "That's a copy of your file, Paul. You can keep it. Good luck with your search." She shook hands all around and walked out to her car.

"Dad, will you help me?"

"Think about it for a couple of days, Paul. If you decide it's really what you want to do, of course I'll help you. Go out with your friends and celebrate the end of school with them, Once all that's wound down, we can talk again. Fair enough?"

"I guess so. But, I'd like to skip the hi-jinx and try to start this."

"Of course you would, but graduation only comes once. Call Tawny and get your arrangements in place for celebrating. We'll talk again in a couple of days and get things set up for you.

TWO
Reservation Run

Three weeks later, Paul arrived at the reserve. Most of that time had been spent on research. It was harder than he'd expected to find out how to get there. He'd made the first leg from North Bay to Thunder bay, then headed north, stopping at every small town he passed through and asking for directions.

Now he was here. In the center of the reserve was a large communal building. The open space was surrounded by forest. He was impressed by how neat and well maintained everything was. The expectations he had for an 'Indian Reserve' were for a lot of squalid, run-down shacks with outhouses behind them. This place seemed to be the opposite of that in every way.

He parked near the big building hoping to find someone who could direct him to his grandfather's house.

He found a door that was marked as 'Village Manager', but it was locked. The sign on the door said the staff would be busy in a meeting until two. It was just one-thirty now. He stretched out on the hood of his car to wait until the office reopened.

The hood of the car was warm and the sun beating down made it even hotter. When he closed his eyes, all he could hear was the wind in the trees and the tick of his engine as it cooled. Off in the distance some kind of crow or raven was yakking away. A song bird was giving an impressive performance somewhere close by. So peaceful.

"Hey, you asleep?" Somebody was shaking his foot gently. He opened his eyes and realized he'd drifted off.

"I guess I did fall asleep. It's been a long drive."

Paul saw the fellow who'd awakened him was around twenty-five. Jeans, black t-shirt, some kind of headband. Cowboy boots. His left eye was lazy and looked off in some random direction. That left the right eye to do all the heavy lifting. Paul couldn't get a read on the guy at all. The eye that was staring at him seemed friendly enough but it was kind 'a hard to tell for sure.

"Where'd you come from?"

"Just drove up from North Bay. Name's Paul Tucker." He held out his hand. The new acquaintance gave the hand a quick shake. Paul could feel hard callouses on the hand he shook, but the grasp was very soft, almost limp.

"John Wilson. Come sit in the shade, that sun's stronger than you think with the breeze coming off the lake."

Paul followed John around to the shady side of the building . They sat together, leaning against the wall. Crickets chirped under the building. A red squirrel scolded in the trees nearby. Paul realized he *had* kind of baked himself in the sun and now felt almost cold in the shade. The grass under his butt felt damp but it was dry when he ran his hand across it.

John seemed to be leaving the conversation up to him.

Here it goes then.

Paul started. "I guess you must know everyone around here, eh?"

"Nobody I don't know. There's only a couple hundred people here."

Paul nodded. "Doesn't seem very crowded. I'm looking for Wallace Grayleg. Know where I can find him?"

"Sure. He's got a cabin on the lake shore. Walk down to the lake, make a right at the water. Wallace's cabin is about a mile down the shore."

That was easy.

"Thanks. Is it okay if I leave my car here?"

"Lock it up; you'll be fine. Maybe put a sign in the window saying 'back soon' or something like that."

"I'll do that. Thanks for the help."

"Does Wallace know you're coming?"

"No, it's a surprise."

John grimaced and wagged his head regretfully. "Wallace don't like surprises. He's a paranoid old prick. When you find the place, stand out in the dooryard and call. Don't step up on the porch before he gets a look at you."

"What's he going to do, shoot me?"

The right eye looked down at the ground then up to Paul's face. The left seemed to be tracking a seagull over the lake. "Nah. Probably not."

Not reassuring.

When he got to the lake shore, Paul found a rough trail following the water's edge. It wasn't quite a boardwalk, but pieces of split cedar, about four feet long had been laid side by side on the ground making a sort of sidewalk. Paul realized that someone had cut the cedar poles to length and then quartered them with a froe. The thought of all that effort just to make a trail gave him a headache.

Wallace's place was impossible to miss. For most of the distance thick brush grew out to the edge of the trail. On the left, the lake came within three feet of the trail. Paul had been walking for about twenty minutes when a clearing appeared on his right. It occurred just beyond a little peninsula and it was invisible until you rounded the point.

Wallace's house was a small shack covered with cedar shakes. A porch ran the length of the front. A big stone chimney rose above one end of the shack, seeming to grow out of the earth itself. A little wind started up now there was room for it to move. Paul smelled the aroma of a stew simmering. Leaves rattled on the trees and the wind blew waves across the ankle high grass in the dooryard. A small dock extended out into the lake. Paul could hear waves lapping at the sides of the canoe moored to the dock.

Just when Paul was going to call out and announce himself, he heard the sound of an ax coming from farther down the shore. He followed the sound of the ax and found himself in another clearing. A couple of trestles had been set up and a small cedar log sat on the trestles.

An old native man was squaring off the log with some kind of broad ax. Paul watched him for a bit. The old man stood parallel to the pole, facing along its length. With every swing of the ax, a large square chip detached itself from the pole.

The old man got to the end of the pole and rolled it over . Now the side he had just faced was on top and he started moving down the length of the pole scoring it with the ax.

A squirrel chattered right beside Paul and the worker looked around. "Who's there?" he called. "Come out where I can see you."

Paul stepped out. "Over here," he called.

Wallace moved straight towards him, holding the ax down at his side. He stopped about eighteen inches in front of Paul. Paul could see every wrinkle and pore on his face.

"What are you doing sneaking around my place?" He stood with his legs apart, almost on the balls of his feet. The ax was loose in his hands across his body.

Paul took a step back. Wallace took a step forward.

"I wasn't sneaking," Paul said. "I came looking for you. I heard you chopping when I got to your shack, so I came down here."

"Who are you and why should I care?"

"I'm Paul Tucker, from North Bay."

"Doesn't ring a bell. What do you want with me? Make it snappy or I'll kick your ass the whole mile back to the center."

"I'm your grandson, Gladys's son."

Paul was expecting some warmth at that point. Instead, the old man's eyes grew hard and brilliant. He raised the ax slightly. "Get out of here and don't ever come back. Get into your car and head back to whatever white place you came from. There's nothing here for you but trouble. That's a promise."

"I just want to know where I came from. Please. Talk to me."

"You only think you want to know. The truth isn't pretty like you think. The best thing I ever did was send you away to the adoption agency. There's nothing for you here, nothing. So turn around right now, go back up the pretty wooden trail and forget all about being native. You can't just pull it on and off. You're lucky and white now, so go play with the honkies." He raised the ax again and shook it for emphasis.

Paul had never seen such anger. Threat of violence rolled off the old man like a bad smell.

"All right, all right. I'll go." He turned and walked back to the trail. After a few steps, he looked back over his shoulder. His grandfather was still standing where he had left him. It was all Paul could do to keep from running. His guts felt loose in his belly.

I never thought I was a coward, but he scares the crap out of me. This trip wasn't my best idea ever.

He didn't break into a run, but the walk back to the village took a lot less time.

What the hell am I doing here?

Paul could feel his heart slowing down, but he still felt empty inside and he found he was panting a bit, When he held his hand out he could see a tremble. Still lots of adrenaline racing around.

"Hey, North Bay, you're back already. Not much of a chat, eh?" John Wilson sat down in front of Paul.

"Old bugger ran me off with an ax. I think he might really have chopped me if I didn't leave."

"I told you he was cranky. What did you do to set him off?"

"Nothing. I just told him who I was and he flipped."

"What, he didn't like your name or something?"

"The name didn't bother him, but when I told him I was his grandson he got hostile."

John locked on Paul's face with his good eye and gave a low whistle. "You're Gladys's kid? No wonder he went nuts. If you want to spend any time here, don't tell anybody who your mom is. Best thing you can do is jump into your shiny red graduation present and head on out of here."

"That's the same thing Wallace said. What do you all think is wrong with me?"

"Ain't you man, it's your mom."

"What about her? I came all this way to find out where I'm from."

"Tell me why it matters so much to you."

Paul ran his hands through his hair and

shook his head. "Look," he said, "I was adopted when I was two..."

John held his hand up to interrupt. "You were three, not two."

"I was? No wonder I was always big for my age. Why'd they do that?" Long pause. "Anyway, my parents were great. Hardly anybody was mean to me at school. But, inside, I never felt like I belonged. You know?"

John nodded. "I know that one, " he said. "I hitched down to Thunder Bay once. I felt like a white crow or something."

Paul nodded. "It was pretty obvious the guy looking back at me in the mirror was no honky. My folks told me I was adopted, that I was Ojibway, but they didn't know anything else. They promised me they'd help me find where I came from after I graduated from high school."

John's expression was a bit softer now. "How long you been working on this?"

"My dad did a bunch of work on it this year. I graduated June seventeenth. We started to work on it for real after Canada Day. It wasn't that hard, but even the adoption agency didn't know much. Long story short: I did a bunch of research online and here I am."

John looked down at the ground, his left eye flitting around like an inebriated bee. He was obviously weighing his options. "Got any money?" he finally asked.

"Sure. Why?"

"Let's go in the center there, grab some lunch and some pop. We can take it down to the shore. I'll tell you a little story."

"Thank you. You won't be sorry."

"I'm sorry already, but I guess you need to

hear your own story. I don't think you'll like it much."

They got a couple of nice ham and cheese buns. John tried for burgers but the girl behind the counter said the grill was already turned off. Paul paid for the buns and a six pack of Pepsi.

There was a picnic table in the shade. They sat on the table with their feet on the seat, facing the lake and chewed their sandwiches . There was a loon calling off in the distance somewhere. A couple of Coots were dabbling around in the mud.

Paul discovered that he wasn't in much of a hurry to hear the story. All the negative reaction had him spooked, so he waited patiently rather than hurrying John along.

John watched the Coots for a while. At last, he gave a big sigh and started in. "Life here ain't like what you might have heard about other reserves. People here are mostly after a quiet life. Everybody goes to church when the preacher comes by. Some drive to Sioux Rapids or Nestor's Falls on Sunday and attend there. All the yahoo alcoholic shit you hear about on other reserves doesn't happen here."

"I noticed everything was clean and neat when I drove in. It surprised me a bit."

John nodded. "I know what you were expecting. That ain't us. 'Cept for your mom."

He fiddled around with a pipe he produced from somewhere in his clothes. Soon clouds of aromatic smoke were winding up into the breeze and drifting in Paul's direction.

"Your mother, Gladys, was a famous slut. She went away to high school in Nestor's Falls. It was a deal where she stayed with a family in town."

John puffed on his pipe while he searched for words. "I don't know what kind ‘a place it was she stayed at. The first year was fine. She came home in the summer happy and healthy. The next summer when she came home she was different and she didn't go back and finish school."

Paul was concentrating hard. "Something bad must have happened to her."

"Probably, but she didn't tell anybody, far as I know." John started fiddling with his pipe again. His eyes were shiny with tears, but his voice was still steady.

"Here's the thing, " he said. "Once she got rolling, there wasn't anything Gladys wouldn't do for a drink. She used to go to town for a couple weeks at a time, come home when she was too tired and beat up and needed to recover. Later, when she got her house, white guys from town would drive in with booze and party at her place. It was about a year after she got her place that you showed up."

"So I might not even be Indian?"

"Well, your mom was, so half for sure. But your dad was probably white."

"Why was my mom named Coldwater instead of Grayleg?"

"Charley Coldwater was always nuts for Gladys. When she came up pregnant he offered to marry her so the kid—that's you—would have a dad."

Another long pause. Paul looked away while John wiped his eyes. The story seemed to be hurting John more than Paul. Paul just felt numb despair as his hopes dissolved.

"What happened to her?" he asked.

"Let's tell it in the order it happened. I can handle it when it's a straight line. If we start jumping around I'll get confused and probably start bawling."

"All right. Pick it up where Charley came in."

"Charley gave it a good try but it was no good. Gladys just carried on like nothing had happened. All being married meant to her was that she had a free babysitter so she could party. Six months was all Charley could handle. He went to Montreal to work the steel and hasn't been seen since."

John paused for comments or questions. Paul just waited.

"After Charley left, Gladys used to drop you off with Wallace whenever she headed out. She never asked. If Wallace wasn't home she just left you on the porch in your basket and went.

"I should tell you about Wallace. He used to be a respected elder before all this went down. One reason this place is so reasonable is because of his influence. After Gladys went off the rails he lost his position in the community. That's why he lives in that shack down the shore instead of in town. People blamed him for not being able to control her. When he looks at you, he's forced back into the bitterest experience of his life.

"After Gladys disappeared, he tried to raise you himself. That didn't work. He said he was angry at you all the time. He knew it was really Gladys who he was mad at, but he couldn't help himself. That's why he adopted you out. He was afraid he was going to hurt you for something that wasn't your fault."

John seemed to have run out of steam for a while. He didn't say anything more. Paul didn't ask anything. They just sat there on the picnic table listening to the waves lap the shore and the loon cry out on the lake. The sun went behind a cloud and Paul felt the chill. He disappeared inside himself, processing everything he'd heard.

"What's your name?"

Paul startled back to the present and looked around. There was a little girl on the seat beside their feet, looking up at him. Her clothes were dusty and rumpled, but her face was clean. She looked to be about ten years old. She was staring up at him with the biggest smile, her face full of curiosity.

"My name's Paul. Who are you?"

"Miigwan. That means feather in the old tongue."

Paul extended his hand for a shake. "I'm sorry I didn't see you show up."

"That's all right. I'm just a little kid. You don't have to notice me."

"Well, I'm glad I did." Just then a humming bird flew past with a buzz and a flash of red and blue brilliance. The little girl jumped down and started off in the wake of the bird. "I have to see where it goes. Bye-bye."

John had been looking on in amazement. "She snuck right up on us, didn't she? " he said.

"Yeah, she did. What a great little girl."

"Everybody loves little Feather, but she doesn't stay in one spot for long so nobody gets much time with her."

"Time to finish the story?"

John nodded. "We're at the end now. Gladys disappeared a couple of weeks before Christmas. She took off with a couple of guys in a van, never came home. They found her frozen in a snowbank when spring came round."

"Nobody knows what happened?"

"Nope. The most popular theory is that it turned out there were some things Gladys wouldn't do for a drink. When her new friends realized that no meant no, they kicked her out in the snow and drove off. Who knows, though? She wasn't wearing a coat when they found her so that makes it seem most likely."

Paul shook his head. "I don't know what to make of all this. I worked really hard to live in the white world, but I never quite fit. Now you tell me I can't fit here either. What the hell am I supposed to do?"

"There's no place for you here, that's true. If you want to know what to do next, you need to have a vision."

"You mean like a dream?"

"It's more than that. You have to prepare properly and follow the ceremony. If you're lucky you'll know what to do after it's over."

"Great. How am I supposed to do that?"

"You have to ask Chayden for help."

THREE
Vision Quest

Chayden turned out to be the local shaman. Everybody on the reserve was firmly Christian but they still turned to a shaman for help when they were dealing with native issues.

Miigwan was Chayden's niece. She lived with her uncle in a wigwam some distance from the village. Living in the traditional lodge instead of a modern house helped keep Chayden on his path.

John brought Paul to meet the shaman at his lodge. He said he was too busy to take on a student. Besides, if Paul was raised in the white world it wasn't likely that he could achieve a vision.

He changed his mind when he discovered that Paul was Gladys Coldwater's son. "Gladys was a good girl. She got trapped because of what happened to her in town. I might have been able to help her, but she never asked."

Paul was happy to find at least one person who liked his mother. "Didn't it bother you, the way she drank and fooled around?"

Chayden looked solemn and seemed to be searching for a way to say what he meant. "Everybody thought Gladys was weak because she drank, but that wasn't it. The world knocked her down. The drinking and the rage was strength, it was her saying 'Fuck you, world. I go my own way now.' The demon had her but she was still good inside."

Chayden agreed to help Paul find a vision. First, he had to build a sweat lodge and learn some simple chants to sing in the lodge. He also had to eat very simple food. The main dish was a thin gruel made with cornmeal and moose jerky, and he had to cook it himself.

The lake became Paul's gymnasium. There was a small island a couple of hundred yards off-shore. Chayden told Paul he had to swim back and forth to the island five times every day and that he couldn't try for the vision until he could manage the swim.

The first time Paul tried for the island he couldn't reach it. Chayden followed him in a canoe. When Paul reached the limit of his strength, Chayden threw him a float , but he wouldn't let him quit until he reached the island. It took three weeks before Paul was strong enough to swim the distance five times.

Miigwan was always around, Sometimes she was in the canoe with Chayden while Paul swam. She saved him from burning his gruel and showed him how to stir it properly and keep the pot on the edge of the fire instead of in the middle. Paul never saw her complain or cry. Her smile could create a light inside him no matter how discouraged he was. And Miigwan ran everywhere she went; Miigwan ran toward life.

By the time a month had passed, Paul’s skin

had darkened in the outdoor sunlight. His body was thin and whip-hard from the exercise and the simple diet. He sweated and chanted for an hour every day. Sometimes, when he was finished with his sweat, his mind seemed so clear that he felt he could explode rocks with his will.

Chayden told him that it was time for him to seek his vision. The first step was to build himself a small wigwam. It had to be high enough to stand up in and twice as wide as Paul's height, and he had to create it without instruction.

"How am I supposed to know how to build it?"

Chayden pointed toward his own lodge with a gesture that obviously meant, "Copy this."

Paul was able to build one. The only difficult part was figuring out how to strip the bark off the birch trees in big enough sheets to cover the walls. Chayden helped him with that part by gathering bark for his own use and allowing Paul to watch what he did.

Chayden told him to stay in the wigwam for a night and a day, chanting and fasting. He had to stay awake, chant and fast for the entire time. Chayden left him in the lodge and tied the door shut. Paul was locked in the gloom with a bottle of water to drink and a bucket to pee in. The only light he had was what managed to sneak through the little holes where the birch-bark attached to the frames. Paul settled on the floor in the middle of the lodge and began to chant.

He started to chant under his breath. The chant was so wired into his brain that he continued to hear it even if he stopped altogether. Somehow he got through the night. He couldn't tell if he was awake or asleep, and no longer knew if there was a difference.

Sometime later little spears of light began shining through the holes in the walls. A woodpecker began to pound on a nearby tree and a new day began.

When Chayden unsealed the door flap he found Paul leaning against the wall just inside. "Go for a little walk," he told him. "Find some licorice root. It'll take the bad taste out of your mouth. I'll set things up here."

FOUR
Datura

When Paul got back to the wigwam Chayden had set up a pile of cushions on the floor that could be arranged into a bed. He'd also installed a large beanbag chair. There was a small table set up beside the chair. A candle sat in the middle of the table lighting the room. There was a box beside the table with some bowls and utensils.

Chayden was sitting on the ground and waved to Paul to sit in the beanbag. "Here's how this works," he said. "You're going to use Datura, Jimson weed, to find your vision. It's the best aid to unlock your inner being. Unfortunately, Datura is painful and violent to use. You have to buffer it and prepare it properly. It also tastes like shit, so there's that."

He put a paper bag on the table. "Mushrooms," he said. "They aren't magic mushrooms. These are angel wing mushrooms. You eat them to take the edge off the Datura. Them you can just chew up dry. Notice you have a big jug of water."

"Datura is really bitter. What you do there is pour a couple of cups of sugar into a bowl and add enough water to make a thick syrup. Then grate the Datura roots into the syrup. You want about half a cup. Be sure you wear the rubber gloves or you'll absorb the juice through your skin. You don't want that. With me so far?"

Paul nodded. His stomach was twisting and he couldn't seem to catch his breath easily.

Not sure I'm ready for this.

"Okay, here's what you do," said Chayden. "Make your syrup and grate the root. When it's all mixed together, eat a couple of the mushrooms, drink some water."

He paused, studying Paul's face. "At some point, you'll hear a ringing in your ears and feel a chill. When that happens blow out the candle. Take a spoonful of Datura syrup. Take one every five minutes or so. When the lights come on put the Datura away. Don't have anymore."

"What do I do next?" Paul asked.

"Fasten your seatbelt and watch the pretty pictures. You ready to go?"

"I guess so."

"You're on your own then. I'm going to close the door flap, but it won't be fastened. Bon voyage."

After Chayden left, Paul followed the instructions he'd been given. It was an easy procedure to follow for someone who aced chemistry in high school.

The mushrooms were white, thin semi-circles. He chomped down five of them. They had a woody taste that washed away with a drink of water.

Sometime later, he heard the ringing in his ears, like small silver bells, then he felt a sudden chill. He took a spoonful of the syrup, blew out the candle and waited for something to happen.

Nothing did. He waited for what seemed like five minutes and took another spoonful.

Still nothing. He was just about to take a third

spoonful of the syrup when the lights came on. The candle was still out, but he could see every detail of the framework of the wigwam in sharp-edged detail. He could see every crack and piece of bark on the bent sticks. It was almost painful. Then everything he looked at developed a warm orange glow and began to pulsate.

He felt very heavy, like an Easter Island statue. He couldn't lift a hand no matter how hard he tried.

The door flap swung open and Miigwan came in. She had a flashlight and the beam seemed to burn Paul's eyes. He let out a yell and she quickly turned the flashlight away from him.

"Don't make any noise," she said. "Uncle told me to stay away but I have a present for you." It was a three inch square piece of stiff paper. It was a photo of her. She held the picture under her chin. At first it was cute, then some weird echo started between her actual face and the one in the photo.

Paul let out a moan because he could no longer tell which was the real face and which was the photo. Miigwan saw he was bothered and slipped the picture into his shirt pocket.

She looked at what was on the table, stuck her finger into the Datura syrup. It was sweet and she dipped out several fingers-full and licked them up.

Paul tried to shout, "No Feather don't, please don't," but his tongue seemed to be made of stone and his lips as thick as tree trunks. He couldn't make a sound and his stone body wouldn't move to stop her.

Miigwan giggled. "I better go before Uncle finds out. Don't tell him I was here." She gave him a quick kiss on the cheek and disappeared through the door flap.

Alone again, Paul went back to watching the rippling of the lodge frame. He knew that something had happened but he couldn't remember what. The orange glow in the room faded to blue. Then came a sudden explosion of bright, white light. He cried out in fear and the Datura took him completely. He crawled out of the wigwam and went off stumbling through the forest.

FIVE
Aftermath

When the Datura released him, Paul found himself lying on a bed of moss under a birch tree. He sat up, gripping the sides of his head. It felt like there were hot wires connecting his temples to his eyeballs. He was one big ache. There was a foul taste in his mouth, and his stomach was rolling.

There was something in his shirt pocket. A picture of Miigwan.

Where did that come from? She must have given it to me when I was out.

He didn't seem to have achieved a vision. He found he couldn't remember anything about his experience with the drug. All he had was a vague sense of flashing colors and feeling very hot. He decided it had been interesting, but the aftermath wasn't worth it.

He was too weak to move very far. Somehow he managed to get as far as the trunk of the tree and leaned against it. The moss he was sitting on was deep and cool. He could hear the leaves rattling overhead . His clothes were soaked with sweat, he stank and he was chilled by the breeze that was blowing.

He had no idea where he was. This was a part of the forest he wasn't familiar with.

Listen, just listen.

There. He didn't hear anything but the wind in the trees for a long time. Then, he heard a loon call. It came from his two o'clock. The call was faint so he could be a long way from the lake. It would be easy going, the forest was quite open here. He started walking, pausing every five minutes for another clue, adjusting as necessary.

When the lake appeared in front of him, he realized he was only about half a mile from Chayden's lodge. He recognized the little island that had been the goal of his swimming in the last month.

There was a bunch of people sitting on the ground in front of the lodge. Chayden was sitting near the door opening, crying.

Alarmed, Paul picked up his stumbling gait.

Drawing closer, he registered that Chayden was clutching a bundle of wet rags as he wailed. No. A tiny wet body.

Dread washed over Paul as he lurched forward.

It was Miigwan!

Had she drowned? What the hell? She could swim like a beaver.

When he stumbled up to the lodge, Chayden looked up at him and just shook his head. One of the young men sitting on the ground jumped up, launched himself at Paul, punching him in the face. Others joined in. When he went down, they formed a circle, taking turns kicking him.

Paul knew they would kill him, but was helpless to defend himself. The kicking only stopped when Chayden called out sharply and sent the young men away.

Chayden helped Paul sit up and brought him water. Paul rinsed his mouth. The water he spat out was red.

The two of them sat on the ground, the old man still holding fast to his little niece. "I'm sorry they beat you," he said. "I know what happened wasn't your fault, but I wanted it to be, so I was happy when they put the boots to you. Then I was ashamed and I ended it. I was wrong. Please forgive me."

"What happened to Feather?"

"She ran into the lake screaming. She went deep and was thrashing and crying. She drowned before anybody could get to her."

"It was my fault?"

"She took some Datura that was intended for you. That wasn’t your fault. I should have kept her in sight while you were having a vision."

"I remember now. She did take some. She came to give me something, saw the Datura in the bowl and took some. I can't remember anything else."

The shaman nodded. "When the drug kicked in she was terrified. If she hadn't run into the lake she could have gotten lost in the forest."

"She would have been hot," said Paul. "The Datura makes you feel like you're burning up. She must have been trying to cool down."

"That's what I think happened. My head tells me this is not your fault. Miigwan was finished as soon as she ate the Datura. The dose was too strong for somebody her size. If she hadn't drowned she would have died of a convulsion." Chayden looked down at the little girl, brushed a strand of hair off her face. "But Paul, you have to leave. Go right now. You are in great danger if you stay."

"Will those men kill me?"

"They won't, but I might. The wolf inside me wants to chop you into pieces with my ax and throw them in the lake." He shook his head. "I'm ashamed of the desire. But listen, I don't think you will have a happy day for the rest of your life. I think you have Gladys's demon inside you. I hope I'm wrong, but I don't think I am. You will spread pain and unhappiness wherever you go."

Paul shook his head and made a pushing away motion. He started to cry because he looked at little Miigwan and needed to see her run and smile again.

"Did you at least have a vision?" asked Chayden.

Paul shook his head.

"All for nothing. then," said Chayden. "What an awful waste." He waved 'go now', then staggered to his feet and took his little niece into the lodge.

Somehow Paul made his way into the village, got into his car and drove south toward Thunder Bay. Chayden's final words held him in a horrific trance. There must have been stops to eat and gas up, but he was on autopilot until he reached the lake-head.

He saw a used car dealer at the edge of town. He pulled into the lot and sold his car for the first price the salesman offered. With the check in his pocket, he walked back up to the highway, pulled his wallet out of his pocket and threw it as far as he could. His cell phone followed.

The he stuck out his thumb and waited for the first ride that would take him west. Before too long, an old blue pick-up stopped. His first ride, of many. Paul climbed into the passenger seat and stared out the windshield, thinking of the way Miigwan went everywhere at a run—always running *toward*, never *away*.

"Name's Bob. What's yours?" It was the driver's voice, seeming to come from a long way away.

"Jacob, " Paul said. He remembered reading once that Jacob meant the supplanter, the one who replaces.

"Jacob Running Feather."

THE END

Glenn Palmer is a retired computer nerd from SFU. He's always lived in a fantasy world. For the last five years he's been writing down what he sees.

The Clockmaker

By Kevin Buchholz

Years ago I met a clockmaker by chance. The ease with which the clockmaker could manipulate time amazed all. Time could stand still; time could fly by. Marvels could appear and disappear in the blink of an eye.

So I say to the clockmaker, "May I join you?" I ask to be with him—"If for a day, then a day; if for longer, then better." The clockmaker asks who I am and I say, "This is who I believe I am."

The clockmaker smiles at my enthusiasm and sees my courage.

The clockmaker warns me. I'm told of the perils, I'm warned of the pitfalls and I'm told of the plight. I laugh them all off for I know who I am. Look how well my clock works. I'm warned I might want to walk away. But I still agree, for the things I see do amaze.

The clockmaker chuckles at my enthusiasm and admires my courage.

The clockmaker says to me one time, "Do you want to know how I do it?" And I say "yes," for I want to know. The clockmaker says, "It's not easy and there will be many trials." And I ask, "How long does it take?" The clockmaker replies, "Everyone is different and some may take longer than others." "Will I fail?" I ask the clockmaker. "Well, if you don't try, you've already failed," is the reply. Then I will try.

And the clockmaker smiles at my enthusiasm and brags of my courage.

The clockmaker shows me how to use my clock. The clockmaker encourages me to take it apart. At first I am afraid, but I soon learned. And in no time I could see all and I was saddened. I ask the clockmaker, “What next?” I ask, “Is this all there is to be?” And the clockmaker replies, "What more do you want?" And I respond, “Just some more time.”

And the clockmaker is saddened by my enthusiasm and hurt by my courage.

“Will there come a time when I won't want to try?” I ask. "If that time comes up, then you will already be out of time," he answers. I then ask, “Why is there a time limit?” The reply is, "There is always a time limit." “But I really want to learn this,” I say. "Then you'll take the time needed to do it." “Ok, I’ll do it!” I yell, exhausted. "You can't say it like that," the clockmaker says. "You have to want to do it, that's how it works." I reply, “It's a lot to commit to.”

And the clockmaker cries at my enthusiasm and hates my courage.

"You've already run out of time," says the clockmaker. ‘Out of time’ is what I hear the clockmaker say. “But how can I be out of time?” I ask. And with that the clockmaker shows me the clock I have made. And I know it to be true. “Not fair,” I say. “I didn't know,” I say. “How can there be a time limit?”

And the clockmaker is damaged by my enthusiasm and broken by my courage.

I'm shown the clock I have made. I'm told sadly that, "It has run out of time." And I ask to wind it up again. Barely in a whisper, the clockmaker says, “But the key is lost." In my anger I throw the clock. I kick the clock and I rearrange its insides. And now the clock is ugly and destroyed and the response comes again, even sadder still. "You've run out of time."

And the clockmaker weeps at my enthusiasm and mourns over my courage.

And I look at the clockmaker and defiantly say, "All I have to do is find the key. And maybe it won't be as great as I remember it. But as long as I keep looking for the key it might just be better than it ever was."

With this the clockmaker smiles at my enthusiasm and admires my courage.

Kevin Buchholz was not born nor raised in Fort St. John, but he has been happily living here for a few years now.

4233.2 (Finding Peace Trilogy)

By Katy Clarke

Four thousand two hundred and
Thirty-three point two
Passing Mile zero, some would tell her, a metaphor.
A river, a momentary arrest taking in the view.
Her silver camel, poised in the stillness, south of the Peace.
A vessel for her life, past and future packed with
Boxes, as well as a freshly stamped parchment
Prophesying her talents.
A two wheeled, red steel chariot
Strapped to the back
Longing to take flight.
She stands, searching for some solace.
Trying to nurture courage.
Her mind giving birth to chapter three.
With trepidation she crosses the vibrating bridge,
Monks chanting as they roll across the singing bridge,
Connected now to the North.

Four thousand two hundred and
Thirty-three point two
A salesman peddling passion,
Lures her into his story of hope.
A glimpse through a tinted lens...possibility.
Having bought what is being sold.
A soul, once cemented in defeat,
Now searches for freedom, as it climbs

On its noble steed,
Each stroke a struggle yet a step forward.
Legs wrapped in fabric that forgives as she shifts gears,
He was
Peddling passion, peddling passion, pedaling passion.
And she found her Peace on a red CCM.

Katy Gray Clark invented enthusiasm and proves it when she rides her bikes, works with kids and especially when writing poems about our cool Peace Country as a 'boomerang' resident.

This Is How I Die

By: Lindsay Jardine

This is how I die…
…on a solo adventure,
on a guided tour in a third world country,
where "safety" is a buzzword to get tourists' cash.

This is how I die…
…in a blaze of glory,
overworked and underpaid, drowning in paperwork,
toiling tirelessly to save the world from its self.

This is how I die…
…in a so called "lovers" quarrel,
with a man with bedroom eyes, rough hands,
and veins full of Latin fire, jealousy and tequila.

This is how I die…
…in a fiery crash,
on the Alaska Highway, in a red convertible,
street racing my father, trying to win his praise.

This is how I die…
…slowly, of boredom,
because I can no longer go on trips, work, love, or
otherwise behave recklessly,
with wild abandon, hair blowing in the wind, sun on
my face, smiling, full of life.

Lindsay Jardine is a rebellious, workaholic, mascara-wearing, left wing, feminist, earth-loving, artist and life-long learner. She likes to travel, read, paint, quilt, golf, garden, and loves the work she does to help people find their path.

Spencer's Ghost

By Patrick D. Ferris

A Snowy Highway

The dreary and tedious winter had long since worn out its welcome. It had been cold and snowy every day it seemed, and was snowing hard again, snowflakes having a mesmerizing effect in the Cunningham's headlights, reducing visibility to almost nothing. Stopping wasn't an option. The highway was far too narrow to safely move to the side of the road to wait out the storm, if they could see where the edge of the road was; plus they were only a few miles from home now—they were committed. Jeff said nothing as his wife Carol concentrated on the road. Their little Mustang car was cool and fast when it was dry but being light and high powered was not the best when road conditions were slippery and dangerous.

"These roads are awful, Jeff. I hate it. It's a good thing Mrs. Wright was willing to walk Spencer home from school," said Carol, struggling to keep the car under control. The center lines were no longer visible.

Silent for a moment, Jeff said, "I applied for my old job at Agassiz Prison, Carol. It—it looks good that I might even get back in."

Caught by surprise Carol said, "Back to being a jail guard? Why? I thought you were happy working on the railroad?"

"It was fun for a while but I'm tired of the hours, supervising people, fooling with train schedules and all that crap. Back at the Agassiz jail, I just show up for work, get paid and go home. We'll get a house nearby. That way it's not much of a commute and cheaper than Vancouver. And," he added pointedly, "No snow. What do you say?"

"I need to think about this, Jeff," Carol said, stunned.

"It's already arranged. It's a done deal," he announced.

Shocked, Carol half-turned toward him, her death grip on the steering wheel lessening for a split second.

A forty-ton logging truck popped out of the swirling snow, flattening the little car as if it were a tube of cardboard.

The logging truck driver was unhurt, but knew something awful had been crushed beneath his wheels. He scrambled out into the blinding snow and crawled under the big truck's tires. Steaming blood ran from the flattened car and pooled on the icy road. The driver had seen a lot in his forty years of driving but was not prepared for this. On his hands and knees he began to cry.

***

Carol and Jeff Cunninghams' nine-year-old son Spencer found it odd his mom wasn't home when he arrived from school. At first he busied himself in his room with homework and watched TV a bit, but by five, he was sitting at the kitchen table, waiting, and getting scared.

It was seven–thirty that evening before Susan Frey, the social worker, and a police officer knocked on the Cunningham's front door. Identification of the victims had been slow; the drive in the blizzard was difficult, making them later than they would have liked.

There was no reply to their urgent knocking.

They could still see the remnants of Spencer's footprints just outside the doorway, so they knew he was in there. Susan had once heard Carol say in conversation that she, and all of Brandon Lake, left spare front door keys under their welcome mats. She lifted up the mat and found the key as predicted. Opening the door, she saw at once there was smoke belching from the oven. She ran inside to turn it off. Grabbing a dishtowel, she pulled a big metal pan out, dropping it onto the counter with a clatter. It was the charred remains of a pot-roast, and what could have been three potatoes and five carrots. Turning away she noticed a collection of a child's artwork stuck to the fridge. It broke her heart.

The police officer was crouched down beside Spencer. The boy was seated at the table between his parents' places, where his plate, fork, spoon and goofy plastic cartoon cup had been carefully placed before him. There was a flower arrangement in the center of the table, a basket of buns and salt and pepper shakers shaped like smiling bears.

Spencer looked very small with his big black glasses, clutching a worn, one-eyed elephant in his arms. He was as white as a ghost. "I didn't know how to shut off the oven. Mommy says I mustn't touch it," he whispered.

"It's alright, Spencer. Remember me? I knew your parents. We met at the picnic at the lake last year," said Susan.

Spencer nodded and pushed his glasses back up on his nose. "Where's my Mommy and Daddy?"

Overwhelmed by sadness, Susan picked him up and held him, tears streaming down her face.

The Visitor

Susan Frey arrived unannounced at the Alexanders the next day. Beth Alexander invited her in out of the weather and fed her a steaming cup of tea. Susan was initially silent about the boy, confining herself to her tea and making small talk. When she felt enough time had elapsed, she told Beth the sad tale of Jeff and Carol Cunningham, both killed in a car accident, the day before. Beth and Joe both knew the Cunninghams from the BCR shop where Joe worked, so the news was especially shocking. Spencer wasn't with them at the time, thank God. He was staying at the local hospital for a few days while Susan found a place for him to live, temporarily. She wanted Spencer to keep going to his regular school so his routine would remain the same.

Susan said, "Didn't I see you and Joe with Spencer at the Railco barbeque?"

"Yes, Jeff was Joe's boss at Railco. I wouldn't say we saw a lot of each other, but we did get together from time to time. And yes we did spend time with Spencer… poor kid."

Susan considered her words before speaking, "We don't have any place for Spencer out here and he needs someone who knows him. I don't want to totally alienate him by sending him away to Vancouver. He has school and his teachers here, so this would be a good place for him at this terrible time. I could set you up as a temporary foster home, Beth."

Beth considered before speaking. "This–this is unexpected. I'd have to talk it over with Joe, first."

Susan sipped her tea, letting Beth take in all the information. "Do you know if Jeff and Carol had any relatives?"

"I don't believe they did. As far as I know their parents are deceased and they didn't have any brothers or sisters. It was a small family on both sides. Carol said Spencer would be carrying on the Cunningham name, single-handed," Beth said.

"That's what we found, too. We were hoping some relative were available but no luck," Susan said.

"So, how exactly do we become a foster home?"

"I have the forms to fill out and you are done. We could speed this up so it's done in a few days. I do appreciate this, Beth. This is a bad time for all of us, but I'm desperate to get him placed."

"That poor boy! It's the least we can do for Jeff and Carol."

Later that very night, Beth explained the situation to Joe and he was in complete agreement. They spent the balance of the evening setting up the guest room for Spencer who would arrive next day.

What do you say to a nine-year-old orphan?

That Friday afternoon, Susan brought Spencer straight from school to the Alexanders'. Spencer got out of her car, with a little old fashioned suitcase which appeared to hold all his belongings. Beth and Joe could feel his overpowering sadness. One look at his innocent, honest expression almost brought them both to tears. They could see both Jeff and Carol in his face. He was all by himself in the world and was now being presented to them. He was wholly at their mercy. It was a crushing responsibility the Alexanders felt they were ill-equipped to handle. They just wanted to run up to him and hug this poor boy but it was not their place. He looked like he had cried all he could until there was nothing left but emptiness. He stood before them, his pale face downcast, his arms slack by his sides, a tiny statue of sadness.

Sue placed her arm over Spencer's slumped shoulders and guided him towards the Alexanders. Joe and Beth smiled and put on a brave face, but they too felt overwhelmingly sad. Beth reached out and gently shook Spencer's limp hand, then invited him inside the house.

When Susan was satisfied Spencer would fit in she said goodbye, and drove away. Watching her out the front window, Spencer tracked her car down the driveway and around the corner until it vanished from sight. It looked to Beth as if Spencer believed with Sue's departure, the whole world had deserted him.

***

The Alexanders showed Spencer around the busy farmyard. He perked up a little when a broken down horse clumped over to him and pushed its hairy muzzle in his neck. 'Buckles' was happy to see anyone and could be depended upon to nudge them in hopes of a carrot.

Rags the dog was next to approach Spencer, wagging his skinny tail. He was fat, old and friendly, always looking for a pat on the head or, better yet, a handout.

The mule was aloof and would not come to say hello at all. He just suspiciously walked around in the snow observing the tour. It was his job to guard the farm which he did all the time. Beth told Spencer she had named him 'Joe' because she thought the mule looked like her husband when he hadn't shaved for a few days. Joe was mildly amused.

The ducks and chickens interested Spencer as they cluttered, quacked and clucked, approaching every obstacle like a comedy troupe, full of excitement, gabbling and squabbling among themselves. After a few minutes and a brief smile, his interest in their antics soon faded. In spite of Joe and Beth's best efforts to make him feel at home, Spencer had a crushing sense of sadness and no one he trusted to share it with.

His room at the Alexander's was nice and bright with a colorful bed, chest of drawers and a pillow. Beth took his clothes from his suitcase and put them in the drawers of the wooden dresser. His stuffed toys were put on top of the bed, including battered Ed the elephant.

The room should have been great, but things were missing. He realized that it was the small stuff he'd barely noticed before. His old room had had some pictures of him on his bedside stand, of his mom and dad, along with a few old birthday cards, gifts, and special toys. They wove together the story of him and his parents and all they had done together. There was nothing here like that and never would be again. Soon tears were streaming down his face. He saw that Beth was crying too. She held him tight and this time, he let her.

The first few weeks living with Joe and Beth were hard but is seemed the Alexanders were up to the challenge. They worked tirelessly to cheer him up. There was nothing Beth wouldn't make, cook or do if he could muster up a smile in response, which he found himself trying to do more often than he'd like, for her sake, even if it was fake. She tried so hard, he felt bad it didn't make him feel better.

As the days and weeks went by, some of his new chores started to feel good to him, like feeding the horse, mule, ducks and the chickens. He liked the way the animals crowded around him when he spread out their food. They scratched, clucked and quacked at each other in barnyard chaos. It was times like these that his smiles weren't fake.

Each day, the school bus would come by the farm to take Spencer to school. The other kids and the teachers were nice to him but he stayed mostly to himself. His marks were steady. Homework was never a problem; he worked just as hard as he did before.

One Saturday afternoon Joe, Beth and Spencer went on a spring picnic. The weather was pleasant so they went off to a nearby lake for a bit of sightseeing and wildlife watching. They built a fire, roasted some hotdogs on home-cut sticks and drank hot chocolate. Later, they went to the edge of the lake to watch for ducks and beavers. Spencer threw rocks out on the thin ice which still covered parts of the lake. The rocks made a high pitched pinging noise as they bounced and echoed across the wide area. Spencer had never heard such a crazy, eerie sound.

As they stood quietly at the lake shore, a breeze came up. Rippling waves crossed the lake, disturbing the thin layer of surface ice. Then one large sheet of ice began moving across the lake, hitting against another large sheet, then slid up on top of it before moving away. The sliding sound of the ice layers produced the most magical sound Spencer had ever heard. They seemed to sing, squeal and chime. He knew he would never forget that sound.

It was a pretty good day.

Spencer had been with the Alexanders for almost a year. The teachers were pleased and the social worker was happy with his adjustments. Sometimes he felt sad, but the Alexanders would get him to do a few chores to bring him out of the funk and back into his new routine. They showed him every day they liked having him around.

Spring and summer came and went, followed by a glorious fall. Spencer and the Alexanders were constantly out and about getting wood for the stove, feed for the little farmyard troupe and planning for the coming winter. Joe came up with a set of cross country skis for each of them, and a toboggan. When the snow arrived they'd head out to the local ski trails every weekend followed by a hair-raising toboggan run down the hill. He loved the feeling of speed as they bounced and scraped on the ice and snow with complete abandon, him and Joe screaming and laughing all the way.

Of all his chores, chopping wood was the one he most admired. It was a grown-up job, one that showed him Joe trusted him. This trust was a new experience for Spencer, one he wanted to earn and keep. And there was the fact that splitting and hacking away on a block of wood appealed to all boys. He jumped at every chance to chop wood. Joe and Beth had been nervous about it at the start, but he'd persisted until they finally gave in. Joe methodically showed him how to chop while being careful not to hit his hands or feet. It was only after Joe was confident that Spencer took the task seriously and would be careful, that he allowed him to take over the task.

Spencer would split the firewood with a hatchet on a piece of an old fence post. He'd select a large piece of wood, too big for the stove, balance it on the chopping block, then swing the hatchet high over his head and bring it down on the wood, splitting it in two. He loved the stretching of his muscles, the satisfying splitting sound as the wood cracked apart, the growing evidence of his hard work piled up in the wheel barrow, all soon to be warming them in the house.

It was a rainy Saturday morning. The woodpile was soaked. Spencer was working on a particularly awkward piece of wood from a tree root that wouldn't stand up by itself. The hatchet bounced off instead of biting into the wood. Frustrated, he changed hands, which did no good at all. Before throwing the chunk of root back into the pile as useless, he gave it one last whack. The hatchet glanced off the slimy wood and went where it was not supposed to go, buried into the mitt on his left hand.

Everything stopped.

The hatchet had sliced through his mitt, and stuck into the wooden stump, cementing the mitt to the block. In horror, he looked at the damaged left mitten, with the hole and bit of blood that splashed in crimson droplets across the snow. He knocked the hatchet aside and gently pulled his hand free of the mitt. There was only a bloody stump where his finger had been.

He opened his mouth and screamed.

Then he saw the finger, lying beside his boot in the snow, bloody at its base, white at its tip. It was so small and so very large, both at the same time. He kept looking in horror at the bleeding hand with the missing finger and screamed and screamed.

Joe came running, followed by Beth. When they saw his hand and the finger in the snow, there was a lot more screaming and commotion.

At the house, Beth quickly bandaged his hand up to stop the bleeding. Joe called the hospital to say they were coming before scooping Spencer up and half-running toward the Jeep. He set Spencer into the backseat, with Beth climbing in after, gathering Spencer's quaking body against her for the ride to the hospital. Through the whole trip all Spencer registered was the relentless throbbing of his hand, and the fact that Joe's tense efforts over slippery, snowy roads toward help never seemed to end.

When they finally arrived, both a nurse and a doctor greeted them at the door of the Brandon Lake hospital. "Did you bring the finger?" the doctor asked. "Sometimes it can be re-attached."

Beth and Joe had never even thought of it.

Once inside a curtained-off cubicle, Spencer lay in the bed while the medical staff bandaged him up on one side and Joe and Beth crowded in on the other. He thought he recognized the nurse from last year when he'd stayed at the hospital after his parents were killed.

The doctor kept Spencer in the hospital for two days for observation before he would pronounce him fit to return home. He couldn't help overhearing how annoyed the doctor was to be handed the pile of forms and all the phone calls he fielded because Spencer was in state care. Susan came by and seemed more irritated than sympathetic about the accident, too.

Beth and Joe alternated staying with Spencer the entire time and were glad to be able to take him home. Joe drove, and just as they had traveled to the hospital, Beth stayed beside Spencer in the rear seat.

It was a few more days before Spencer was back into his routine. He finally felt well enough to go outside and resume a few light farm chores but first he went over to the chopping block to see if his finger was still there, but it had vanished. A cat or a fox or even Rags might have grabbed it and had taken it away. The thought made his stomach churn and he almost lost his lunch out in the dirty snow. He looked at the stub, where his left index finger used to be, and missed it. It felt as if part of his life had been taken away. First his parents and his home and everything he depended on. Now even his body was irreparably damaged too, an important part gone forever.

***

Susan Frey's boss was furious the Alexanders had exposed Spencer to harm while he was under their care.

Apparently a newspaper had found out, allowing the critics of the Family Services department to make some political hay from the incident. Susan would have to move him to another foster home.

She felt awkward about the whole situation as it had been her personal request the Alexanders look after Spencer. She felt guilty for pushing them into a situation they might not have been ready for. Now, from Vancouver, she could give them very little support in their bid to keep Spencer after the finger incident, in spite of the fact he'd made a complete recovery and was thriving in their care.

Her supervisors had other ideas, other priorities, more concerned about how the accident made them look, than poor young Spencer's adjustment.

They ordered a 'fresh start'.

Clara

Susan, the social worker, took Spencer to a foster home in Williams Lake for a night.

Next day a new social worker picked him up, driving him into Vancouver, explaining they were finding a place for him. He sat quietly, clutching his possessions.

The second social worker handed him off to a third, who took him across on the car ferry headed to Victoria.

Under any other circumstances Spencer would have found the ferry ride exciting as he had never experienced such a thing before. He said very little, spending his time gazing out the windows as the social worker read a magazine. Finally, they re-boarded the car and drove off, arriving at the front of a creepy old fence surrounding a gigantic, very old, ivy-covered, decrepit mansion.

"Here we are, Spencer. Home-sweet-home until we can get you a place. You'll only be here a week or two and then we will get you a nicer place."

Spencer hesitated, then asked, "Do the Munster's live here?"

She smiled, "No, but it's the original Ross Bay Orphanage and is over a hundred years old. It was a home for foundlings, orphans or children from single parents, usually mothers, who couldn't look after their children. The mothers would leave their kids for the orphanage to look after while they worked. When they could, they would come visit them."

"Am I a foundling?" he asked, nudging his cheap oversized-glasses back up his nose before grasping his beat up suitcase tighter to his body. It felt better knowing Ed the Elephant was close to his chest. Yeah, he was ten now, and it was babyish; he didn't care.

The social worker looked back at him, and it occurred to Spencer she might be seeing him for the very first time. After a moment of silence, she murmured, "No, you're not," and placing her arm around him, another first, guided him to the main entrance.

Spencer looked at the giant old building, obviously neglected and appearing to be ready for some renovation to convert it into a school or college. The brick work was shabby, dirty with ivy barely clinging. The old window sills had not been painted for years but looked odd because big silver tubes extended down to the ground making the irritated old building look like a monstrous octopus.

The building was the size of a high school, and seemed mostly empty. It reminded him of a creepy old horror show mansion on TV. Eventually he was registered, then escorted by a friendly, elderly nun who hobbled along on a cane and showed him around. His assigned room contained four bunk beds, though it seemed he would be the only occupant.

"There you go, Spencer. You have a room all to yourself," she gasped out.

"How many kids are here?" asked Spencer.

"You can call me Sister Ann, young man. We have room for five hundred but currently only have forty children. The orphanage is being phased out. The children are to go back into homes in the community."

"Have you always been here?"

She smiled, "I've been here for forty-five years…a very long time."

Spencer had no idea what it all meant but understood there were only a few kids like him in the building.

She stood there for a few moments as Spencer looked around the room, then added, "You can just come and ask me if you need anything. There's a bell for meals, down in the main room. We do school during the weekdays, nine to three. After school you can explore the grounds but don't go outside the fence."

"What are those big tubes at the windows?" he asked.

"Those are fire escapes. You open that window and jump into the slide to escape the building. We have four of them around the upper floors."

"Can I try it sometime, Sister Ann?"

She sighed, "Not today but you can use it if there is a fire."

He looked at the window and the slide escapes for a few moments, "Where am I going from here, Sister Ann?"

She gasped and wheezed, obviously thinking, then replied, "Usually they decide where they are going to send you. That will be a foster home somewhere. In the meantime, you can stay with us. We like having you here." She smiled kindly, then clumsily tapped him on his shoulder and hobbled away.

Spencer looked around the old room. He had an old steel bunk bed and thin mattress with bedding but no pillow. The floor was covered with old, chipped linoleum and the walls were covered with old, tattered wallpaper. After looking around, he sat on the bed and opened up his suitcase, found Ed and placed him at the top of his bed as a pillow, but couldn't bring himself to unpack—not yet.

Curious, he stood to look out the window that didn't have the slide escape, through the rusty bars to the front parking lot. There were big lawns with old trees on either side, all enclosed in a high, metal fence. Over in the far left corner was what looked like a cemetery with cracked headstones. It reminded him he was an orphan.

After the evening dinner in the cafeteria, a bath, and reading a bit of a Hardy Boys novel he'd found in a book bin in the library on the second floor, Spencer went back to his room and climbed into his bed. The old bed springs creaked as he settled in. It seemed sad not having Joe and Beth here. He'd come to like being around them. The image of Beth's tear-streaked face appeared in his mind unbidden and he quickly banished it. He didn't have anyone to say goodnight to, so he simply said, "Good night Ed," and was fast asleep.

The next day, his first full day at the orphanage, was uneventful, so he took his book and went out into the grassy lawn near the cemetery, sat down and leaned his back up against one of the jagged oak trees. There was an annoying squadron of geese honking at him but a few sticks and rocks tossed their way scattered them nicely. He settled down to read his book, to transport himself away from this tenuous, difficult world.

"Wha'cha readin'?"

Spencer jolted out of his reading trance, "Pardon?"

"Wha'cha reading, I said."

He looked up to see a girl about his age standing nearby. She was about his height, very thin, with long stringy hair and was wearing an old fashioned dress, though it was shabby and patched.

"I'm reading a Hardy Boys Book."

"Oh. Do you like to read?"

"I do. Who are you?"

"I'm Clara... Clara Hutchinson. Who are you?"

"I'm Spencer Cunningham."

They stood in awkward silence. Then Clara sat down near him and asked, "Could you read your book to me, Spencer?" He looked at her as she pursed dry lips, her unblinking eyes staring down at the Hardy Boys novel.

'Why not', he thought, sat down himself and started to read aloud.

She listened, as if entranced, then asked, "Who are the Hardy Boys?"

"They're a pair of boy detectives trying to solve a mystery. They call it 'a case'."

"For real?"

"Not really. This is a make believe story. It's meant to be fun, to take you to a different world, so you can forget about your own life for a while."

She said nothing, so he started reading again. He lost all track of time, concentrating on doing the best narration he could.

The dinner bell startled him. He looked up and Clara was nowhere to be seen among the trees or buildings. Maybe he would see her at dinner.

There weren't that many other kids at the cafeteria but he couldn't see Clara. He was so busy looking for her that he dropped his tray of food on the floor with a crash. Everyone looked up and some laughed, which, to his horror, made him cry. Here he was, all alone in a strange place with nobody, and he was blubbering like a little kid in front of everyone.

Sister Ann hobbled over to help him. After stopping the laughter with a fierce glare to the other children in the hall, she ordered someone to clean the floor while she took Spencer back to the line for more food. Soon he was seated with his new supper and Sister Ann sitting next to him, with her arm on his shoulders, though he was still hiccupping and shuddering, wiping at tears that just wouldn't quit.

"It's okay Spencer. Go ahead and dig in." She dabbed up his tears with her handkerchief which made Spencer feel a bit better. Who cared what the other kids thought now? They'd already seen his meltdown. He tried a mouthful of macaroni and cheese, found that he liked it and kept going, surprised he was still hungry.

Sister Ann patiently waited with him, trying to cheer him up. "So Spencer, you had a day off school. Were you able to find your way around here? We have some books you can read, too."

Spencer spoke between mouthfuls. "I took a book and read it on the front lawn."

"What was the book about?"

"It was a Hardy Boys mystery. I liked it and so did Clara."

"Clara?"

"Yes...she came up to me and asked if I could read it to her, so I did."

"Hmm...I didn't think we had a girl named Clara here. What did she look like?"

Spencer chewed while he thought. "She was kinda my age, as tall as me, long hair, thin and had an old dress on."

Sister Ann said nothing but watched him eat.

He read until lights out; said goodnight to Ed. Clara was on his mind until he fell asleep. He dreamed of home, sitting at the dinner table with his dad on his right and his mom on his left, laughing and telling stories about their day.

After the church service the next day he went back to his spot on the lawn and read. It was Sunday and the sun was out in force. He looked around to see if anyone was nearby. He was alone. Before he sat, he made sure there wasn't any Canada goose poo on the grass. Opening the book, he was soon off in the Hardy Boy world.

It wasn't long before he heard the now familiar voice of Clara. "Hello Spencer. Would you read to me again?"

Annoyed, he looked up at her, but immediately felt guilty about it. She could be lonely, just like him; besides she was nice company. "Sure."

Eventually he was thirsty and had to go to the bathroom. "Guard my book from the geese until I get back, Clara. Want a drink or something?"

"I can watch your book but no drink, thank you."

Spencer ran back to the washroom, picked up a glass of water. Walking back to the lawn He saw a goose picking at his book and Clara nowhere to be seen. He grabbed up a stick and chased the hissing bird away. Puzzled, he sat down, re-organized his disheveled book and started to read again. It wasn't long before he saw Clara's feet in the grass standing nearby.

"You left my book. The geese were pecking at it," he accused.

"I'm sorry. I wasn't sure you were coming back so I left."

She looked even sadder than usual so Spencer relented. "It's alright Clara. Do you want me to read to you again?"

She nodded and sat down, looking at his book with big eyes.

He read to her for an hour straight, coming to the exciting conclusion. "The end."

"Is the story over?" she asked.

"It's over. It's the end and they all lived happily ever after."

"What does that mean, Spencer?"

"It means they all got what they wanted, the bad guys got caught and Joe and Frank move on to their next case."

"Will we live happily ever after, Spencer?"

"I don't know. I'm not sure where I'm going. My parents are dead."

Clara thought, then spoke. "My daddy died in the Great War. Mommy is coming for me but I haven't seen her for a while. She loves me, you know."

"I'm sure she does."

"Do you have anyone, Spencer?"

"No. It's just me and Ed."

"Ed?"

"Ed is my stuffed elephant. I've had him for ages. Ed's family."

He turned his head when the dinner bell rang. When he turned back, Clara was gone. Weird.

He stood up, gave the geese a dirty look, pointing at them and headed off for lunch. Once again, he didn't see Clara at the cafeteria. He saw Sister Ann sitting alone at one of the tables so brought his tray to sit beside her.

"What have you been doing, Spencer?"

"I've been reading my Hardy Boys book to Clara, near the cemetery. It's sunny out.

"That sounds like fun. What's Clara's last name?"

"It's Clara…Clara…Hutchinson," he remembered.

Sister Ann smiled, and watched him as he finished his lunch. He was glad for her company.

"So where are you off to now, Spencer?" she asked.

"I'm getting another book to read to Clara."

"Good for you. I might join you, later."

Spencer put his dishes away and dashed up to the library and the book bin, retrieving another Hardy Boys book. He then battled the annoying goose for his sitting spot, cleaned off a fresh poop, totally disgusted, then sat down and started to read, hoping Clara would meet him. Soon he was lost in the world of his book.

After a while he heard footsteps. He looked up, expecting to see his new friend, Clara. "Oh. Hi, Sister Ann."

"Hello Spencer. Did Clara come to see you?"

"No. I guess she was busy."

"Come with me, Spencer. Bring your book. I want to show you something."

Puzzled, he stood up and followed Sister Ann's limping trail across the lumpy cemetery grass to the second to last headstone on the front row.

"What did you want to show me?"

Sister Ann squinted then pointed to a small, worn stone, laying on the ground and barely readable.

Clara G. Hutchinson
1910 - 1920

"Clara died forty-five years ago, Spencer."

Spencer looked up at her, bewildered.

"Clara's father was killed in the Great War and her mom struggled to raise her, leaving her at this orphanage for long periods of time. Her mother died in the great influenza epidemic and that's why Clara waited and waited for her to come but she never did. Later Clara died from the 'flu herself in 1920."

Spencer was shocked. "But I saw her—I spoke to her."

"I don't know who she was, or why she'd tell you her name was Clara. This Clara died a long time ago. I looked up the old records. It's true. I'm so sorry about your new friend." Sister Ann rested her arm on his shoulder.

He did not know what to say. For sure he wouldn't be telling Sister Ann that Clara had been real, and was maybe even a ghost. They just stood together in silence thinking about a young soul that passed away unnoticed, so long ago. It reminded Spencer yet again how alone he was.

Spooked and sad, Spencer left the lawn area and went inside. He looked around the ancient old rooms and halls, imagining all the children who had been here before him, imagining all their stories. He knew the cemetery had stories to tell and wondered if there were more ghosts.

Eventually he got his courage back and headed to the place by the tree, book in hand, Ed under his arm for comfort and reinforcement, ready to do more reading. It was a warm spring afternoon with the sun out and flowers blooming, such a contrast to the winter weather he'd seen at Brandon Lake. It was a bit chilly so he'd worn a sweater. He wondered why Clara only wore a thin dress but supposed ghosts didn't get cold, then stopped himself.

Did he seriously believe Clara was a ghost?

Maybe he'd day-dreamed Clara? This thought was immediately troubling. He'd known her real story before Sister Ann had told him the truth.

The goose was nowhere to be seen, so he sat down, determined to forget about Clara. Soon he was solving mysteries with the Hardy Boys. He made it through thirty pages and was quite proud of himself when he heard something and looked up, right into Clara's face. Surprised, he jolted and so did Clara. He blurted, "You scared me, Clara!"

Clara gave a wan smile, "Sorry, Spencer. I thought you wouldn't mind if I sat beside you."

"I – I guess I don't mind."

"Is this Ed?" She pointed to the bedraggled elephant, this time she wore a big smile.

"Yes, this is my old buddy Ed. We've been through a lot, together. Do you want to hold him?"

"Well... I actually can't... but will you read to me?"

"Sure." Spencer settled Ed into the grass beside her, not understanding her reluctance to hold him, but glad for her company.

He read to her for an hour, feeling pleased he hardly missed any words. Sadly, when he looked up from his book, Clara was gone. He stood and looked over towards the cemetery stone Sister Ann had shown him and said aloud, "You left Ed, Clara." There was no reply. He was sad, but he wasn't surprised.

It was late. Disappointed, he collected Ed and went to his room.

From that day forward, he went to that reading place every day for the remainder of his stay, but he never saw Clara again.

It was two weeks later when Sister Ann saw the social services government car pull up in the driveway as she had so many times in the past.

"I'm here to pick up Spencer Cunningham," the worker told her.

Sister Ann handed over Spencer's file as well as a transfer form to be filled out.

The Social Worker filled in the blanks until the last box on the page, "How was Spencer? He's been through a lot in the past year."

The sister smiled. "I think he's a nice boy and he works hard. That'll help him through the tough times."

A Rolling Stone

Forty years later, Spencer stood on the street corner in his postal uniform, mailbag in hand, reflecting back on those days, the Alexanders, the orphanage, and the many foster homes that followed. He remembered being forced to move again and again, the spark of human touch he extended to each new family growing dimmer and fainter with each attempt.

His bundle of belongings grew smaller and smaller with each move. Even the pajamas his parents had given him when he was nine were abandoned, at last too small and too worn. Somewhere along the way, he lost the old suitcase, too.

It was as if his soul shrank as well, finally extinguished after the twelfth home in seven years. He'd learned to depend on himself and nothing more, nothing less.

Each foster home was often busy, and crowded. It seemed at least one of the other foster kids was causing trouble and commanded a great deal of attention, the home full of stress. If Spencer had his own room, he'd eagerly stay there with the door closed, reading or doing his homework, a welcome respite from the chaos. The other kids were temporary, he was temporary, the foster home was temporary. Even the Social workers, who shifted from caseload to caseload, were temporary. It became sort of a shell game. Under which shell would Spencer be this month?

Spencer quickly learned the difference between a normal home and a foster home. In a normal home, there was undoubtedly some sibling competition, but love was unconditional. There was no real threat of banishment, just hurt feelings. Things were different in a foster home. In a foster home, there existed a continuing competition for food, for shelter, and for attention. An orphan's fate could rest on a whim, or a mood. Maybe this would be the day Spencer's unkempt room or unmade bed would be the last straw and he would be sent on his way. He was an outsider, in a game of musical chairs. Sometimes the sheer coincidence of a transfer could confirm his irrational fears.

He never got used to the shock of being told he was being moved, regardless of how many times it happened. The reasons and excuses could be made with a smile and an apology. The home he was in might seem sad to see him go but the sick feeling of packing up and saying goodbye was more or less the same. This was utterly out of his hands.

He didn't bother making friends at the various schools he attended, even when tempted. He never brought artwork, or the stories he sometimes wrote to the home he was currently assigned to because nobody was going to look at it or show it, anyway. Nobody was going to put a foster kid's artwork on the fridge. He just crumpled it up and threw it away.

Sometimes he would think of Clara and wondered if she would be willing to hear his stories. Since there was no one else interested, he crumpled his stories up too and threw them away. It made him sad nobody would see them. It was the story of his life.

After a while he had a little contest with himself on his numerous family transfers to see how little he told them about himself or how much evidence would remain of him after he was gone. It was as if he was never there.

Spencer kept it all to himself like a bottle with a cork. He worked hard enough in school to pass everything, which, instead of helping, could work against him as he often would be put into a foster home that was a bit overcrowded. Because he appeared fine on the surface, he seemed to be the first one sent away to give more time to another foster child who was having trouble adjusting.

When his latest case worker seemed overworked, or claimed she was, Spencer would smile and be polite during the interview as she hustled through the paperwork and transferred him once again with barely a second thought. He never considered how there were never enough of these foster homes to go around and how much these open, caring, loving people did for kids like him. Each home did make an effort to welcome him.

Each Christmas was traumatic at the foster homes. Spencer knew the ropes—there would be a few gifts from the parents and a dinner, not bad things. The hard part was when some of the kids were expecting to be picked up by parents or relatives. They would be told by the social worker that a parent or relative would be picking them up, and this is where the trouble began—Spencer had seen it time and time again.

Danny, a boy who shared his current foster home, and who was around the same age as Spencer, had been told that his mother was coming for him today at one o'clock. Spencer watched him as he waited in a chair looking out the front window watching for her to come.

Spencer could see Danny had his hopes up and was now vulnerable and wide open. His heart waited for his mom to come, desperately needing that human connection and fearing she wouldn't appear. It seemed to Spencer that Danny would only allow himself to believe it when he saw it but still hope upon hope as his mother's arrival time came and slowly drifted away from him.

Still, he remained at the window and Spencer suspected that he was praying that the next car would stop, that he and his mother would still have Christmas together, just this once.

Eventually the foster mom came and sat beside Danny, putting her arm around him. Danny, who normally resisted any physical display of affection because he was the home tough-guy, leaned his head on her shoulder and wept, quietly, the very picture of abandonment and hopelessness, stood up again, like so many years before.

It was crushing to witness his belief that this year might be different being destroyed.

Once a girl sharing one of Spencer's foster homes traveled for eight hours to High Level on a bus, only to find there was nobody there to take her in for Christmas as had been arranged. Her hopes for love and affection were rebuffed in the cruelest way. She ended up sitting on her suitcase in the gas station that served as a bus depot until the RCMP found her early the next morning. She was devastated, and spent days sobbing in her room after her return.

Afterward, Spencer overheard the foster parents whisper to each other, appalled and disgusted the parents could treat their child so cruelly at such a vulnerable time in her life. This girl had opened up her jaded and disappointed heart once again, hoping for any crumb of affection and had been destroyed. Spencer told himself that would never be him because he would steel his heart from hurt forever. He took the safe route, turning himself inwards, never sharing his thoughts and feelings with anyone anymore. It was easier than making a few connections with other people only to have them torn away when he was uprooted again and sent on another journey.

Looking back, it always felt peculiar when he arrived at a new home where everyone already knew his history, his parents' demise and the fact he was an orphan. Parents and the other kids would crowd the doorway of the house to greet the new arrival, the children's faces poking through any available viewing space. It was like being a zoo exhibit. They would look at him sadly, speak to him with pity and sympathy. Spencer knew it was not meant as derision but he still didn't like it.

Spencer was always an outsider, wherever he lived, never part of the family.

The foster parents' children were often suspicious of the new foster kids, fearing they were at worst trouble makers, druggies or thieves which was seldom the case. At best, these new arrivals competed for the parent's time and affection. This all made for a general feeling of insecurity. Everyone was temporary. Fear of this quiet boy with the 'active imagination' sped him along to the next home, taking his suspected deeper issues safely away with him.

Spencer made himself a promise that someday he would have a stable place to live and a stable job and stay with it until he retired. He'd had enough with the day to day circus that was his life.

He had to admit his final foster family did manage to get through to his heart. The Williams family ran a little rural post office from an old bunkhouse trailer, next to their home. They were kindly and helpful people who noticed that Spencer showed an interest in what they did. They set him up sorting the mail and doing local deliveries on his bike. He found he enjoyed the work and it earned him a bit of pocket money. It was an active job, got him out of the house and was something he could control after years of being shuffled around without options. Soon the Williams were trusting Spencer to run the post office while they were away for a day or an afternoon.

The Williams family also remembered his eighteenth birthday, and planned a surprise party for him. Spencer came home from school as usual. He finished his homework in his room and then came down for supper. They had dinner as usual and were just thinking about dessert when Mrs. Williams brought out a big chocolate cake with eighteen candles burning brightly. The other five kids sang Happy Birthday. He blew out the candles and they all had as much cake as they could eat. Later they talked, laughed, and joked around, wearing paper party hats.

The Williams's gave him a wallet and a shaving kit for a birthday and farewell gift. The truth was, this was a going away and birthday party combined— Spencer had finally aged out of the system.

Everyone hugged him and wished him well. Despite himself, he had a lump in his throat. The Williams had wanted to give him a heartfelt send off and they'd done it.

With his eighteenth birthday Spencer's time as a ward of the government was at long last over. It was time for him to go out on his own, to make his way in the world. The Williams put in a good word for him at the Regional Post Office and when an opening came up in the mail depot in Donvegan, nestled on the edge of the Peace River, he was offered a job as a mail delivery person starting after school ended. While thrilled about the new prospect, Spencer dreaded having to relocate to the unknown one more time. Hopefully this will be the last one, he thought.

Barney and the Hearse

Almost forty years later Spencer still loved the fact he went to sleep every day knowing where he was, where he'd be, who he'd see, year after year. Nothing ever changed.

Delivering mail was as dull as dishwater with a delicious sameness he craved. Each day was the same as the first. This job would never change or abandon him or make him feel uncomfortable, unlike his past life. Yes, it had turned him into a loner with most contact with his fellow workers minimized, or, if he could arrange it, avoided. Privately Spencer couldn't have cared less about his co-workers. It wasn't that he hated them; it was simply that he preferred to keep to himself and do his job, get paid and go home. He couldn't imagine it any other way.

Barney worked to the left of Spencer's sorting station at the post office for eighteen years. Spencer hardly knew him other than to mumble 'Morning' to him, and only if hard pressed. Barney was a friendly guy who chattered away about this and that with Spencer barely listening. He was about the same age as Spencer but after that, had little in common. He was tall and thin with a little scraggly goatee, a gregarious family man, full of stories about his wife and the antics of their seven active kids. According to Barney, all his kids were good students, avid figure skaters and hockey players.

Spencer thought all this family stuff sounded expensive, with the kids' sport costs and all. Barney never took a sick day because he simply could not afford it. He worked any overtime hours he could find at the post office as well as moonlighting for the local funeral home.

"Morning Spencer! How are you?" said Barney, looking him in the eyes.

"Um...fine." Spencer looked away, ignoring him.

Barney was tenacious. "Boy, I had another tough night driving stiffs around for the funeral home. Want to hear about it?"

"Not really..."

"I'm glad you asked! They pay me to drive this huge Cadillac hearse up to Fort Mac and back and it's so quiet you could hear a heartbeat from inside a coffin... if there was a heartbeat in a coffin. That's a 'Craig' joke. He's the funeral guy up there. Funny fella or at least he thinks he is."

"I can imagine..." mumbled Spencer, wishing Barney would shut up.

Clark worked on Spencer's right as he had done for twenty-five years. As far as Spencer knew or cared, he was a single guy, about three years younger. One of Clark's annoying favorite antics was to find an interesting postcard and read it to everyone in the building. He'd call out for everyone to listen while he read the private contents with batting of eye lashes, gesticulation, animation and great theatrical flourish. Today was one of those days.

"Hey, everyone! We have a postcard from Deb in Vegas. Listen up!"

'Dear Marge! Saw Tom Jones in Vegas concert so I took my panties off and threw them on to the stage. Jim was so mad at me! Well I didn't want to be left out. Maybe Mr. Jones will send for me or something. Oh well, what happens in Vegas, stays in Vegas, right? LOL! Deb.'

Everyone roared their approval of Clark's selection then drifted back to their workstations. Spencer had watched the proceedings with embarrassment for the poor lady in the postcard. He grabbed another handful of letters and continued sorting.

"That Clark always cracks me up," grinned Barney as he put his crutches to one side, gracelessly slumped into his chair beside Spencer, then grimaced in pain. "Aw!"

Last week Barney had slipped on a patch of ice very early into his mail route. Heavily laden with two big mailbags, he fell awkwardly, twisting and hitting the ground. He'd shared the experience with Spencer in excruciating detail—claiming to hear the bone in his thigh snap like a dry stick. Unwilling to move, he'd stayed down and called for help. Three other nearby post office delivery people came to him to offer assistance but Barney wisely declined, waiting for the ambulance. At Barney's insistence, the three postal workers split up his route mail, each claiming the mail that was nearest their route and put it in their own satchels and departed. He used his cell phone to stay in contact with the post office while he patiently waited for an ambulance to arrive. According to the doctors, he had a compound fracture of the thigh bone and would be in a huge cast for fourteen weeks. It was a bad break.

Even Spencer couldn't ignore Barney's new cast. Barney wasn't able to drive or walk normally for some time and was currently doing light duty at the post office depot. Despite Spencer's indifference, Barney insisted on keeping in touch with him during his rounds.

Barney always stood a bit too closely for Spencer's comfort. "Hey Spencer, a friend of mine owns Giebelhaus Funeral Home and she needs a driver to go to Fort Mac and return to Donvegan on the weekends. It's usually a Saturday or Sunday night. It's easy money. As you can see, I'm out of commission, but the funeral home still needs a weekend driver. Did I mention it pays real well? You could get a new computer or a big screen TV!"

Spencer's go-to answer—'NO'—stuck in his throat at the thought of his ancient computer locking up for the hundredth time. "I don't know. I'm not sure I'm a funeral home kind of person."

Barney sensed his change of heart, and jumped in. "It's an easy job. You'd be transporting someone who doesn't make any trouble while you're driving the nicest car you'll ever have the pleasure to drive while earning a few one-hundred-dollar bills. This holds the job open for me, too, so I can step back into it when I heal up. What's not to like?"

It was not like Spencer had a busy life on the weekends. His evenings were usually him and his dog snoring on the couch until it was time to go to bed. It sounded like it could be easy money. The more Spencer thought about it, the better it sounded. He gave the funeral home a call and offered to do the job for three months. They assured him it would be the odd weekend or two, mostly night drives.

After work, Spencer had a call waiting for him on his voicemail. This was unusual. A loner doesn't get many phone calls. "Hello, this is Cathy Belson from the Funeral Service with a message for Spencer Cunningham. Barney told us about you and we'd like to interview you at five o'clock, tomorrow. We hope to see you then."

The next day he arrived at the funeral home still dressed in his post office uniform. Stopping at the door, he took a deep breath before walking in.

A plump, middle-aged woman greeted him with a pleasant smile. "You must be Spencer. Come and sit down in the meeting room. This won't take a minute."

Following her, he saw at once that he would be facing four interviewers, each seated at an elderly wooden table. Did they think he might be someone to fear, and they needed the distance for protection?

The woman indicated that he should sit on the single wooden chair set up on the opposite side of the table. He pulled it out and sat. It was covered in old vinyl and made the requisite farting sound every time he shifted on it. Good to know. He stopped moving, and glanced around. The room was overly large for its purpose, surplus, unused, old, and smell of formaldehyde.

"Thank you for coming. We found your references acceptable and helpful," the woman said, her chair screeching as she brought it closer to the table, making more farting sounds as she squirmed, seeking comfort that would never be, all echoing in the large empty space. "To my right or …sorry ...I meant my left, is Gary Jones, the local manager, then Marino Julio, office manager, Ina Smith, shipper and Hank Reynolds, chief embalmer and furnace manager."

"You mean 'Hank of the Hell Fire department? He's the cream of cremation," laughed Ina.

"People! Be professional. We are trying to have a position interview here. Head Office demands a proper interview," she scolded.

"Tell him who you are, Cathy," Hank said dryly.

"Oh yes, I'm Cathy Belson, co-office manager."

Spencer immediately regretted applying for this job and considered making a run for it, but they all watched him now, like spiders on the wall, so escape was not an option. Yet.

"I guess I'll open this discussion up and ask you, Mr. Spencer. Have you ever done this line of work before?" Cathy asked, making another farting sound as she moved forward to speak. Did they not hear this?

"Mr. Cunningham. My name is Spencer Cunningham, ma'am."

The panelists all looked at each other and at their papers, bewildered for a few moments.

"Of course you are Mr. Cunningham. I'm very sorry."

"Shit," Hank Reynolds murmured. The one named Gary tipped his water bottle. He lunged forward to rescue it, then screeched the chair back and retreated to the washroom for paper towel.

"Sorry. Let's begin again, Mr. Cunningham. Perhaps you could tell us your name and present occupation," Cathy said, flustered as Gary bumped back into his chair.

"I'm a mailman with Canada Post. I've been there for forty years."

"Married Mr. Cunningham?" asked Ina.

Hank blurted out, "Ina! You can't ask that anymore. Sorry Mr. Cunningham."

"It's alright. No, I'm not married."

"Looking for a date, Ina?" teased Hank.

Cathy ignored them. "I trust you have a clean driver's record and no criminal record?"

Hank added, "We can't have you stealing our dead people, Spencer."

Spencer fought a smile. Okay, so that was funny. "Yes, my driver's record is clean. And no criminal record." He handed over the two documents Barney had told him to bring.

"Have you ever driven a hearse before?"

"I've driven vans that are about the same length but not a hearse."

"I have a few questions our headquarters suggested...let's see...when was the last time you had a conflict with your supervisor and how did you resolve it?"

The truth was Spencer never had an issue with any of his bosses. He was as quiet as a mouse at work. They barely knew of his existence. "Well, I've never had an issue. They give me the mail, I sort it and drop it in the mailboxes."

Spencer could see the panellists leaning over towards him, anticipating some type of story. He was almost sorry he had none to tell. He added, "I suppose I do have the odd problem with a customer during a delivery of their mail."

Cathy seemed quite excited about this. "Really? Please tell us about it."

"Well, I was making my rounds when a customer's dog bit my finger when I put their mail through the slot in the door." He held up his left hand with the missing finger.

The people on the panel gasped in horror.

"Oh, sorry…he bit my baby finger, not the missing one."

The panel expelled a collective sigh of relief.

"How did you resolve this biting dog thing?" she asked eagerly.

"Well, next day, I waited for something that looked like a cheque, then held it in the slot so the dog would wrestle it out of my hand and chew it up. The next delivery day the dog was gone."

Hank laughed so hard that tears ran down his cheeks. "You're hired, Spencer!"

Spencer blinked in surprise, relieved the interview was over.

Cathy leaned across the table and gave him some keys. "There you go, Spencer, the keys to the hearse. I'll be calling you when the next delivery comes up."

"What exactly will I be delivering, Ms. Belson?"

"Why caskets, of course."

"Will there be someone in them?"

"I hope so, Spencer."

Easy Money… With a Catch

All he had to do was drive a nearly new Cadillac hearse up to Fort Mac and then drive it back again. The road was deserted. There was hardly a house or living soul on the two-hour drive. It was on an empty road with only a few deer to dodge. He did nothing but drive and daydream. The best part was four hours of solitude for four hundred bucks. It was all cash money, under the table. No taxes or T4's. Pure profit.

He'd left right after work, arriving in the early evening. The drive up was pleasant enough. The hearse was terrific to drive. It was so luxurious, quiet and smooth he hardly knew it was moving. It wasn't until he arrived at the funeral home in Fort Mac, that he began to have second thoughts.

He did as instructed, driving up the sloping hill and backing up to the second story roll doors for the pickup. Even though he'd been told where to find the funeral home's doorway it still seemed odd it was located over the town bowling alley. Climbing from the hearse, he could hear the sounds of balls rumbling down the alley, the banging of a strike followed by yells of triumph. Yup. It was a bowling alley.

"What an awful racket," he muttered as he approached the entrance. The attendant surprised him, flinging open the door as Spencer was about to knock. The Fort Mac office was staffed by a part-timer named Craig, and this must be him. Barney had warned Spencer that Craig was a bit odd. Apparently he fancied himself something of an amateur comedian, with emphasis on the amateur. He looked to be in his late twenties, stood about six-foot tall, had a medium build and was missing two front teeth.

"Oh, you're here. Back up and I'll open the roll door," he commanded with a surprising and pronounced lisp–caused by the missing teeth, no doubt—then slammed the door in Spencer's face.

Surprised, Spencer did as he was told, honking his horn as a warning and backing up. The attendant rolled the garage door open, waved him in and closed it behind him.

Transferring a coffin was private business, apparently.

As Spencer got out, he found that the attendant had already opened the big rear door of the hearse. Abruptly it dawned on him what this trip was all about…bringing back a dead person! Yikes!

At first, Spencer was not sure if he was supposed to help with the loading process or not, so just stood and watched. He couldn't help but notice that this particular casket was pretty beat up and rough, not your usual gleaming affair. The smooth wood surface and ornate corner brass work had numerous scratches, chips and dents in it. This must be the traveler version for transportation.

Craig wore faded blue coveralls, red croc flip flops on his feet and a green baseball hat that simply said 'Runs like a Deere'. It was a strange outfit to wear in a funeral home, even in Fort Mac. Craig got the casket in the back of the hearse, easily accomplished with the gurney. All that remained was to secure the casket to the floor of the hearse so it didn't hop around during the long drive.

Looking around the funeral home bay, Spencer couldn't help noticing how stark and unfinished it was. The open roof beams were laced with cobwebs and the walls, while insulated, were as yet unclad. The concrete floor was unpainted and puddled with water and mud. This grubby, rented garage was the sorry end of the line for someone.

Craig woke him from his thoughts, staring at him as if expecting Spencer to say something. It was an awkward moment before Spencer found his voice and spoke.

"I should introduce myself. I'm Spencer," he said, offering his hand. Craig grinned, took his hand, giving an overly firm, clammy and protracted handshake with far too much eye contact.

"Rule #1, Spencer, is don't shake hands with someone who handles dead people." Craig grinned and winked.

Spencer pulled his hand back in horror, then stood rooted in embarrassment as Craig laughed. The attendant's lisp made the word 'someone' sound like 'thumb-one' and 'rule' sound like woo-ull', like an Elmer Fudd cartoon. It was then Spencer saw his discolored teeth and a telltale sign of chewing tobacco as it dribbled down his chin, and couldn't contain a shudder.

"It's okay, I'm just pulling your leg!" From Craig's mouth, 'pulling' sound like 'poo-ing'. He handed Spencer a clipboard with papers to sign.

"What am I signing for?" Spencer asked.

"It's not so much 'what' as 'who' are you signing for," Craig replied.

"Is there a body in there?"

The attendant smiled at him and said, "I hope so. We can pop the lid and look, if you like!"

"No... No... that's okay. I'll take your word for it."

"This is Gordon Smith from Lethbridge. Gord, meet Spencer. He will be your driver for this evening," said Craig announced grandly, introducing the casket with a sweep of his arm. After a moment's pause he added, "Apparently he's not going to shake your hand so this is as good as a greeting."

"What happened to him?" asked Spencer, compelled to know.

"Gord had no arms and legs and was a bull fighter with fatal results," the attendant deadpanned.

The lisp made it sound like "Goad had no awms and wegs …was a boo fightah…"
Funeral guy humor? Spencer didn't get the joke.

Craig looked at him expecting a reaction and not getting any. "Gord? Gored? Get it? You don't get it? Never mind. I hate explaining jokes to people. Gord's loaded up, signed for, and you both can be on your way," he said with a lisp. A bit of tobacco spittle escaped from the corner of his mouth.

There was no turning back now, Spencer was committed. He climbed back into the hearse. Craig opened the big roll door and Spencer drove off into the night, following the deserted road without a house to be seen for miles.

The hearse was wonderful to drive. It was smooth and quiet with a terrific sound system so Spencer could play his music as loud as he wanted. It was a nice way to make a hundred dollars an hour and he didn't have to talk to a living soul. He decided he liked this job enough to help out regularly.

Life

The Alexanders enjoyed taking in foster kids. It was like a new chapter in their lives, helping out these needy children. They came in all ages and sizes. Joe put an addition onto the house so they could accommodate three at any one time. They became attached to all the kids and believed that each one truly enjoyed being there. When the kids left, it was a tearful affair, but Beth always made an effort to keep in touch, send them a birthday card or little Christmas gift. She loved them all.

On Beth's 35th birthday, she surprised Joe with the announcement she was pregnant. They had long given up thinking about their own children but surprisingly they were to become parents after all. Kirstin was born healthy and happy and enjoyed a continuous line of foster brothers and sisters as she grew up. There was always an endless supply.

Eventually the Alexanders retired and moved from little Brandon Lake, up to the bustling town of

Donvegan to be closer to their daughter. It was nice, living in a larger center with all the city amenities, yet the town was not yet big enough to lose its small town charm. They didn't go out often, but it was nice to have the option if they wanted it. They had a bigger, newer house, all on one floor so it was not an effort to go up and down stairs. Once in a while, they would go back to Brandon Lake for a visit to see all their old friends.

Certainly, Beth and Joe were getting older. Both of them were now in their mid-seventies. They were spry and cheerful, making every effort to get out and enjoy the day with exercise or some activity. With Kirstin, her husband Jason and their two children so close now, it was easy to meet up somewhere, or have them over. Beth and Joe's network of foster kids, now adults, would drop by when they were in town to visit, the Alexanders always glad to see them—and their children. It was like a large, great extended family.

Once in a while, Joe or Beth would ask the other about that first orphaned boy, Spencer, who they'd taken in so long ago. 'What do you suppose ever became of Spencer?'

Mail

After a walk to work, Spencer's day at the Donvegan Post Office started at the early hour of six o'clock in the morning. The depot itself was an old three story stone building, situated in the middle of town. The building's stonework was old and weathered with winter-killed ivy hanging off the walls, their gnarled brown stalks like withered fingers. The windows were all filthy, covered with mud and bird excrement. Nobody was concerned about the state of the building as it was irrelevant to its function. There were only the postal workers, a few front office clerks and a supervisor. They had no time or interest to look out the windows anyway.

Coming in from the pretty Donvegan street, Spencer found the back entrance door open and walked in. The thick steel door had big locks at the sides and a heavy cross bar to keep out prowlers who continuously tried to break in from the alley.

The workers got to work as soon as they arrived. The sooner they were done, the sooner they went home, the sooner the days, weeks, months and years went by, the sooner they got to the age of sixty-five and could retire. It was an urgent, never-ending treadmill of mundane tasks but came with a solid pay check. They started in the dark, early morning, sorted their own mail routes in an hour or two and were on their way through the streets of Donvegan.

Spencer sometimes wondered what kept him in Donvegan after all these years. Sometimes he fancied moving somewhere exciting but the move never took place. His last foster home with the Williams family had been in Fort Mac and he'd moved directly to Donvegan when the post office hired him on the Williams's recommendation. He didn't think much of the town, but had fallen into a routine that suited him. The people were kind enough and the town was rural enough to offer anything he needed. Houses were affordable. It was a pretty place with all the four seasons. Once he'd bought a house, Donvegan became his home.

Spencer entered the huge, cluttered mailroom filled with mail carts, sorting boxes and bustling postal workers. Both the postal boss and the postal union steward watched the proceedings closely for signs of trouble or contract interpretations. Spencer was of two minds of the postal union. While the union seemed confrontational at times, something Spencer disliked, they did make sure the workers were paid a healthy wage and benefits package for something the private postal contract delivery people and sorters got pennies for. Considering how simple a postal workers job was, on a technical level, they enjoyed job security and received a good wage. The postal union had looked after them very well, over the years.

Once at his station, Spencer grabbed his pile of mail from the mail cart and sorted the envelopes into the little 'pigeon holes'. The 'pigeon holes' was a wall of wooden dividers set up in rows. The rows of slots were stacked next to each other in the order of the houses up and down a street on a mail run.

The wooden mail slot cabinets were beat up, dirty thin plywood, built decades ago. Even though Spencer spent a huge part of his working life here, it never occurred to him to request a simple coat of fresh paint or any kind of simple renovation from the shop steward. The man would be sure to refuse him.

Spencer was a handy guy who could fix something beat up and make it look better than new, given the opportunity. He sometimes passed his sorting time imagining how he could refurbish these mail slots into something beautiful, functional and marvelous to look at. A simple built-in light alone could make sorting so much easier for everyone.

Maybe he would do it on his last day before retirement. By the time the union steward spied the improvement, Spencer would be long gone.

But that would be one day. For today, he had his deliveries. He refocused his attention. Each little divider had just enough room for a few envelopes and some individually addressed junk mail. Each divider represented a mailbox. A mailbox represented the people who lived at that address. Each divider's mail was their contact with friends, family, creditors, merchants, catalogue sales and scam artists.

Lately, Spencer was hearing rumors about the new centralized sorting system the post office was trying out. All the mail would go to giant sorting stations in the major cities and was sorted by hand or machine into the street routes using the postal codes on the mail. Immigrants, contractors, out-of-country cheap labor or anyone else could get the contract to sort the tons of mail that arrived daily. There was no need for highly paid union workers to do such a simple task when it could be done by untrained cheap labor at a central location on a large scale. The public demanded the cheapest prices for everything including the price of a stamp, while demanding to be paid top wages for their own work, he thought wryly. These two concepts did not mesh.

It didn't take a rocket scientist to see there were going to be layoffs. They would be a well-paid dinosaur, slowly becoming irrelevant in the age of email and the internet where the post office was transitioning into a service for junk mail, flyers and bogus winning sweepstakes applications, which in itself was considerable. It all required postage for delivery.

A few folks played pranks on the postal system, usually student-loan poor university students, if they were too poor to pay for a stamp. They'd mail the letter without a stamp, with the 'return' address as the destination and the actual mailing address in the upper left corner reserved for the 'return'. The little 'return' address was in fact their destination address where the stampless envelope was eventually sent. The mailer of the letter got a free delivery! It was a lot of work to save the cost of a stamp but it was always good for a laugh for someone.

Such were the politics of his workplace. Every job had them, each unique unto itself. Spencer would work around them just as he had for years. He just kept his head down and did his job well each and every day.

Outsider

Digging through his mailbag at the station Spencer remembered back to those first few days on the job when all he had to say was, "Nice day!" or "Sure cold, today". Nobody wanted to talk much, they just wanted their mail. His co-workers at the post office didn't say much either; they were all in a hurry to get their deliveries done. They were paid for an eight-hour day, so if they hustled and skipped lunch and breaks, they could be done in seven hours. With an early start and quick step they could be home by one in the afternoon. It was a hard, nonstop seven-hour race, but the rest of the day was theirs.

"Spencer, what are you doing this weekend?" Barney asked.

"Oh, I don't know. I guess I'll decide when it comes along," he replied, marching out his usual evasive, non-committal answer.

"You know, there are a few of us going to Casey's, afterwards. You are welcome to join us."

"Yeah...Well, maybe. I'll think about it," was his reply. They both knew he wouldn't go.

Spencer stuffed his mail into two big sacks. He put the two registered letters in the special side pocket of his postal bag. He disliked registered letters because that meant he would have to carry on a conversation with the recipient while they signed his receipt form. The post office was sticky about getting the required signature. He made sure he had the necessary black ink pen which also meant less talk and discussion.

The post office door opened and slammed shut constantly with posties heading into the dark, damp outside world. He took his turn through the door, taking a moment to take in a breath of the cold, morning air. As much as he enjoyed the predictability of his indoor chores, he much preferred the solitude and independence of outside. Nobody even looked his way as he trundled up and down the streets with the mail.

After years of experience, Spencer was very efficient at delivering mail. His stocky physique was well suited to the heavy trudge of carrying mail long distances—his daily route on the North West side of town. There were industrial drops, a few apartment buildings, houses old and new as well as a couple of mansions on the edge of town that bordered a big park. The route was well paved with sidewalks and streetlights. The fall air was fresh as he crunched along his way.

The first house was a tiny, rundown old house, surrounded by deep, uncut grass. A very old, fragile man named Sam LaPointe lived there, although Spencer had only seen him once coming out the door as Spencer put his mail in the box. Deftly, Spencer reached into his pack for Sam's mail. Sam's mailbox was stuffed from last week so Spencer had to squeeze in a few bills, a flyer and a personal, hand addressed envelope before he was on his way down the street. Was the old guy away? He'd soon have to stop delivery.

"Quick and painless with a clean get away," he muttered grimly, and headed back to the street. As per postal regulations regarding uncollected mail, he would hand in a little card that requested a home follow-up.

Seeing Things

One extremely cold winter Saturday morning, the Giebelhaus Funeral Home sent Spencer back up to Fort Mac, in a pickup truck this time, instead of the hearse. Traveling in a pickup was a bit of a disappointment. Mind you, the pickup was nice enough, bright red, nice interior with a powerful V8 engine and stick shift on the floor. It was snappy and cool with a sound system loud enough to make his ears bleed.

The pickup's beige interior was beautiful, though cramped, with bucket seats and a wide shifter console. It was an older, non-extended cab so there was no room for Spencer's coat, boots and emergency pack which he'd had to pile in a heap on the passenger seat beside him.

Other than being very cold, the drive up was uneventful. He did see a work crew out surveying on the side of the road and pitied the poor flagman having to stand there, all day. Spencer knew what it was like to be out in the cold, but at least when he worked, he was on the move and not having to stand still.

When he arrived at the funeral home in Fort Mac, Craig sent him over to the government coroner's office instead. Spencer guessed there was something odd about this particular body's circumstance, and shuddered.

Once there, a man wearing a grubby white smock came out and waved him around to the side of the building. Spencer hopped out, grabbing his coat and gloves, just in time to see the frozen body.

"Dead?" he blurted, recoiling in horror.

"Frozen hard as a gargoyle," the grim coroner confirmed. "The body was frozen in this sitting position. Apparently, late in the evening, he had too much to drink, became belligerent and the hotel bar bouncers threw him out into the cold. He staggered around a while, then, we think he decided to hide behind some empty crates so nobody would bother him and went to sleep at forty below. He froze to death. Nobody knew him or cared to look for him, I guess. Three days later a police officer discovered his frozen body."

Spencer was aghast. The victim was fully dressed in faded jeans, a blue lined jean coat and had a blue 'Maple Leafs' baseball cap slouched over its eyes. An ordinary guy you'd meet on the street. It looked as if he just went to sleep and never awoke.

The coroner said, "I haven't the time or the place to thaw him out and put him in a coffin. If you'll assist me, we'll secure him in the back of the pickup and he'll be fine for the short drive home."

What? Spencer couldn't believe he'd heard the request correctly and couldn't believe he was actually helping the man put the crazy plan into action. Together, he and the coroner each took an arm and a leg and loaded up the frozen corpse, placing it in the open box of the pickup with the corpse's back fit against the cab. They secured it with bungie cords until they were both satisfied it wasn't going anywhere. Weirdly, the seated body fit perfectly into the corner.

"He sort of looks like a full size garden gnome," Spencer remarked, instantly regretting his heartless choice of words.

"Yes, and still looks very life-like, sitting there," agreed the coroner, apparently not appalled at all.

Spencer stood for a minute, looking in disbelief at the frozen, seated body with its eyes frozen open. It looked as if he could jump up and yell 'boo!' as if this was all just a cruel joke.

After signing for the frozen man and collecting the transfer papers, Spencer got in the pickup and drove towards home with his frozen passenger in the back. Morbid fascination made him glance often in the rear-view mirror, repeatedly checking that the inert body was still there. All he could see was the back of a dirty baseball hat. Fortunately, the frozen statue never moved as long as he watched it. This distracted him so much he almost went off the road a few times, so he cursed himself and concentrated instead on the road ahead. After a half an hour of driving the lonely cold road, his music blaring, he forgot about his horrifying cargo.

Ice fog developed, making it harder to see the road ahead and took up all of his attention. He drove on, rarely seeing another vehicle on the road, even though it was late afternoon. It was just miles and miles of desolate snow and bush. Not a moose or deer stirred; even the ravens were strangely absent. The hoar frost on the trees and brush gave the route a ghostly look.

Eventually he came to the Toad Creek Bridge crossing, slowing down after seeing construction signs on the edge of the road. Finally, a winter-clad flagman stopped him to allow a nearby work crew to squeeze into the back of a truck. They promptly drove off, forgetting their faithful flagman. He was pissed!

Alarmed, the flagman hailed Spencer, who unrolled his window, just a crack. He knew what was coming, and already didn't like it.

"Hey buddy. Could you drop me off at the camp? It's a mile on your route." The guy was dressed well enough against this cold, with heavy boots, a thick balaclava over his head, gloves, but he was filthy with dirt and oil. Spencer couldn't let him sit inside this nice clean truck. He couldn't leave him stranded, either.

Spencer stammered, "I suppose, but…"

"Thanks, buddy!" The heavily dressed flagman thumped the side of the truck with the flat of his hand. He jumped into the back of the pickup for the short ride to camp and sought a sheltered place for the short ride beside the frozen gnome. Perhaps the fellow thought he was going to be friendly to the frozen guy in the open pickup bed. Maybe he knew him!

Spencer was horrified but it was too late to tell the flagman about the body he was seated next to. Hopefully he will think the person was drunk or asleep. In the rear-view mirror, Spencer could see the flagman was actually chatting to the dead body, trying to be friendly. The dead body ignored his conversation attempts and sat like a stone.

Spencer drove as fast as he dared, hoping the flagman wouldn't notice his frozen passenger. But, just as they got to their destination and Spencer slowed down in the camp yard, the flagman suddenly spun around and put his hand over his mouth, possibly screaming, but the rush of air rendered him soundless. He jumped out without waiting for a full stop and ran to the camp entrance.

Spencer drove by him and yelled out the window, "It's okay! He was dead, already!" And he was on his way home. Spencer couldn't keep from grinning at the whole experience. Since he didn't get out much, this qualified as excitement in his world. He felt pleased with himself for getting this well paid side job. It turned out to be a bit of harmless adventure.

Eventually winter hesitantly turned to spring and Spencer was sent to Fort Mac for another weekend's macabre delivery. Craig had his usual smart ass remarks, one-liners and lame jokes with his Elmer Fudd lisp. Classy.

"Who do we have, tonight, Craig?" Spencer asked, already dreading the answer. He had to ask, unfortunately.

"Brad McLean, motorcycle driver."

"What's his problem?" asked Spencer.

"He's dead," said Craig, not his usual wealth of icky information and puns.

"How?" asked Spencer, amazed he was even asking.

"Decapitation! He was headed back to the camp in the dark and hit a tow cable strung across the road. His body got here by ambulance, his head by motorcycle. He's a head on a Honda!"

"Good one, Craig."

"Spencer, you are catching on in this business." Craig grinned, flashing the spaces in his tobacco-stained teeth.

Thankfully all Brad's body parts were already in the coffin, secured in the hearse and Spencer was off on the long drive home. It was another quiet night on the open road without competing houselights to the headlights of the hearse. They were the only eerie illumination on the road.

The warm car and deathly quiet made Spencer feel a bit sleepy so he tried the car radio to see what he could pick up. It was a cool night with a brilliant dome of green and blue Northern Lights overhead, which meant he might pick up an American station to revive him. He fumbled with the dial only finding a radio evangelist on a rant. "Repent your wicked ways and find the way of the Lord or you will burn in Hell!" The radio blared, and then faded.

"Not a minute too soon!" Spencer announced with gusto.

Silence returned but not a restful one. He felt uneasy which turned to a creepy feeling in his gut, like he was being watched. The hair on the back of his neck stood out but he dared not look in the back of the hearse. He heard an unmistakable sound he had not heard since he was ten years old—the magic sound of ice, like tiny wind chimes. Spencer couldn't help but wonder if this was some harbinger of things to come. Nothing came. Spencer chalked it up to the coffin driver's jitters and pushed it from his mind. By the time he saw the Donvegan city lights it was forgotten.

It was the following Fort Mac trip a few weeks later that creepy things began in earnest.

His 'passenger', Brian, was an older man, mid-50's, car accident victim. He'd died a long way from home, living in a camp, sending his earnings home to his family. He'd died on a lonely road where no one cared to know him and was now going home in the proverbial 'pine box'.

Spencer could not imagine why these older men would choose to work endless long hours, so far away from home working in camps for months, sending money away to a house and a spouse somewhere far south. The wife would get the money and a daily routine unencumbered by his actual presence. He couldn't help wondering if this poor fellow wouldn't be missed as much as his pay cheque.

He drove on in silence, regretting he had forgotten his music. The roadway was dark, straight and utterly deserted. He might as well be driving on a giant demented treadmill. It was a road from nowhere to destinations unknown. It was even hard to see the stars; it was so black. Then, he heard the sound of those tiny wind chimes, the sound he'd remember the shifting lake ice had made, all those years ago. The chime sound kept going for a few minutes until…he heard the sound of a voice coming from inside the coffin!

The voice asked, "Where am I?"

Spencer stiffened in his seat. He gripped the steering wheel until his knuckles were white, the hearse swaying drunkenly on the deserted road. He held his breath, just feeling his heart pounding in his chest, then the sound was gone. The car was quiet, again, except for wind noise around the hearses' extended roof line.

"I didn't hear anything. That was the wind making noises," Spencer said aloud, trying to calm himself.

"Hey!"

Spencer jumped in his seat.

"Can you hear me out there?" the insistent voice repeated, clearly coming from the coffin area of the hearse.

Spencer's grip on the steering wheel tightened, twisted. The voice was real and sounded very close—like right behind him!

"The radio! It's the radio!" Spencer said aloud, groping for the dial and finding it already turned off.

He took his foot off the accelerator, slowing to a stop. He sat in stunned silence praying for his heartbeat to return to normal. Gradually, he could breathe normally again. More importantly, the voice had stopped. It had to have been some radio show coming in while he was driving. Maybe something was wrong with the radio so it worked even when it was shut off. He couldn't convince himself completely that it was just a radio voice. It actually sounded like it was coming from the back of the hearse.

"How would it be a voice from the coffin?" He asked aloud, daring the voice to reappear.

At the end of the trip, Spencer did his best to get out of the deadhead business but the funeral home owner was insistent.

"I need you for another two months, until Barney gets back," she pleaded. "Please..."

"I'm awfully busy these days and I just don't have time, anymore," lied Spencer. He refused to admit being haunted by ghosts.

"Come on, Spencer. You aren't that busy. You're a single guy and have lots of time. I know you don't want to let Barney down. I'll tell you what...I'll give you a fifty-dollar bonus for every trip," coaxed the funeral director.

She was right, Barney needed him to hold this job for him. How could he refuse? "Well ... I suppose I could," Spencer heard himself saying.

He didn't dare tell her about his experience with voices from the coffin. Who would believe him, anyway? Maybe he was just tired or had been daydreaming on that trip or had a leaky exhaust pipe. It was probably something on the radio that he heard that night. His hearing was playing tricks on him, surely. Craig must have had some type of battery speaker in the coffin to pull a prank on him and was laughing his ass off right now. There had to be a logical explanation because there were no such things as ghosts! Yeah—that had to be it. He felt angry with Craig but relieved he wasn't going crazy.

He agreed to keep driving until Barney returned, which was only a month and a half away, barring any healing complications.

The following day, Spencer walked along the houses and delivered some flyers and a New York Times newspaper. He crossed the street, all the time mulling over the coffin runs and the possibility he might actually have met a ghost. After a few sleepless nights, he resolved to forget the whole matter.

The funeral director called him up for a Saturday pick up at Fort Mac so off he went at five p.m. after an early supper and putting his dog Porky outside. He made sure he brought his music this time, loud, rocky, take no prisoners music.

"Maybe a little AC/DC music will scare away the ghosts," he chuckled.

The drive up to Fort Mac was so uneventful Spencer chided himself for believing the 'voices'. Craig wasn't his usual witty self so he and Spencer simply loaded up the coffin. After Craig went into the office, Spencer had a close look at the coffin for wires or speakers, making sure he wasn't the victim of one of Craig's pranks. Confronting Craig was not his style. Satisfied all was well, he drove off into the night.

The coffin apparently contained an elderly lady named Enid Bauer. She was very old and died of natural causes, while coming through on a bus tour to Alaska. She'd taken ill and passed away, overnight.

All was quiet so Spencer just drove on, listening to his music. Eventually he tired of the music he'd brought and thought he would take a chance on the radio, instead. He picked up a few bits of radio stations but annoyingly, they kept fading in and out. The only solid signal was some crackly US talk show which was replaced by silence. There was a long pause, followed by the familiar eerie sound of ice tinkling and squeaking. Then came the familiar sound of the wind chimes.

Oh no.

There was a pause and a raspy voice, "Bus driver?"

Spencer gave a start.

"Where are we, bus driver?" the voice continued with an edge of exhaustion. "Are we stopping, soon?"

Fighting to keep the hearse safely on the road, Spencer couldn't utter a word at first, then managed to stammer, "Go away! You are a dream or something! Craig? Are you doing this to me? Stop it!"

The irritated old woman's voice spoke again from the passenger seat. "Young man I'm right here and don't be silly. Didn't they teach you any manners at that bus driving school?" she demanded.

"Holy Shit!" Spencer shouted, barely keeping the hearse in control. "Aren't you supposed to be deceased?"

"No, I'm not deceased. Look at me! I'm sitting here beside you…and watch your language!" she scolded.

Spencer slowly stopped the hearse in the middle of the dark deserted highway. He turned his head right to see where the voice was coming from. First he saw a hat on a head of gray hair then saw it was attached to a prim and proper eighty-year old woman! She was crinkled and old, well dressed, complete with a veil, hat and clutched a purse in her lap. And she was translucent …

Spencer's mouth fell open. "No ma'am, I think you're possibly dead and could be a ghost. Are you here to haunt me?" he managed to mumble.

"Dead? Now that you mention it, I do feel a bit queer. Land sakes, my hands look kind of pale. But I do feel better than I have in years. Do you suppose I'm dead? Are you St. Peter or something?" she asked, looking at him intently.

"My name's Spencer, not St. Peter."

"Saint Spencer? What happened to Saint Peter? Have I gone to Hell?" she demanded. "God knows that endless bus ride felt like Hell. Have I spent all those years in church for nothing? Lord, I did try to lead a good life and prayed every day…"

Spencer interrupted her lament, "No ma'am, I think you passed away and have somehow turned into a ghost or a spirit."

The elderly ghost sat wordlessly, considering her situation, taking in all these shocking details and facts. She turned and stiffly looked towards the rear of the hearse, particularly at the black ornate coffin. The ghost then glanced back at Spencer and settled into her seat with a sigh. She stared down the lonely highway for some minutes before speaking again.

"Now I see what you are saying, Spencer. I remember now. I wasn't feeling very well and they took me to the hospital and I must have died."

"Yes, ma'am that could be what happened. And now I am the hearse driver transporting your body...er...you to the city. I presume your relatives will have you transported back to your home in the states."

The ghost said nothing for about five minutes. She just sat quietly, staring down the bleak highway, sighing every once and awhile. Spencer thought she might be considering her options, her plight, before trusting herself to speak to a total stranger. By this time Spencer realized this was a harmless apparition so released the brake and resumed the journey. Occasionally a passing car's headlights would pass through the windshield. The sudden light made the old woman's body vanish, then reappear.

Just when Spencer hoped she had vanished for good, she was back and in the mood to talk. "My name's Enid, Spencer. So it finally happened after all this time. After eighty years I've gone and died. Just like that!" she declared, "And what do I have to show for eighty years of existence? I'm not sure. I have no family. I was single all my life. What do you suppose they will do with my body when I get home? I'm not sure there's anyone who would even come to my funeral," she added sadly.

Surprised at this admission, Spencer offered, "There must be someone to receive you. You must have had friends, extended family, someone."

"There's no one. I kept to myself. I just worked and lived day-to-day. I'm not much of a people person, you see. I've probably told you as much as I've told anyone in my whole life," she confessed.

Spencer was unsure how to talk to a ghost. Maybe ghosts could turn into the devil and blow flames out of their mouths or something, but somehow Spencer didn't think so. The old lady just seemed lonely and needed someone to talk to. Since speaking to people wasn't Spencer's style, he sat in silence, unsure of what to say. He was a lonely, private person too. Thirty years from now Spencer could imagine himself saying these very words.

He was spared further communication efforts as she just vanished after an hour of painful silence while he agonized over how to comfort her. He couldn't help feeling he'd failed her, not knowing what to say to a helpless old woman during her last hours on Earth.

He drove into town and dropped off the hearse and the 'passenger'. He was shaken but didn't tell anyone about the apparition. Edna's ghost had said things that hit too close to his heart.

On Monday he walked along doing his deliveries, deep in thought about that visit from Edna's ghost. Was he losing his mind? Perhaps being alone all these years was taking its toll.

The ghost of Edna got to him. He had actually carried on a conversation with her! She'd told him things he had never considered about being alone and being forgotten. He could not imagine how anyone else, let alone a spirit, could know the things he felt. Perhaps, a trained medical person might be able to help or at least look him over to see if there was something wrong with him. Maybe it was a brain tumor or some kind of slow food poisoning. Perhaps his house had lead pipes and it was making him crazy.

He went to the doctor for a complete examination but of course didn't mention the real reason he was there. He just said he felt a bit funny, ringing in his ears and vertigo or something. It had been ten years since he'd last had a medical.

The young doctor checked his heart, blood pressure, looked in his mouth and poked his tongue and looked in his ears. At last the doctor checked his prostate. All this time, Spencer thought a prostate gland was in his armpit.

Apparently not.

At last the doctor told him to put on his clothes. She looked at his medical records and pronounced him healthy and fit as a fiddle. He thought the physical could have qualified as one of the better dates he'd had over the years. Spencer was confident the doctor visit cleared him of any tumors or circulatory issues. He wasn't sure if he should be happy or sad.

As additional insurance he crawled under the hearse and tightened up all the exhaust system clamps and bolts to make sure exhaust fumes weren't causing hallucinations.

Spencer went back to work vowing to never tell a soul about his ghostly encounters.

Candy

The following weekend trip to Fort Mac was uneventful… going north. It was the trip south with the coffin that strange things happened on a level he couldn't have foreseen. The office had specifically instructed him to go directly to the coroners' office for the pickup, which meant there was some legal, criminal or dreadful issue with the body.

After Spencer arrived at his office, the grim coroner helped him load up the temporary coffin into the back of the hearse.

"Who do we have, tonight?" Spencer really did not want to know but was required to confirm the pick-up.

The coroner answered without a hint of emotion, "We have an American stripper murdered in the Drake Hotel. It's still under investigation. She's going to Donvegan, then on to Edmonton for further examination."

Spencer carefully tied the coffin down so it wouldn't move if they went into the ditch. It would be too ironic if he were killed by a flying coffin.

The coroner added, "Make sure the legal seals are not broken on this coffin lid or there'll be holy hell to pay."

Spencer asked, "Do the seals hold well enough so the body can't fall out?" Or climb out, sit beside me and carry on a conversation. He shuddered.

"Of course! These legally sealed lids are anchored down so the contents can't get out, even if you flip over the car," the coroner explained.

Apparently we're just 'contents' when we are dead. How cold was that?

Spencer did not want to think about being trapped for a night in a car after a body had fallen out of a coffin. He could imagine frantic Emergency

Responders squeezed in beside him, busily trying to revive it. 'I think I gotta heart beat over here, Vern!'

With that cheery thought, he drove down the chilly highway. The reassuring town lights were quickly lost behind him and it was back to the blackness of the night, illuminated only by his headlights.

To fill the silence, Spencer started up the music once again, filling the vehicle with rock. He cranked it up louder.

"Wow, I hope it isn't loud enough to wake the dead!" He forced a laugh he didn't feel.

After thirty minutes of loud rock and roll music and the 'Hells Bells' climax, a soothing quiet took over the car and the darkness outside. Spencer thought the silence was a nice change from steady rock and roll so didn't press replay. Perhaps rock music scares away the demons, he thought.

He found himself enjoying the silence. Occasionally headlights of passing vehicles would dazzle and flash past him. The quiet power and smoothness of the car soothed him. All he could see ahead was the cone of his own headlights drifting ahead, piercing the darkness. He adjusted the seat back a little as he relaxed. The first hour went smoothly by.

Then Spencer began to get that creepy feeling. He tried his best to ignore it but soon realized it was going to happen, no matter how much he didn't want it to. Soon he heard the peculiar wind chimes sound. Not a good sign.

"Fuck me…it's starting again!" he cursed aloud, miserably, slouching in his seat, already lifting his foot off the accelerator.

"I could arrange that, honey," cooed a sweet reply.

The source of the voice was sitting right beside him. He looked down to see a ghostly hand on his right leg. The hand led to an arm and a shapely pair of bare legs all attached to a very pretty girl, early twenties, in a very pink and very short dressing gown covered with what appeared to be spattered blood.

This must have been what she was wearing on the night she was murdered.

She looked like a pinup girl from a playboy magazine, strikingly pretty with long curly brunette hair that draped her ample breasts. Spencer couldn't be sure about her height but she sat about a foot shorter on the seat than he did. He slowed then stopped the car.

The girl tucked her legs up, bringing her head to the same level as Spencer's, likely so her bare feet would not be on the cold hearse floor. Do ghosts get cold feet?

She looked at him, her eyes brown, her skin pasty white. Spencer couldn't help but notice goosebumps on the skin of her exposed cleavage, nipples straining the thin dressing gown material.

Drafty outfit, he thought wryly.

He reluctantly looked into her eyes.

"A blow for the road?" she cheerfully said, returning his gaze intently and sporting a huge grin.

Her smile lit up the car, lips wide and red with perfect rows of snow white teeth, obviously her well-practiced 'show' smile.

"Well, big boy? What do you think?" she asked. "I see you have big feet! You know what they say…"

Spencer could not believe his ears or his eyes. He was being propositioned by a ghost to do unspeakable things! "Sorry Lady. You couldn't blow out a candle in your ghostly state!"

"Ghostly state?" She was obviously shocked he would turn her down. Her gaze fell to her arms, noticing something was amiss. Her translucent body and legs had to appear odd to her, unprepared as she had to be. Amazed, her mouth fell open as she studied her body for a few minutes. "Oh my...you can see right through me?" she gasped, "What's happened to me? I don't understand! Am I ... Am I dead?"

"Yes, lady, you are deceased and possibly are now just a spirit."

She put her hand up to her mouth in horror, "No! I still have two more shows to do! I can't be dead. I'm talking to you, so I'm alive, right?"

"Not necessarily," Spencer cautioned, "You were killed, apparently. Turn around and look in the back. See that coffin? That's you in there."

She slowly turned and looked, studying it for some minutes.

"No, I can't be in there! I'm right here!"

"Pinch yourself. Feel anything?"

She tried pinching her arms and legs. He could see she felt nothing, her fingers and flesh had no substance. Tears filled her eyes and poured down her cheeks.

Spencer gave her a Kleenex from the dashboard dispenser. Do spirits shed tears? The answer would be yes.

She dabbed her cheeks and sat quietly for a few minutes, deep in thought. Then she looked at herself again, for some minutes before finally speaking.

"Am I really a ghost?" she asked in a hushed tone, "Do I have to be dead to be a ghost?"

"Unfortunately, yes."

The stripper was quiet for a few seconds then seemed to change her mood. "Cool! Am I still pretty, even though I'm a ghost?"

Not the sharpest tool in the shed. "Yes, you are very pretty in a see-through sort of way."

She moved her left arm to rest on his shoulder. It was like she was looking for comfort from Spencer.

They sat quietly for a few moments, thinking about their situation, which was either being a ghost or talking to a ghost. Her face was close to his, which Spencer found disconcerting, being a loner. Not to mention, alive.

She studied his face, waiting for a response.

Spencer gave up and broke the silence, "Well, yes...you are very pretty even though you are a ghost. That is, other than the bullet hole… I mean."

"Bullet hole?" asked Candy.

"Yes, you have a bullet hole in your forehead... you know... "

She sat stunned for a few seconds. "Oh, yeah! I forgot about that!" she exclaimed, straining to look into the hearse's rear-view mirror.

She stuck her index finger in the bloody rimmed hole in her forehead and giggled, "Kyle was a coke head but he was a good shot!"

"Lucky you."

"Thanks! My mom always said I sure knew how to pick 'em!"

"I'm sure she did."

The ghost situation seemed to calm down, so Spencer put the hearse in drive and started moving on down the highway. She leaned gently against him. He sensed another change in her mood.

Shoulders slumped, her bubbly personality faded. As reality set in she asked, "What's your name?"

"Spencer Cunningham. Think of me as your driver, tonight," he said, trying to soften the fact he was her hearse driver.

"Hello Spencer."

Spencer hoped for silence but instead the girl began telling him the story of her life, tired and defeated. "My show name was Candy Kane but my real name is Barbara Stellina. My manager said men aren't going to pay to watch a 'Barbara' so I had to have a name of something they could imagine licking. How lame is that?"

"Did you have a choice, Barbara?" asked Spencer, more to be polite. He did not want to know but he still wasn't sure that these ghosts didn't have some kind of power to turn him in to a goat or ornate chair.

"I guess I never thought about it. I could have got married out of high school and had a half a dozen kids by now. Heck, I could have had my own trailer in the trailer park but that was no future. I wanted excitement! I was pretty, everyone said so, so I thought I might as well cash in on my looks. It was fun for a while. I got to travel to different cities and see different men all the time. I could buy the best clothes …" She faded off with a grimace. "I just didn't get to wear them for very long."

Then she perked up. "All the money I made paid for a boob job, braces for my teeth and my coke habit. That's how I met my fiancé, Kyle. He looked after me."

"So Kyle was your pimp?" asked Spencer, already sorry for his choice of words.

"Yes, I suppose that's true, though I always referred to him as my manager, agent and bodyguard."

"No offense but he didn't do a very good job protecting you, did he?"

"He was the one who shot me! Kyle was always a jealous type with a crazy bad temper and didn't like it when other men came to visit me." She giggled.

"So, he shot you? Your own boyfriend shot you?" Spencer said in amazement.

"Right between the eyes! Right here!" Barbara said proudly, putting her face uncomfortably close to

Spencer's again and sticking her index finger in the hole again, as far as it would go. "See?"

He looked away, feeling nauseated.

Her excitement faded. They drove along in silence, the sad ghost of the dead girl seated close to Spencer, her arm still resting on his shoulder.

"Are there any women in your life, Spencer?" Barbara asked in a flat tone.

"No, I'm unattached at this time," Spencer replied grandly, hoping the conversation would end. It didn't.

"Are you gay?"

"No," he blurted out. Is that what people think of me?

"Do you still live with your family at home?"

"I live alone, with my dog, and I like it that way," he declared, hoping his tone indicated he didn't want to talk about this anymore. "I don't have any family and my parents are dead!"

Rebuffed, Barbara fell silent, still leaning on his shoulder but after a few minutes quietly asked, "Have you always been lonely?"

Spencer thought about it for a bit, and then replied, "I've never *felt* lonely."

"Even when you were young?"

"My parents were killed when I was nine years old. They had no living relatives so I went from foster home to foster home. I learned to be self-reliant, to live alone. It's the only way I know now. As the line in the old song says, 'Alone but never lonely," Spencer said, feeling proud of the clever 'old song' line.

That statement seemed to annoy her. "Alone is lonely! Don't ever kid yourself. I've felt alone all my life. People around me had no meaning, no substance. My life, my occupation has been all about other people's fantasies. I fit into their make-believe world. I might as well have been a blow up doll for all that I am. It's as though Barbara never existed. You want to hear how my life ended? I just finished my last dance, picked up my clothes and went to my dressing room. The hotel owner was there wanting a 'freebie' because it was his hotel and was kind 'a feeling me up when Kyle came in. There was a fight and Kyle just looked at me funny, pulled out his gun and everything went black. Now, here I am, a ghost."

"That must have been terrible!"

"I'm alone and died alone. I'm probably going home where nobody knows me or cares, anymore. Without someone to remember me, my gravestone, if I even get one, will be just another piece of stone in a field. It will mean nothing more than a rock on a beach."

Spencer felt profoundly sad. Without reply he sat beside this depressed and lonely ghost without warmth to give her. It was cold comfort for both of them.

"So Barbara, what was life on the road like?"

Barbara looked down the road in silence for a time. She seemed content to sit close to Spencer and lean on him. "My life was awful. My job, mostly, was dealing impersonally, for the entertainment of lonely men. Some were single, ugly, awkward or an outcast.

Some were older, married and far away from home or were maybe locals, frustrated with their sex life at home. They had become irrelevant. Begging or hoping for brief, predictable, infrequent, inconvenient sex with a busy and bored wife just didn't work for them, anymore. A fling with a nice looking 'pro' devoted to what and when they wanted was, to them, a breath of fresh air at a fair price. One of them even told me a night of 'pro' sex with me was cheaper than an alternator he had just replaced on his wife's' SUV, but way more fun with a lot less arguing about it."

Spencer said nothing, trying to imagine what she'd gone through.

"Do you plan to be alone, forever, Spencer?"

He hadn't thought about it before. He'd become a day-to-day guy and never considered the future—not seriously. Being alone was all he knew or thought he would ever know.

"Forever is a long time. I suppose until I die, anyway."

Barbara sharply pointed out, "So when you die nobody will remember you? No one will visit your tombstone. It will be as if you never existed. You'll be just like me. People won't forget us because it'll be as if we never existed in the first place. You have to live and be with people and have relationships to belong."

"I live with people, all day long. It's just the closeness that I avoid. Isn't that enough?" said Spencer.

"Unless you try to make connections with the people around you, meaningful ones, you'll always be alone. In a way, you and I are the same. We meet people on a superficial level, do our jobs, then move on. We miss the emotional contact and the risk it takes to get close to someone. Without closeness, it's all superficial. You're already a ghost others barely see, Spencer."

He was surprised how perceptive she was. He risked turning to her. "You know Barbara, you're much more intelligent than you ever let anyone know."

"I suppose," she said ruefully, "And I waited until I was dead to use it. Don't wait too long, yourself!" It sounded like a death sentence, especially coming from a dead person.

"Maybe I've waited too long already."

They drove along in solitude, Barbara's arm still resting on his shoulder. He could not feel it but could sense it. For once, he didn't mind offering comfort to someone, even if it was a ghost.

Ironically, of all the men who'd spent time with 'Candy', he was probably the only person who took the time to actually listen to her and truly learn something about her.

Spencer couldn't say at what point she vanished. She just did. He suddenly felt badly that he hadn't said goodbye, not even offering the barest of soothing words to a ghost of a lonely person. The radio played a gentle Tom Waits song, 'Closing time', triggering something, deep down in his hidden, unappreciated soul. He slowed the hearse to a stop once again, this time pulling over onto the shoulder, tears streaming down his face. He hadn't cried like this since he was a teenager, shuffled yet again to another foster home. He'd always make sure to cry only when nobody was around, fearing someone would laugh at him or tease him or worse, someone would ask him earnestly about his feelings and actually want to listen. His sense of privacy would never allow it.

All those feelings of loneliness and sadness flooded over him. It had been thirty years since he had felt this way. He had been successful at keeping his sorrow in a little compartment in his soul, never to be opened. Until tonight.

'Candy' and Barbara had somehow found the key to his soul and had unlocked it. His feelings were out and raging for release and would never go back into hiding.

He arrived at home feeling as empty and alone as the ghosts who had visited him. He was a shell of a person. Nobody knew if he was there or not. Normally, he wouldn't have cared if they did, but today? Today was different. Today it mattered. He was determined to never be lonely again. He would become part of a family, somehow. Maybe he would find someone to care about him and who he could care for.

He just wasn't sure how to go about it.

***

It was nine-thirty in the morning and Spencer walked along his route on the wide, paved quiet street. It was a warm, spring day. He was making good time today while thinking about his situation. Was being a loner such a good idea in the long run? It had served his function of protecting him from being torn away from new people, but ultimately had come at a great cost.

He'd observed many relationships from a distance over the years, and thought he understood them, but observing is not the same thing as experiencing. He had never offered anyone a relationship, and in fact had rebuffed all offers coming his way, probably as far back as when he'd left Brandon Lake. He'd left all his school friends and contacts there, when they moved him away and into the system. The last good relationship he'd allowed himself to experience with any warmth at all had been his brief, strange friendship with Clara.

It was depressing to realize he had told the hearse ghosts more about his feelings and thoughts than he'd ever told a living human being.

Lost in thought, Spencer continued his delivery run on automatic pilot, approaching each home and dropping off their mail bundles, barely registering the day go by.

Beth Alexander heard the mailbox lid lift then clink shut outside her front door. She walked over and opened the door just in time to see the back of a postman walking away, on his appointed rounds. Spencer did not hear her as he was lost in profound friendship thought. She had no idea their postman was that sad lonely boy they had met so long ago at Brandon Lake.

Approaching his own house after work, Spencer could hear Porky barking. She knew the sound of his steps and wasted no time letting him know she was excited he was home. A flood of warmth came over him.

Porky was the one exception in Spencer's private existence. She had arrived unbidden at his doorstep three years ago, shivering and hungry without a collar or markings. There were no notices around town about her being lost. When Spencer thought about it, he recalled seeing her on his route, as she wandered aimlessly around the area before arriving on his doorstep. His first impulse had been to push the mutt away, but something in her upturn face and pleading eyes had stopped him. He'd thought back to the days when he was an orphan and had needed help himself. This dog was reaching out to him, asking for his help. He couldn't refuse her. The dog was so grateful, and he was so touched that a bond formed between them within a week. This dog had such an amazing grunting and snuffling sound when she ate that Spencer started calling her 'Porky' and the name stood.

Porky was a mixed breed of some kind. She was medium size, built thin, but not skinny, and was mostly black with some white spots. While certainly no purebred, neither she nor Spencer cared. It appeared she was an older dog and was house broken, which sealed the deal.

Spencer's house was not big, by anyone's standards. He liked the fact it was well made, older with some character, and on the edge of town overlooking a large park. He could look out the kitchen window and see deer, moose and birds out in the wooded areas amongst the trees and in the tall grass. It had the added bonus that he could run Porky around the area to her heart's content.

It had been a big purchase, twenty years ago, but now it was worth triple the price he had paid. It had been a huge decision and he'd agonized for weeks over buying it, but he'd hated renting more, having to talk to a landlord about anything his place needed. His own house would safeguard his precious privacy and security. The settlement he'd received from his parents' estate mostly paid for the place so it was a good deal for him.

He looked over his property as he approached from the sidewalk. His yard had an agreeable fluffy green hedge covering the tough, impenetrable old chain link fence inside it, rather like his personal feelings; outwardly benign but came with a hidden barrier.

"Hello, Richard," smiled his neighbor, busily raking his leaves.

Spencer nodded in response, though the neighbor had his name wrong and Spencer didn't know his, either.

Spencer glanced at his two bay garage in the backyard, one containing his well-equipped workshop and the other his precious Lexus car. He was a thrifty guy most of the time, but when he did buy something, it was top quality and kept for a long time. His 1995

Lexus was in perfect shape, despite its age, purchased when it was a couple of years old and looked better than it had when he bought it. He'd fixed any little scratch or dent immediately. Mechanically, it was as good a car as any collector would expect to see.

As Spencer entered the gate, Porky excitedly circled him, wagging her tail, almost grinning. Spencer petted her as he went to the front door. It was an older, eight hundred square foot place, with a grey stucco exterior. As he unlocked the door, he reached into his own mailbox to retrieve the mail and the local newspaper.

He held Porky outside, gently, with his knee and a smile. "You can stay outside, Porky! It's a nice day," and petted her head once more.

The interior of the house was nicely finished with original hand-hewn wood floors. The old wooden window seats were refurbished to perfection. The elderly majestic stone fireplace sat there, waiting to be started. Spencer had long since converted it to natural gas. He'd had a bad experience chopping wood he wasn't eager to repeat. The house had a couple of old built-in china cabinets which he refurbished to perfection. Even the kitchen had its old-time charm but he gently brought it up to modern standards with a granite counter top and a dishwasher.

Spencer was proud of his house. He'd done almost all the work himself. It took a lot of time, but he'd carefully researched every part of the project beforehand. He'd bought the best materials and parts.

Eventually, he'd built a very good workshop in his garage, complete with all the power tools he needed. As it turned out, he was a very handy guy when it came to refurbishing wood furniture. He was naturally gifted and it showed.

The only labor he'd brought in was an electrician to improve the old house's electrical service panel to bring the wiring up to the latest building code. As he could afford it, he'd brought in a plumber to add more piping and drains for an improved bathroom upstairs and a new one, downstairs. It was a first class job.

Slowly he'd added various pieces of furniture from the same time period as the house. Each piece was lovingly refinished and recovered, all matching and looked terrific. Even the kitchen table and chairs were redone to match the rest of the house. The only exception to the antiques was the big screen TV set up on the wall. That was courtesy of driving the hearse. Sadly, other than Porky and himself, nobody else had ever seen these masterpieces or had so much as sat in one of his beautifully refurbished chairs.

After letting Porky in, he headed for the kitchen, turned on the kettle then dug out some dry dog food, poured it into the dog dish and put it on the floor for Porky. Opening the fridge, he pulled out a frozen lasagna, opened it up and put it into the micro wave. By that time the water was boiling for his tea. Red Rose tea was his favorite.

He walked into the bedroom he'd converted into a study and turned his new computer on. He consulted a couple of news feeds to see what had taken place in the day, then it was back to the kitchen to dish out his supper which should be hot by now. Porky ate her dinner while Spencer sat at the kitchen table and ate his own while absentmindedly picking through his mail.

Afterwards, he brought a second cup of tea into the living room, sat down in the big chair with Porky at his feet. He turned the TV on to the news and they both slowly drifted off to sleep. At ten o'clock he awoke with a snort, sent Porky outside, showered, brought the dog back in and went to bed, ready for the same routine tomorrow.

His schedule rarely changed except for weekends. He got up a little later for a leisurely breakfast. Instead of going to work, he would take the dog for a long walk in the park. Spencer might take a thermos of coffee with him to sit on a bench and listen to the wildlife if the weather was nice. Unless it was garage sale season, then he'd get up early and would drive to the various flea markets and garage sales looking for certain types of old furniture for his house. Last month he found the perfect end table for his bedroom. It was beat up and abused but he knew how to fix it up. He was out in his workshop in the evenings and on weekends working on it. To repair the old wood, he carefully took it apart, stripped off the numerous layers of paint and dirt. The base was trued up, drawer runners fixed and the table reassembled. At last, the ancient wood was carefully sanded and re-varnished with a number of coats, to look like it was new. Admiring his handiwork, he thought, it sure could use a lamp from the same time period. He would have to consult his computer to find some type of lamp from the 1900 era yet could be modified to use a modern electric bulb.

Tomorrow was Saturday. Maybe he could spy one at a garage sale. He set his alarm clock.

The Sale

Beth and Joe Alexander had accumulated a lot of old stuff from their retirement move from Brandon Lake. They were not much for throwing anything away, regardless of how old and beat up it was. They would good-naturedly accuse each other of being hoarders.

"The difference between us and a hoarder is we don't have enough storage space to hoard!"

They had an accumulation of old skiing gear, old books, furniture, shoes, clothing, china and general flotsam and jetsam. They felt guilty about throwing stuff out and considered it wasteful. Their parents had survived the Great Depression whose thrift had been imbedded in their children. Perhaps a garage sale would be a better idea. They could give their old stuff a new home and get a little money for it along the way. They were getting older now and it was time to downsize their possessions. It would be a good Saturday project. In the meantime, they would poke through it all and sort it, with every piece telling its story. There is a fine line between junk and treasure and a sale sounded like fun.

They wondered what fair market value was for each piece and what they should price it at. Worth is subjective. Friends told them everything needed to be priced cheap or you get to take it to the dump when the sales over and get nothing for it. They took all this under advisement and worked on the garage sale items for a few weeks until the sale was ready to go.

A Saturday date was set and suitable advertising was placed in the local paper. Joe had even stapled a few posters to power poles about town.

Early in the morning of the sale they slid the table full of sale items out of the garage and into the sunshine. They added a few pieces of furniture, some old car tires, a hanger stand loaded with clothes and boxes brimming with books—all were placed along the driveway by six a.m. Customers came in like vultures.

The Alexanders were surprised the garage sale people were so serious about it all. They drove like maniacs, some zooming past the Alexanders' yard display but kept going. Many of the shoppers, noticing their mistake, would then jam on their brakes and back their cars wildly and erratically up the block, like crazed, blindfolded firemen arriving at a fire.

More and more people arrived, digging through their stuff with fierce determination, looking for specific items like jewelry, china and kid's toys. A few argued about prices. A few skinflints wanted to haggle over some cheap articles. Joe just told them with a smile, to take them, if they were that 'hard up'.

Both Joe and Beth enjoyed the day and made two hundred and seventy-five bucks. It was a good haul for a bunch of junk.

At about one o'clock in the afternoon an older white Lexus car drove up, parked and a man of about fifty got out. He walked up to the garage sale area, obviously looking for something specific. Joe and Beth said hi to him and he shyly said hi in return. He looked around for a few more minutes, then noticed an old lamp sitting on the ground. He picked it up, and had a good look at it.

"How much you asking for the lamp?"

"Fifteen bucks," replied Joe, "But just so you know, it doesn't work. It's pretty old."

"I may be able to fix it. I pull the insides out of it, refurbish it and put in a new lamp core. I'll take it."

He approached Beth but suddenly got a pained look on his face as he patted his pockets fruitlessly. "No wallet! Damn!" he said, "Would you mind holding this for me while I go home and get my wallet? I'm sorry about this."

"Please go ahead and take it. Come back and pay us later," Beth said, thinking his face was vaguely familiar. Did she know him from somewhere?

"Oh, I couldn't," he said. "I'll be back in a little while."

He returned to his car and drove off.

By the time Spencer got back to the house, it was after three p.m. He went into the garage and put another coat of varnish on his latest wood project and set it down to dry. Timing of the coats was important. Being close to supper time, he went into the house so he and Porky could get something to eat. They took a walk afterwards, then hunkered down in the chair in front of the TV falling fast asleep. When he woke up he realized he had forgotten all about the lamp.

The Lamp

Beth and Joe Alexander were at the breakfast table, early as usual. They had their favorite breakfast of eggs, toast and fried potatoes, just as they always did.

"Did you get a look at the fellow who wanted that old lamp, Joe?"

"Not really. Why?"

"I think that might have been Spencer Cunningham."

Joe stopped eating, sitting upright in surprise, "Are you sure? He'd be mid-fifties by now. You aren't getting dotty, are you?"

"No."

"The first thing I thought when I saw him on Saturday was, 'Hey, there's our mailman'," Joe pointed out.

"I'm not a hundred percent sure, but he looks like Spencer, or at least how I imagine Spencer would look today. He said he'd come back to pick up the lamp so we'll see. I can't get over bumping into Spencer Cunningham, at a garage sale!" said Beth.

"If he's really Spencer," Joe cautioned. "Oddly, I picked up that very lamp at Jeff and Carol's estate sale."

"I wonder if Spencer would appreciate knowing that? Should we be going slowly with this? It has been a long time. I don't know where he's at with all this. He may be shocked or he may prefer his privacy or he may not want to have anything to do with us," Beth said, looking at Joe.

"Yes, that's true. He may prefer to not say anything to us. It may bring up some painful memories he may not want to stir up," said Joe. "We *are* the ones who decided it was okay for a ten-year-old to chop firewood."

Beth shuddered. "Don't remind me. What we didn't know about children back then. After all these years, I'd like to think we know a lot more about how to deal with all this, certainly more than we knew when we took him in. In a way, we are all very different people."

"Yes, I think we are certainly older and wiser than we were. What do you suggest?"

"If he's delivering our mail, I'll leave it to Spencer to decide how he wants to approach this, if he wants to at all—if it is him. I can be out working on the garden when he comes by. I won't trap him."

"Sure, say hi and leave it to him to start a conversation or not."

"This might be a little like making friends with the stray cat of the neighborhood," she warned.

Discovery

"Morning, Spencer."

"Good morning, Barney," Spencer greeted him with a smile. "It's a nice day out there."

Barney's face registered surprise. "Wow, that's the most you've said to me since you started working here."

"That's because I'm relieved you've taken over driving the hearse. It was both a lucrative and very creepy experience."

"Well, I'm glad to be back. My leg's finally good to go."

"I'm glad, too. Oh… Ah … Did you ever see things or hear things when you were doing the 'deadhead runs' from Fort Mac, Barney?"

"Not a thing. Why?"

"Oh, no reason. Hey, we'd better get sorting. Look at the time."

Standing side-by-side, as always, they sorted their mail for the daily run. After Barney was done, Spencer put on his coat, hat and thin gloves and headed for the door himself. The sun was just cresting the horizon, a pretty sight to start his daily rounds.

Monday had been a long day and Spencer was glad to be home. After supper both he and Porky were poised to drift asleep on the couch, as usual. Suddenly he snorted and sat up with a jerk. Porky jumped up in alarm.

"My lamp! Porky; I keep thinking about that old lamp from Saturday! Should we try phoning the lady to see if we can still get it?" He grinned and leaned over, petting the dog who was quite excited but didn't know why.

Spencer rarely used the phone but for some reason he was extraordinarily drawn to that old lamp. He looked up the name from the garage sale. "Alexander," he announced, then dialed their number.

"Hi. Mrs. Alexander?" He gave Porky a thumbs up. "I was at your garage sale on Saturday and was the one looking at an old lamp. Remember me, the guy without his wallet? I hope you will forgive me, but once I got home, I forgot all about it. Do you still have it?"

The answer was yes. He grinned. "When would be a good time to come by and get it?"

"It's only 7:30 now. You could come by and get it tonight, if that works for you," Mrs. Alexander offered, her voice sounding as if she was happy he'd called.

"Sure, I'll be right over."

Soon he was there and knocking on their door.

Mrs. Alexander opened the door. "Come on in!"

"I don't want to be a bother." Face to face, he felt suddenly shy, but Mrs. Alexander insisted he come in.

While she went to get the lamp, Spencer stood awkwardly in the hallway. Standing inside someone's home was a rare social event for him, one he would normally avoid, but he felt almost compelled to get that antique lamp.

She reappeared. "Here you go! I hope this is the right one."

"That's the one!" He reached into his pocket for the money. "Thank you very much!"

He handed her the fifteen dollars. Turning to leave, a framed photograph stopped him. It was of the Alexanders, much younger here, standing in front of a different house with four kids of varying ages beside an ancient jeep wagon. Everyone was grinning.

"That looks very familiar," Spencer remarked, then surprised himself by asking, "Where was this taken?"

"Oh, that was our old house in Brandon Lake," Mrs. Alexander remarked, seeming to be watching him closely.

Spencer stood in stunned silence for a few moments, recalling the house. It—it couldn't be. After years of guarding his feelings, he hastily covered his thoughts, glanced over at Mrs. Alexander, then quickly away. "Thank you," he blurted and was off to his car.

***

Beth Alexander stood in the window and watched Spencer walk to his car and drive away.

"Joe!" she called.

Joe came out of the study and asked, "What's wrong? You look spooked!"

"Almost… I'm … I'm almost positive that was Spencer Cunningham! He recognized the picture of us and the house at Brandon Lake!"

"Did he say anything about it? How do you know it's him?"

"He recognized the picture but tried not to let on that he knew it. And... and he has a missing finger on his left hand!"

***

Spencer drove off, his mind swimming with memories firing at him from all sides. Was that the foster people from Brandon Lake he had first stayed with, so long ago? He was fairly sure it was, but what should he do about it?

It was a sleepless night for Spencer. Rediscovering his first foster parents, the Alexanders, from so long ago left his mind a jumble of confused thoughts and murky memories, and with them came a flood of images and incidents from all the years and all the different foster homes of his past.

He thought back to his foster home days, only this time, his memories were truer. This time, he saw some of the good things that had happened along the way. Perhaps he should not have been too hasty to condemn it all.

He remembered one family in Abbottsford. The lady used to sing while she cooked amazing meals for her foster kids. It was a delight for them to arrive at the table to see the delicious meals.

There was the father balancing a jumble of children on his knees and on the arms of his chair, reading them stories such as 'Call of the Wild' and 'Nancy Drew' stories, thrilling them with a deep, baritone voice making the stories come alive with tales of Mounties' dog teams and mysteries.

Another foster family would pile all of them in a big, old van and take them out for a day at a lake. They all went swimming and fishing and anything else they wanted to do. Afterwards, they had a huge picnic of potato salad, cold cuts, pop and homemade buns and pickles around a campfire. In Victoria, one couple took all of them to see the museum and the Butchart Gardens. They'd explored the Harbor walkways afterwards.

Some homes made sure all the kids had bikes to ride. Others made sure skates were available if the kids went to the arena. Some had fishing gear for everyone to fish the nearby river.

In hindsight, all the foster homes were not so bad. Perhaps Spencer had been looking inward more than he should have. Personally, he seemed to have turned out alright. He was no axe murderer.

He glanced down at his hand and grimaced. He'd only been a danger to himself, all along.

In fact, he was reasonably well adjusted, other than occasionally talking to ghosts.

Eventually he fell asleep. All too soon, his alarm clock went off at 5 am, and he was up and ready to meet the day.

He had his coffee machine set to start on a timer, so it was ready. After sending Porky out into the yard, he cooked himself two eggs, a slice of toast and added a glass of orange juice to complete his breakfast. Then it was into his uniform and out the door and off to walk to the Post Office. Spencer felt strangely happy and optimistic, for no apparent reason.

The post office station was a busy place, as usual, full of hustle and bustle. Mail was going in all directions in the big mail carts, the union steward was crabbing at the post office supervisor. Barney and Clark were yammering on about their weekend and Spencer didn't mind. For the first time in many years, he heard it all and enjoyed it. It was the sound of life going on around him. He could choose to be a part of it, listen to it or choose to ignore it. It was his choice and he was listening!

Clark was sifting through his mail when he grabbed a post card, looked at it and called to everyone to listen:

'Dear Jane,

Having a great time at Betty's. There is a cute guy that comes to pick up her trash Monday and Thursday. I tried talking to him but he always seems too busy, so next garbage day I'll meet him wearing something revealing! That should improve my sex life! Ha-ha. Sabrina

The crowd laughed and cheered its approval of Clark's selection of the postcard. Even Spencer laughed, which was very unusual.

Spencer was off doing his rounds, whistling as he walked. Eventually, he made it to the Alexanders' house. As he walked along, he realized he had been anticipating this particular delivery all morning and was nervous at the prospect of seeing the Alexanders in the yard. He was not sure what he would say to them or even if they were, in fact, his first foster family after all these years. Family. He thought he liked the feel of it but this was unfamiliar territory. He stepped through the gate and headed for the mailbox.

Beth Alexander was working in the garden. Spencer had to have been by their house thousands of times, delivering their mail, yet this was the first time he noticed the amazing roses the Alexanders grew. They had all types, spread all over the yard and up in trellises.

Beth stood up, her face flushed and said, "I'll take that." Then she asked, "Is that actually you, Spencer Cunningham, after all these years?"

His heart sprang up into his throat. "Yes, it's me, Spencer! I had no idea it was you. I could hardly remember your names. It was a long time ago and those were such dark days for me."

"We are just so pleased to see you after all this time, Spencer. We wondered where you were and how you were doing ..."

"I've been well. I had some adjusting to do. Got kind of shuffled around a bit but here I am, healthy and happy."

"I can see you are healthy and happy," Beth replied. "Will we be seeing more of you in the future?"

"Yes, I'll be delivering the mail until I retire," Spencer said, knowing that wasn't what she meant, but powerless to react in any other way. "Must go. Duty calls."

"Of course you have to go back to work," said Beth, patting him on the back as he turned and left. With that touch, Spencer remembered suddenly that she'd often shown affection by patting a person she liked on the back. It was gentle, informal contact, and it pleased him more than he could describe. With her touch, good memories of his time with the Alexanders flooded into his brain, into his heart.

He made his rounds and then headed home. Porky was thrilled to see him, dancing around him, wagging her tail. Spencer went in the house for his usual dinner time routine. Afterwards, he went out to his workshop to work on the old lamp he'd acquired from the Alexanders. Porky went in and out of the open shop door to keep him company as he worked. It was almost ten o'clock when he finally finished and went to bed.

The next day, late into his delivery run, he came to the Alexander's, again. He opened the gate and walked through, headed for the mailbox. Both Beth and Joe were at work, moving plants around their garden, but they stopped when Spencer came through the gate.

"Hello Spencer. Nice day, isn't it?" Beth said.

"It's a very nice day," confirmed Spencer, pleased to take a moment to talk to her.

"Spencer, I have someone here I'd like you to meet. It's my husband, Joe. Do you remember Joe?"

Spencer looked at Joe for a moment, trying to find some features to recognize. Joe was about medium height, medium build with a big nose and a face that always seemed to smile. He had less hair than Spencer remembered, but his expressive bushy eyebrows remained. He extended his hand to Joe.

"It's been a long time, Spencer. It's good to see you after all these years! I see you never found that finger!"

"Nope. It still might grow back, though," Spencer chuckled.

They all laughed about it. For a minute or so, all three just stood in the quiet and enjoyed each other's company before Spencer saluted them both and was off on his mail run.

***

Spencer worked on the antique lamp for a week. Carefully, he took it apart, noting the pieces he needed. He cleaned the shade and used steel wool to clean the rust off the metal parts. Later in the week, he went to an electrical parts supply store and picked up some internal replacement parts to make it work like a modern lamp, yet still retain its antique look.

Each day, he would go by the Alexander's on his run. He would exchange a few more pleasantries with them and then be on his way.

Finally, on Thursday night, he had the old lamp all together. He plugged it in, turned it on and it worked like a charm. It had a beautiful antique look with modern efficiency. Spencer was very excited with his project. He showed Porky the new lamp. She wagged her tail because she was easily impressed by anything Spencer did.

For some reason, Spencer was a little down, having completed this project and not having anyone to share it with. Normally, this didn't concern him but today it did. Then he had a thought he had not had for decades. He picked up the phone.

"Hello Beth? This is Spencer Cunningham. How are you?"

"I'm fine, Spencer. How about you?" She sounded excited to hear from him.

"I just wanted to tell you that I just finished that old lamp you sold me! It came out very nicely," he said, suddenly nervous. What if the Alexanders weren't interested in the old lamp—or reconnecting with him? Normally he held himself above trying to impress or make other people happy, but the Alexanders were different; they mattered.

Before he could think about it anymore, Beth answered, "Why, that's lovely, Spencer! You must be very clever. That was a very beat up lamp. In fact, I think that might even be a lamp from your parent's house, from long ago."

Spencer literally felt the blood drain from his head. He slumped back into a chair, abruptly unable to maintain his own weight. Porky cocked her head to one side, her expression puzzled. He raised a shaking hand and stroked her head unsteadily. He had not thought of his parents for decades. They had vanished from his memory. He did get a settlement with interest on his twenty-first birthday but he thought everything had been sold off.

"Spencer? Are you still there." Beth sounded worried.

"Ah … yeah. Still here. It's just been a long time since I thought about them. So … you think this lamp was actually my parents at one time? That … that would be incredible."

"I believe it is. Spencer, what are you doing tomorrow evening? Joe and I would like to see the lamp. Why don't you come over? Better yet, how about having supper with us?"

Spencer took a moment, thinking. His first impulse was to say no, like he always did, to escape social contact, but he resisted the old urge. "Sure...what time?" he answered, his voice a bit shaky.

"Come over about five-thirty. Do you still like meat loaf and mashed potatoes?" asked Beth.

"Yes, I do," he answered, scarcely believing he was doing this.

"Bring your lamp and come on over," said Beth. "We'd love to have you."

"I'll be there."

Spencer thanked her and hung up the phone. He was surprised he had the courage to say yes. He hadn't accepted a dinner invitation since he'd left the last foster home when he was eighteen years old. Leaving that home had been his birthday present. His last one.

He remembered that day well. The Williams family had celebrated his birthday and given him a wonderful send-off while they were at it. How had he allowed himself to forget their kindness? Despite himself, he had a lump in his throat just thinking about it. It was funny how fondly he remembered that day, after all these years.

Dinner

Spencer was nervous about the dinner with the Alexanders. He thought back to his foster home days, the years in which he'd sat and had dinner with other people. He hadn't shared a meal with anyone since.

At five-thirty he made it to the Alexanders' carrying his lamp. It was a nice, warm summer evening. The moon was full, showing itself long before nightfall. Spencer enjoyed the scent of the Alexander's rose garden as he made his way to the front door and knocked. Joe Alexander was there to let him in and take his jacket, hanging it in the closet. He invited Spencer to sit down in their living room. Spencer looked around and marveled at all the family photos displayed on the table tops.

Beth came out wearing an apron and said, "Welcome, Spencer! It's so nice to have you here! The last time we had you for dinner was when you were ten years old." Her expression was a happy one, recalling the memory.

"Wow, that's true. I didn't think of that."

"Is that the old lamp?" she asked.

"Yes, all fixed up."

"It's just like new! It's better than new! You've done a wonderful job, Spencer."

The Alexanders both marveled at his workmanship. Joe was completely impressed. He and Spencer talked about the way Spencer did the refurbishment, right down to the technical details about the transformation.

Soon, Beth had them come into the dining room to eat. Supper was wonderful. Spencer found he was enjoying the company. It had been so long since he had eaten with other people, he'd forgotten the fellowship of the foster homes. Everyone felt welcome when they ate together. It was a warm feeling, long forgotten. Afterwards, they had their coffee in the living room. Spencer sat on the big, comfy couch while Joe and Beth sat in nearby chairs.

After a bit of small talk, of Donvegan, Brandon Lake and the old days, Beth brought up the subject of Spencer's parents. He could sense she was being careful of his feelings.

"I don't know if you know this Spencer, but we were friends of your parents when you lived in Brandon Lake."

Spencer was still for a few minutes, considering this. He had not talked to anyone about his parents, other than a few social workers, in decades. It was not that he did not want to say anything, more that he did not know what to say or think about them anymore. As a boy he'd kept his feelings tightly under wraps while he was at a new home. The government people were the only ones who ever asked, usually just prior to a transfer interview. Beth and Joe were the first ones truly interested, outside of the social workers.

"I never knew you and my parents were friends. All the time I was at your house, I never made the connection. I was so distraught it was all just a cloud of gloom."

"Your dad and I drove the trains together. That was how we met them," said Joe.

"My dad was a train engineer?"

"Oh, yes. We both drove GM Diesel Locomotives. They were great, powerful beasts," Joe said, proudly, then added with a twinkle in his eyes, "We even got to blow the whistles at the crossings!"

"That would be fun."

"It *was* fun," Joe confirmed.

Spencer summoned his courage and asked, "Do … do you know what happened to my parents?"

"Well, you were in school for the day, of course. Your mom picked up your dad at the train yard and they were coming back into town. The roads were icy with blowing snow, just like the day we took you to the hospital for your finger, remember?" Beth said, "They slid across a corner in front of a logging truck. I'm pretty sure they never knew what hit them, which is merciful, at least."

Spencer was trying to imagine this happening. He had put the past in a tight fist in his heart. The fist was never unclenched and those dreadful moments would not be relived. Here, with the Alexanders, Spencer felt safe and at home. Here, the fist in his heart opened with all the past thoughts flooding out. He remembered when his parents were killed. It was a moment he'd tried not to re-live. To re-live it was to have no one to shelter him, understand and console him.

It was so many years ago, yet it was absolutely clear to this day. He remembered when the grim-faced social worker and policeman came to his house with the awful news. He remembered being devastated, numb and disbelieving. The adults were so grim and white-faced that he knew they were not joking.

Who would feed his pet fish? How would he get dinner and get to school? Nobody would be waiting for him at home, ever again. It would forever be an empty, silent house. Then he just crumbled into tears. The social worker took him to the hospital for a couple of days while she looked for a place for him in the interim. The nurses were busy but kind. They sat with him at every opportunity and just held him. They had children of their own and knew what it felt like.

He remembered when the social worker picked him up from the hospital and took him over to the Alexanders'. She did say they were friends of his parents but he did not know them.

"I never did hear the full story. It does make me feel better knowing that," said Spencer, finding the lump that formed in his throat made it difficult to speak.

Beth and Joe came to sit on each side of him, putting their arms around him and the three of them just stayed there.

After that day, Spencer went over to the Alexanders' quite often. They soon showed him family picture albums of his parents, their own huge extended family and their daughter Kirstin and her family. It was as if Spencer had been adopted into a big friendly family he never knew he had. He was back in a circle of hearts and thoughts.

Spencer remembered all those restless years of living in a house and a city that just felt temporary and empty. After reuniting with the Alexanders, it all suddenly felt like home.

Home had been with him, all along.

Good Bye Clara

When he was in Victoria on a retirement course, Spencer drove past the old orphanage. He parked, then strolled down the sidewalk and looked over the old place. The front of the building was thoroughly repainted and modernized. The sign in front said it was 'The Ross Bay Condominium'.

The grotesque old fire escape tubes were long gone. For a fleeting second he missed them, thinking how fun it would have been to slide down them just once while he was there. Oh well.

He noticed the sad little cemetery was still in the corner of the front lawn but the remainder of the area was well manicured with rows of flowers growing everywhere. Even the cemetery looked good with the lawn cut and edges trimmed. The annoying geese were still there, standing guard. He could not resist going over to see Clara Hutchinson's headstone.

He stood for a few minutes, listening to the geese gabbling and fussing, enjoying the flowers and the quiet. Clara's headstone was so weathered he could barely make out her name. After a while he saw a bench nearby, and headed over to sit for a while. Spencer thought he'd just enjoy the moment after being packed in a noisy seminar all day. Lately he was on a classic story binge so opened up an old copy of 'Treasure Island', enjoying its simplicity of time and antiqueness. He even enjoyed the texture of the elderly book and its musty smell. Soon he was lost in adventures of boys and pirates, wishing that could have been his childhood instead.

"Spencer. Will you read to me?" A nearby voice requested weakly.

He froze where he sat, still recognizing her voice after all these decades. He raised his eyes to see a nine-year-old girl with a patched old dress standing before him. "Clara?" he whispered, afraid to scare her away.

"Yes, it's me, Spencer," and she sat down beside him.

Not knowing what else to do he just started to read to her. Clara said nothing and watched the book as he read aloud, trying his best to speak perfectly as he made his way through, page after page.

"Hello young man. What are you up to on this lovely evening?"

Spencer looked up from his book, surprised to see an elderly woman tending the flowers nearby. Clara had vanished. "Oh, hello. I was just reading my book."

The elderly woman smiled and said, "I see you know Clara Hutchinson."

"Clara?"

"Yes, the little girl you were reading to. I often see her, too."

"You can see ghosts?" asked Spencer, very surprised. He hadn't been the only one to see Clara.

"I'm glad to finally meet someone else who sees ghosts. My son would say I'm dotty and put me in a home but I'm managing at ninety years old and don't plan to move. How long have you known Clara… Mr …?"

"Cunningham but please call me Spencer, Ma'am."

"And you can call me Katherine. Pleased to meet you, Spencer."

"Pleased to meet you Katherine. I first met Clara when I was ten years old, when this place was the Ross Bay Orphanage, nearly fifty years ago. I was only here for a couple of weeks before they shipped me off to a foster home."

"Same story, here," said Katherine. "We were both orphans here, Spencer."

"Yes. I eventually moved around to about a dozen different homes until I aged out at eighteen, then got my own place. It's been something of a journey."

Katherine said, "Yes, life is a journey, isn't it? After ninety years I have to say we become the people we meet along the way. You seem like a good fellow. What kept you going, home-to-home?"

Spencer pondered her question for a minute. "I haven't thought about that. I guess I took each day, one at a time, believed in myself and became self-reliant. For a long time, I thought there was no time for tears and I hardened my heart to everyone. I had to undo all that and came to appreciate the people around me. Now I know many of them did the best they could for me and I plan to find as many of them as I can and personally thank them for it."

"You have found a wisdom that most people miss."

"Wisdom is hard to come by. I feel sorry for those who can't move on, like Clara," said Spencer.

"What happened to Clara, so long ago?"

"An nun looked up Clara's history and apparently her father was killed in the Great War. Her mother was forced to work and left her in this place. She visited Clara when she could, which wasn't often, until the 'flu epidemic killed her. Clara waited here for her until the 'flu got her, as well. After ninety-six years she's still waiting for her mother to come. I wish there was something we could do."

Katherine listened, thinking before she spoke, "I might have a suggestion for Clara. Could you come back tomorrow evening and meet here? At seven? I might have something we could do."

Puzzled, next evening Spencer was waiting at the cemetery, quietly reading aloud to Clara when Katherine and another woman arrived. Clara vanished with the sound of visitors' voices.

"Oh, hello Katherine. I was just reading to Clara," said Spencer.

"I know. Please come out to see us, Clara. It's alright, Clara," Katherine assured.

Clara appeared in front of them, looking downcast.

Katherine smiled, "Hello Clara. How are you?"

"Fine, ma'am."

"Clara, this is my friend Gladys. She's a medicine woman from the Songhees Nation and lives in the building in the next condominium to me."

Gladys smiled, "Hello Clara."

"Spencer, Gladys and I are all worried about you, Clara. Are you alright?"

"...my mom is coming for me. I'm fine, thanks."

Katherine paused, then said gently, "Gladys can help you see your mom and dad again. Is this alright with you?"

"...I suppose..."

Katherine nodded to Gladys who knelt to the earth with great respect, gently chanting, while building a tiny nest of special grasses and tobacco in her hands. As she chanted ancient words the handful of special plants of the earth started to smoke and smudge harmlessly swirling and following its own path around Clara, who watched with wide eyed wonder. The smudge went around and around her.

Clara raised her arms, smiled and looked back at Spencer. "I'm going home, too, Spencer," and she slowly faded away. Clara was gone.

They stood in stunned silence until Spencer spoke. "Thank you Gladys and Katherine for helping Clara finally join her parents. Everyone deserves to be with the ones they love."

Spencer hugged both of them before they went on their way, leaving him standing alone by the forlorn graveyard. He went to Clara's headstone, wrote something in the front of the book he had been reading to her and placed it on her final resting place.

To Clara,

I hope you've found Peace,

Your friend, Spencer

THE END

Pat Ferris was born in Winnipeg, Manitoba on a chilly January 11, 1954 day. His family eventually moved to Victoria where he spent his formative years but pined away for those sharp, cold winters buried deep in his DNA. In 1975 Pat moved to Fort St. John for six months to experience the burgeoning natural gas industry and feel the cold winters he sorely missed. Forty-one years later he's still there, now turning his hand to writing romance/adventure novels such as; 'Gypsies' and 'A Gypsy

Engagement'. You will find this short story a turn from Pat's usual fare. 'Spencer's Ghost' is a persistent tale that has haunted him for a decade and would not be here had it not been for the persistence of his friends who pestered, cajoled and encouraged lonely Spencer to see the light of day.

Sunday Peace

By Marie Gerald Bernardin

She turned,
"Peace be with you!"
Offered her hand,
I shook it and replied
"And also with you."
She smiled,
Blue eyes twinkled,
then winked.
She turned to the next person
"Peace be with you!"
Again the smile.
Then the next person,
The person in front,
And the one beside them...
Then the service continued.
I sat quietly through the psalms,
Words of the hymns sprung from memory,
And I joined the choir, the congregation
In responses and words of praise,
And, at peace,
I remembered my father,
Seated on the aisle, with 5, 6,
Then 7, 8, 9, 10 children near,
And Mom holding the latest babe,
Quietly beside him.
As the sermon droned on,
His eyes drooped lower,

Peaceful at the very start of the week.
A subtle elbow would bring him back.
And the memory spread peace around me.

Marie Gerald Bernardin is a professional procrastinator extraordinaire, with a flair for words while juggling life.

63477876R00210

Made in the USA
Charleston, SC
05 November 2016